DISQUALIFIED

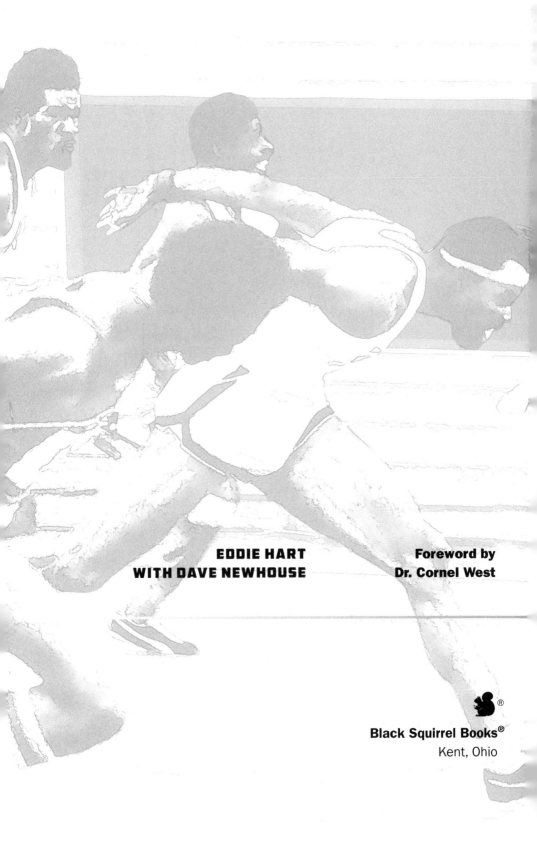

EDDIE HART
WITH DAVE NEWHOUSE

Foreword by
Dr. Cornel West

Black Squirrel Books®
Kent, Ohio

DISQUALIFIED

EDDIE HART, MUNICH 1972, AND THE
VOICES OF THE MOST TRAGIC OLYMPICS

Text © 2017 by Eddie Hart and Dave Newhouse
Foreword © 2017 by The Kent State University Press
All rights reserved

ISBN 978-1-60635-312-7
Manufactured in USA

Black Squirrel Books®
Frisky, industrious black squirrels are a familiar sight on the Kent State University campus
and the inspiration for Black Squirrel Books™, a trade imprint of The Kent State University
Press. www.KentStateUniversityPress.com

Cataloging information for this title is available at the Library of Congress.

21 20 19 18 17   5 4 3 2 1

To my beloved parents, T. J. and Florence Hart: my father taught me to be a husband and father, and the value of what it means to be the best; my mother raised me with an undying love and desire for my physical and spiritual well-being. Without them, there is no Eddie Hart.

To my precious family: my wife, Gwen, who helped me understand the meaning of love, and who is the mother of my children and the person with whom I have grown spiritually; to Paris, my firstborn, who is truly a gift from God and whose unconditional love and joy have brought more happiness to my life than I deserve; to my son, Eddie Jr., who is my right arm, continuing the tradition of the Hart legacy, bringing both honor and dignity to the family, and who has made me the proud grandfather of Eddie III, from a previous marriage, and James and Bella by his wonderful wife, Tara, giving me three beautiful grandchildren.

To my brothers and sisters: Catherine, John, Alfred, Evelyn, and David.

To Stan Wright's family for their continued support, background information, and the genuine heartfelt love they extended to me in the process of writing my book.

—E.H.

To Phyllis Newhouse: a gold-medalist sister and fashionista.

—D.N.

CONTENTS

FOREWORD

DR. CORNEL WEST

Eddie Hart is one of the great exemplars of spiritual integrity and athletic excellence in our time. He is one of those rare persons who combine undeniable dignity and unquestionable achievement.

In the 1970s, Eddie Hart was well known as "The World's Fastest Human"—co-holder of the world record for the 100-meter dash. And for those of us who have known him for more than four decades, he is the embodiment of moral greatness.

I was blessed to first meet Eddie in 1969. He was the good friend (or "elder brother") of my only blood brother, Cliff West. They were roommates in Berkeley, where they were teammates on the University of California track-and-field team. Eddie was the reigning emperor of the "Mad Pad," their famous apartment, and he was the major force behind Cal's NCAA track-and-field championship team of 1970. Together, Cliff, Eddie, Kerry Hampton, and Mike Lyons were loving and supportive comrades in the Mad Pad, and the West family—especially Dad and me—became close adoptive kin to our brother Eddie.

The first thing I noticed about Eddie was his grand style—in music, clothes, walk, and talk. Along with his quiet dignity and deep wisdom was his sophisticated "Pittsburg style," rooted in black southern sensibilities, tested and triumphant in urban West Coast realities. In other words, Eddie is first a product of the black spiritual nobility of the Hart family, especially his father, T. J. Hart, and his mother, Florence Viola Hart. The sublime Hart family represents the best of black church tradition—charity to all, malice toward none, and a willingness to persevere and keep on pushing regardless of the circumstances and consequences. The brute fact that Eddie Hart also became one of the greatest athletes of the twentieth century reinforces his family's proud commitment to compassion in the face of catastrophe and dignity in the face of adversity.

The Eddie Hart story is a story of familial piety—the ways his beloved mother and father, grounded in a trusting God, constituted the fundamental sources of good in his life. This powerful acknowledgment of his debts of gratitude to them becomes the model for his own blessed family, with his marvelous wife, Gwen; their loving daughter, Paris; their loving son, Eddie Jr.; and their three grandchildren.

In our age of cupidity and mendacity, Eddie Hart enacts a life of piety and integrity. Like the Sankofa bird, which looks back to recover the best of the past in order to succeed in the present toward a better future, Eddie Hart builds on a rich tradition of love and perseverance. His courageous response—not reaction—to his heartbreaking experience of disqualification is a life lesson to all of us as to how to be spiritually fortified and morally majestic. And with the multilayered context of the 1972 Munich Olympic Games—barbaric terrorism, double-standard racism, athletic heroism, and technical chicanery—this book intensifies the drama of his life.

My life is enriched because of the life work and spiritual witness of Eddie Hart. I salute Eddie and Dave Newhouse for unleashing this grand drama into a world hungry for integrity, excellence, and dignity.

ACKNOWLEDGMENTS

The authors wish to thank all of the book's participants, Olympians and otherwise, who relived the tragic story of the 1972 Summer Games in Munich, Germany, where a massacre and gold medals merged amid the background noise of terrorists' rifles, police sirens, getaway buses, whirling helicopters, and sniper fire.

Dave Newhouse, together with Eddie Hart, interviewed these 1972 Olympians: Mark Spitz, Rick DeMont, Barbara Ferrell, Tom McMillen, Bob Seagren, Tom Hill, Marilyn King, Klaus Wolfermann, Rey Robinson, Tom Dooley, and Gerald Tinker.

Other Olympians, from games before and after Munich, also contributed: Lee Evans, John Carlos, Jimmy Hines, Stephanie Brown Trafton, Dave Maggard, and Ollan Cassell.

The authors' trip to Munich included further interviews pertaining to the 1972 Olympics: Irmina Richter, Friederike Wolfermann, and journalist Michael Gernandt. Additional conversations in Munich occurred with Alexander Bock and Eddie Hart Jr. Olympian Dick Fosbury arranged two of these Munich interviews.

Adding credibility to this book were Newhouse's telephone interviews with Shaul Ladany and Shlomo Levy in Israel, both of whom escaped the Black September terrorists after the September 5, 1972, assault on the Israeli living quarters at Connollystrasse 31.

Further interviews from Eddie Hart's and Stan Wright's lives included talks with Nanette Mercurio, Rodell Johnson, Bert Bonanno, Jack Albiani, Cliff West, George Wright, and Toni Wright Hartfield.

Eddie Hart Jr. documented the Munich trip by taking photographs and film footage. William Love offered psychological expertise.

Dr. Cornel West and his family have enhanced the life of Eddie Hart Sr., who expresses his gratitude to others who contributed to this book: Blaine Robinson, Carl Ray Harris, Howard Carter, Roy Finks, Donald Payne, Patricia Warfield, Tam Harris, Harold Winston, Larry Winston, Art Mijares, Carlis Harris, Don Pierce, George Scott, George Brooks, Randy Williams, Wyomia Tyus, Clarence Taylor, Rosie Bonds, Ron Wilborn, Chuck Dybdal, Vince Ferrate, Mort Laudsberg, and especially Dave Newhouse, who brought structure and clarity to Hart's life journey.

The authors are indebted to the Kent State University Press, and especially Will Underwood, Mary Young, Susan Cash, and Carol Heller, for believing in this book project and pushing it to fruition. Go Golden Flashes! And much appreciation goes out to Erin Holman for her expert editing of the book.

Making this book visual was David Petranovic of Montclair Photo (Oakland, CA), digitalizing the photographs in the book.

Patsy Newhouse, the perfect wife, stood by patiently as her husband devoted himself to the project, both home and abroad, over a two-year period. Son Casey Newhouse; his wife, Michelle; and grandchildren Callan and Campbell were a valuable source of encouragement.

The authors couldn't have written this book without any of you.

INTRODUCTION

The first Olympic Games were held in, and named for, Olympia, Greece, in 776 B.C.; these classic origins echoed many centuries later in the tragedy that played out in the 1972 Summer Olympics in Munich, Germany.

No modern Olympics—which first commenced in Athens, Greece, in 1896—has experienced anything like Munich did, with the brutal killings of eleven Israeli athletes and coaches by eight Arab terrorists known as the Black September group.

The city, determined to erase the bitter memory of the Nazi-controlled 1936 Summer Olympics in Berlin, presented a "Cheerful Games" in 1972. Thus Olympic Village security was lax in the daytime and nonexistent at night, which made it an easy target for the eight Arabs. Undetected and wearing ski masks, they climbed over a six-and-a-half-foot fence that lacked the protective barbed wire that customarily surrounds an Olympic Village. Carrying concealed rifles in sports bags and murder in their souls, those men committed the first terrorist attack at a sporting event.

Before the carnage of September 5, 1972, was over, five terrorists and one Munich policeman were killed, along with the targeted eleven Israelis. Three Black September members managed to flee the country and weren't ever prosecuted for their crimes. Israeli race walker Shaul Ladany, who escaped, is one of many Munich Olympians who were interviewed for this book. Shlomo Levy, who also contributed, was an interpreter for the Israeli team. He also fled the terrorists, then witnessed the massacre at Building 31 while photographing its sequence from a safe hiding place across the street.

But this is Eddie Hart's book, an inspirational story of dejection and recovery, understanding and forgiveness, and civility beyond comprehension.

Hart was an American sprinter who, along with teammate Rey Robinson, had tied the 100-meter-dash world record of 9.9 seconds at the 1972 Olympic Trials in Eugene, Oregon. But it was Hart who was co-favored, with the Soviet Union's Valery Borzov, to win the 100 in Munich. Then the inexplicable happened. USA sprint coach Stan Wright received the wrong starting times for the quarterfinal heats, and Hart and Robinson were disqualified after arriving late to the track. Borzov then won the 100 and also the 200, while Hart found the inner strength to anchor the USA's 400-meter relay team to victory in world-record time, beating Borzov to the finish line. Robinson, unfortunately, was entered only in the 100 and left Munich medal-less.

Unlike in the very first Olympics, when winners received olive wreaths, every modern Olympian strives for the gold medal. But winning gold in a relay, even though it's a career milestone for some runners, still isn't comparable to winning the Olympic 100-meter dash; for with that distinction comes the title "World's Fastest Human." And Hart was in peak condition in Munich, at the apex of his sprinting career—to this day the envy of other Olympic gold medalists.

"Of all the sprinters I've seen, including myself, Eddie was like the complete sprinter," said Jimmy Hines, who won the 100 meters at the Mexico City Olympics in 1968. "Eddie ran almost the perfect race. He had a great start, a great middle part of his race, and he had a great finish. I was a great sprinter, but not a complete sprinter. Eddie had it all, including the mental approach. If he had gotten to the [Munich] finals, it probably would have been a world record. He would have won without a doubt; he was faster than Borzov."

Alas, Hart was victimized by a rare Olympic disqualification and thus sat in the stands, forlornly, watching Borzov dominate the field in the 100 final with a time of 10.14, much slower than Hart's 9.9, yet well ahead of Robert Taylor (10.24), the silver medalist and the lone American to make his 100 quarterfinal race—barely.

"I can try to imagine how devastating that was for Eddie Hart and Rey Robinson," said Lee Evans, the 400-meter gold medalist at Mexico City. "If it happened to me like it happened to them, it would have been more than four years before I could talk about it. Have you ever been through a divorce? It's very traumatic, man. You don't want to talk about a divorce. I really felt for Eddie and Rey, and how they felt, and I didn't want to talk to them either. I'd see Eddie and keep walking past him."

What Evans didn't grasp, along with other gold medalists, was that Hart evaluated what had befallen him in the 100 and what was left—the 400-meter relay. He refocused faster than most athletes could have in approaching the tail end of their competitive careers (Hart retired right after Munich). The chance to become the World's Fastest Human was lost, but Hart wasn't about to drop the baton. He had an obligation to his relay teammates and was their only chance at gold. He couldn't, and wouldn't, quit on them. Devastated, yes, but Hart wasn't a quitter.

John Carlos, the 200-meter bronze medalist at Mexico City, who is linked with gold medalist Tommie Smith for their Black Power salutes at those 1968 Summer Games, is a fan of Eddie Hart—a super fan.

"Eddie kind of reminds me of Clark Kent," said Carlos, "mild-mannered, but fearsome as a competitor. An easygoing personality, but once he got into the starting blocks, he knew about taking care of business. He was an arch competitor for anyone. I don't think any sprinter was more competitive than Eddie Hart."

Hart is unique among most sprinters, and most humans, in another capacity: he is completely devoid of malice. He could have held Stan Wright accountable for capsizing his track career, which happened on the planet's biggest stage. Even if Wright wasn't directly responsible, and Hart never saw him as that, the coach was in charge of the American sprinters in Munich. Ever since, Wright's critics have held him guilty, despite his own selfless admission of wrongdoing, choosing to fall on his sword for everyone, including his interrogator, Howard Cosell, to see.

Rey Robinson, however, wasn't like Eddie Hart following their disqualifications. "I don't care, the man is a coach, he can say he's sorry," Robinson said at the time. "What about three years [of training]? What about torn ligaments, pulled muscles, a broken leg? He can go on being a coach. What can I go on being?"

Robinson's sprint career peaked, like Hart's, in 1972, only without a medal to show for it. Can Robinson's attitude toward Wright perhaps have softened in a new century? In this book's epilogue, Robinson and Hart discuss this delicate subject in a conversation. But, let's not rush. For besides being the most tragic of Olympics, Munich also had the most captivating storylines, as individual heroism and personal conflict collided in athletes' pursuit of gold medals.

This was the same Olympics in which swimmer Mark Spitz won seven golds and set seven world records, in the greatest Olympic medal haul until Michael Phelps's eight gold medals in swimming at the 2008 Beijing Games. Also in Munich, American swimmer Rick DeMont won the 400-meter freestyle—but had his gold medal taken away, because a prescribed drug he was taking for asthma, which the U.S. Olympic Committee had approved, was disallowed by the International Olympic Committee.

But, then, in terms of politics in sports, there is nothing comparable to the Olympic Games. As classic proof, the USA believed it had won the basketball gold medal in Munich by defeating the Soviet Union in the championship game. Then, inexplicably, three seconds were added to the clock after the game had ended, enabling the Soviets to sink a basket for the official victory—the biggest Olympic gold medal heist ever. Incensed, the Americans refused to accept their silver medals.

With the controversial nature of the Munich Olympics, the book's authors deemed it imperative to add the voices of the men and women involved in the fields of battle, both in the Olympic arenas and at Connollystrasse 31, the building where the Israeli massacre occurred. Besides Ladany and Levy, Newhouse interviewed Spitz, DeMont, and Tom McMillen from the USA basketball team, along with Bob Seagren, who encountered his own track-and-field mishap, and pentathlete Marilyn King, who offered an insightful perspective on Munich 1972.

But, predominantly, this is Eddie Hart's book. And his personal story, before and after Munich, is most compelling. His father, T. J. Hart, was stationed in the Navy in 1944 at Port Chicago, California, where the biggest munitions explosion in American military history occurred, taking 320 lives, including 202 African Americans. Though the elder Hart was uninjured, he became part of history as that horrific incident brought military racism to the forefront and resulted in systemic change.

Though T. J. Hart's education ended in the third grade, he and his wife, Florence, reared six children, including son Eddie, who graduated from the University of California, Berkeley, before earning a master's degree from California State University, Hayward, thus leading to a career in teaching, coaching, and philanthropy. (The Eddie Hart All In One Foundation benefits underserved youth through education, life skills, sports and career-related clinics, and fundraising activities. The foundation's founder, you see, is a giver.)

Eddie Hart also is success in motion, though that success didn't come without hard lessons. His entry into track and field didn't immediately suggest that a gold medalist was growing up in Pittsburg, a blue-collar town forty miles east of San Francisco. Only through a slow process did Hart build a path to Munich.

Then in March 2015, forty-three years after the Olympics, he returned to Munich, to fully comprehend the events of 1972. He traveled with his son, Eddie Hart Jr., and coauthor Newhouse to retrace his past, and to give it substance, with the son as photographer and videographer. Eddie Sr., giving his book further relevance, honors important people in his life, including his wife and teenage sweetheart, Gwen; his son, Eddie Jr.; and his daughter, Paris, who has a developmental disability and lives with her parents. Eddie and Gwen also have three grandchildren. Married forty-three years in 2016, they have a loving relationship and a loving home, built on faith. The husband is a devout man who teaches Sunday school.

Eddie Hart is a special individual, filled with kindness and forgiveness. He remained friends with Stan Wright long after Munich. Hart is soft-spoken but sincere, a man of his word. You couldn't ask for a finer role model or a better friend. He remains an integral, though heartbreaking, part of Olympic lore. Eddie Hart is Munich, and Munich is Eddie Hart. They are tethered forever.

And this is their story—one man, one city, one unforgettable Olympics.

—D.N.

TUNNEL VISION

I can see it, sadly, sixty feet away. The 100-meter starting line is that close, and so is that same ageless angst. Here I am, Eddie Hart, forcing myself to relive that crushing day all over again, standing in that same dark tunnel in 2015, reimagining the sprinters kneeling in their blocks, anxiously awaiting the discharge from the starter's gun. It's like 1972 was just yesterday, only it's forty-three years later.

The painted starting line is still visible, the proverbial light at the end of the tunnel. Nothing has changed, including the acidity in the pit of my stomach that tore at my guts in 1972, when I heard the gun go off, and those seven sprinters, minus one, bolted from the blocks and hurried down the track with a gold medal in mind. The gold medal I had imagined for myself.

I can't forget that horrifying feeling: was it my 100-meter quarterfinal heat that just went off, or was it the heat of an American teammate, Rey Robinson or Robert Taylor? For the three of us, it was sprinter's roulette, death by disqualification. We had arrived late, regardless, because of a scheduling foul-up. The three of us, plus our sprint coach, Stan Wright, hurried like madmen to the Olympic Stadium, knowing the four quarterfinal heats already were underway, but unsure of which heats we were assigned to and fearful that we were all too late.

Returning to Munich for the first time since 1972, I'm experiencing that same paralyzing feeling that froze the four of us like statues the exact moment when the starter's gun exploded in our ears. Robinson's entire Olympic involvement was tied to that 100. Taylor and I still had the 400-meter relay, though no absolutes existed in that event either. One faulty baton pass, and our whole Olympics could collapse.

My heart was racing in the tunnel in 1972, faster than my feet could run. Finally, the four of us nervously approached the starting line, which I'm doing again in March 2015 with that same trepidation, remembering the frantic conversation between Stan Wright and the 100-meter race official. "Which race was that one?" Stan asked. The official replied, "Eddie Hart's. Rey Robinson's race was run earlier."

There's no scripted way to react in a moment of crisis. When Rey heard the devastating news of his disqualification, he tossed his hat aside and said, "Wow!" The summation of an Olympic career: a one-word epitaph.

And my own goal of becoming the World's Fastest Human just went out the window or wherever lifetime goals go when they fly off and disappear. Ten years of training, gone—poof!—all because Stan Wright had been given the wrong 100 quarterfinal heat schedule.

Robert Taylor's heat hadn't gone off yet; it was next up. Robert only had time to take off his sweats, do some quick stretching, and settle down into the blocks. He qualified, when all three of us would have made it easily to the next round. It only took a time of 10.4 seconds, and Rey and I already had run 9.9 to tie the world record. We could have advanced into the semifinals in our bathrobes and slippers. If only I had gotten there two minutes earlier . . .

Stan Wright, naturally, felt excruciating pressure right away, for the sprinters were his main responsibility. He asked that same official, "Are there lanes open in a subsequent race, and could Rey and Eddie fill them?" His request was denied. Thus Rey and I were disqualified, a dreaded word in any sport. But Rey and I weren't disqualified for having done something illegal, like two false starts or running out of our lanes. We were disqualified, innocently, before the race had even begun. How could such a gross error in judgment happen?

The 100-meter schedule works this way at the Olympics: the first heat and the quarterfinals are run on one day, followed by the semis and the final the very next day. I was more than ready to compete for the gold. I had no worry of injury, and my body was loose. I had a great start in that first heat. At the ten-meter mark, I had a one- or two-meter lead. At the fifty, I was ahead by five meters. The field wasn't that great, so I increased my lead even after slowing down. I crossed the finish line comfortably in front in a time of 10.44 seconds. The time wasn't great, but I was running at only 80 percent. I was pleased, regardless.

After I finished that race, I thought to myself that this is what the Olympics is all about—the Olympic torch is lit, seventy thousand people are there, full capacity, the Olympic flag is flying with its five rings. And I'm about to write my name in the history books. I wanted that title, the World's Fastest Human, more than life itself. I hadn't trained diligently for a decade, giving up life's comforts, to come up short now. I wanted to place my name alongside those of Charley Paddock, Jesse Owens, Bob Hayes, Bobby Morrow, and Jimmy Hines, all great American Olympic 100-meter champions.

After I won, I looked into the stands, and it was incredible; people were cheering and looking back at me: one man focused in everyone's lenses. I had competed in five other Olympic cities—Helsinki, Antwerp, Paris, Stockholm, and Los Angeles—and the cheering and atmosphere in each of the five couldn't begin to touch Munich. I was on a natural high that morning, thinking of my parents and how proud I wanted to make them. I practically floated out of that stadium back to the Village.

Rey and Robert also qualified that morning. Then the four of us, including Stan Wright, returned to our lodgings. I didn't check out the schedule for the semis; that was Stan Wright's job, not mine. So I wasn't concerned about our race times. He told us three to get some rest, and we would get together in a few hours and go back to the stadium for the quarterfinals later that afternoon.

So I was back in my room, sitting on my bed, idly thumbing through a packet of information. That's when I noticed that the 100-meter time schedule in the packet was different from Stan Wright's schedule. But, I wasn't alarmed. I went down to Stan's room and said, "I'm sure you have the right schedule, but this schedule is different from the one you have." He wasn't alarmed either. He said, "Just to be on the safe side, go get Robert, and I'll go get Rey, and we'll head over to the stadium."

The Olympic Village in Munich was made up of huge apartment complexes, with all these different buildings. At this one gate, where we'd catch the bus to the track stadium, a television monitor was set up. You watched what was going on at various Olympic sites while waiting for your ride. At that particular time, the men's 100 was being shown. Someone said, "Is that a replay of the races that were run earlier?" And one of the ABC people said, "No, this is live. It's going on right this minute."

Now I was really alarmed. We found ourselves in a nightmare, and here it was the middle of the day. We jumped into an ABC studio van and made a hectic dash to the stadium, traveling the wrong way on a one-way street. A German policeman threw up his arms to stop us, but we went around him and kept going. I retained hope, even with time working against us, that my race hadn't gone off yet.

I tried not to panic. Barbara Ferrell, a USA gold medalist in the 400-meter women's relay in Mexico City and who competed in Munich in 1972, told me later that there was concern at the stadium when she and her American teammates didn't see me, Rey, or Robert warming up on the track before the 100 quarterfinals.

"We were all asking, 'Where are Eddie and the rest of the guys?'" she said.

From left: Robert Taylor, Larry Black, Eddie Hart, and Gerald Tinker show off their 400-meter-relay gold medals in Munich. (Photo courtesy of Eddie Hart)

"We then heard that you were still at the Village, or on your way to the stadium. We knew something was wrong. We were all a team. We worked hard, you guys worked hard, and you should be at the stadium. So what can we do to get you there?"

However, this anxious sprint to the stadium was too late for two of us sprinters. "We finally saw you running in, Eddie," Barbara continued. "And that was confusing. You had prepared all those years for this moment, so it was do or die."

It was do for just Robert, and die for Rey and me. But let me say this about sprinters: we're different from other track-and-field competitors. We come off as cool and collected, like everything is under control. Believe me, that image is only external. Internally, there's a hurricane of energy. Before getting to the track, your body starts to metamorphose; it's shunting blood away from your stomach into your muscles. That's how you get ready to compete, because you're preparing for the 100, a sprint, and you don't have time to blink. Nine-plus seconds, 10 seconds max, and it's over. Thus you must be excited to run the 100, which explains all the trash talk that goes on around the starting blocks. Right there is your internal hurricane fully unleashed.

After the four of us got to the starting line and discovered that Rey and I were disqualified, that hurricane turned into an earthquake. Our whole world crashed, and we felt those tremors rumbling inside our bodies. So how were we supposed to react? With the aftershock of disappointment, how would we go on with our lives?

Eddie Hart takes the baton from Gerald Tinker on the final leg of Olympic 400-meter-relay gold-medal win for the Americans. (Photo courtesy of Eddie Hart)

That's when I heard my father's voice: "Eddie, show perseverance. We didn't teach you to quit. There are no silver spoons in life. If you want something, you've got to go out and get it. Don't give up. For sure, son, you'll win the relay."

My father, T. J. Hart, was my chief advice-giver and my main source of inspiration. If I had even thought of giving up and coming home from Munich after the 100-meter mishap, my father wouldn't have approved. I am my parents' son, and they taught me that there are two ways to handle any situation. One is to react; the other is to respond.

Let me explain the difference. A reaction is an immediate reflex. If someone hits you, you hit him back. A response is more controlled, built out of preparation. So I was prepared for what happened to me in the 100 in Munich even before it happened. That's because of the life I've led, and the teachings of my parents: to respond, not react. My response to my disqualification was that I still had the 400-meter relay ahead of me.

Some people might not get that, but there still was a gold medal waiting for me and for relay teammates Larry Black, Robert Taylor, and Gerald Tinker. I wouldn't get to face Valery Borzov in the 100, where the two of us were co-favorites. But I would see him in the relay, once three baton exchanges took place. Track and field, basically, is an individual sport, but there exists one team aspect: the relays. Larry, Robert, and Gerald were counting on me. We had formed a brotherhood, and though I still was in considerable agony, I had to be there for them just as they had been there for me, emotionally, after my 100-meter misfortune.

I had to live with what happened to me in the 100, but I couldn't live with it for long because there were two heats and the final in the 400-meter relay coming right up. People asked me, "How could you flip a switch like that so quickly?" It wasn't so much a flip of the switch as it was the way I was brought up and how I was taught to deal with disappointment. And that was not to carry myself negatively in public.

"Eddie," my father told me, "we don't fall out crying. The Harts don't do that. That's not our way." I can't tell a lie, though. There was plenty of sorrow after I was disqualified. But it was strictly private. I showered for an hour and a half back at the Village, and I cried the whole time. It was painful, like I had lost a part of myself that I wouldn't get back.

But I still responded the way I'd been taught my whole life. My faith played a strong role in that, too, because I never place anything I do above my God, my savior. Regardless of what happens on this Earth, He's in control. My running that 100, it was something that just wasn't going to happen, but I'm not a fatalist. That's not how I think, and that's not how God works. Thanks to my

Eddie Hart with Robert Taylor
awaiting an interview with Howard
Cosell at the Munich Olympics.
(Photo courtesy of Eddie Hart)

parents, and my faith, I learned and grew from that disqualification. I really found out who I was and what I was about. I learned that I could take disappointment and that I could deal with it. And from that, I gained strength. You go forward or you don't. I went forward.

I walked away from that 100 ordeal believing I couldn't have handled it any better. I didn't say anything afterward that I regretted saying. I got on the bus with Rey, Robert, and Stan Wright following those 100 heats. A reporter recognized us and got on the same bus. He started to ask Robert and me a question, and Stan Wright went right after him. "Leave those guys alone," he said. "Don't ask them anything." So the reporter sat down. I kind of felt sorry for him. That was a big story, and he had an opportunity for a scoop, for what happened to us was only the biggest sports story in the world that day.

I did do interviews afterward. Howard Cosell interviewed Stan Wright and then Rey and me. As devastated as I was feeling, I kept it inside. I'm a Hart, after all. I just told Howard, "I'll get over this." I remember when the Kennedys, John and Robert, were assassinated. I think it was Ethel Kennedy, Robert's widow, who said, "The Kennedys don't cry in public." Jackie Kennedy held up the same way after her husband, the American president, was shot and killed. Even the Kennedy kids held up in public afterward.

When my brother's wife died, a nurse was so impressed with how well we Harts controlled our emotions. I told her, "We don't welcome death, but death is not a stranger." It's something we all have to deal with. Death is part of life.

But my Olympic "death" was temporary. My chance at rebirth was the relay. There was symbolism in a potential victory here: the finish line was the same for the 100 meters and the 400-meter relay. After Borzov won the 100 and the 200, we met, finally, on the anchor leg of the relay. I quickly set aside the 100 debacle because I'm not a spilt-milk, sour-grapes person. I'm not built that way. You have to live the rest of your life regardless of disappointment, Olympian or otherwise.

"Eddie," my dad advised me multiple times, "always do your best, regardless."

And that's what I did after being disqualified. The 400-meter relay soothed that hurt, thanks to Gerald Tinker, who on the third leg took sprinting to another level by building a five-meter lead. Some people said I increased that margin on the anchor leg. I don't know if that's true, but a five-meter lead with 100 meters to go usually is insurmountable. Borzov wasn't going to run me down, regardless, any more than I would have run him down if he had built the same lead, unless one of us pulled a muscle. Again, it's not how you react but how you respond, and I responded perfectly on that anchor leg. The World's Fastest Human is a higher achievement than winning an Olympic relay, but a

Eddie Hart hits the tape in world-record time as the United States wins the 400-meter relay in Munich, with Valery Borzov hidden behind him. (Photo courtesy of Eddie Hart)

world-record relay time of 38.19 seconds isn't too shabby. The best response: I can always say that I'm an Olympic gold medalist.

Coming back to the Olympic Stadium in 2015 engendered a feeling of sadness, because half that relay team is gone. Larry Black had an aneurism and Robert Taylor a heart attack, and they died in their fifties. Coming to Munich was like attending their funerals, which I couldn't make. Then, a couple of years ago, Gerald Tinker had a stroke. I was really nervous, but he bounced back. Eddie Jr. and I went to his sixtieth birthday party. Life to death, there's an eternal bond among the four of us; we're in one another's hearts forever.

Returning to Munich after forty-three years, and coming here with my son, it has been really special. I'm enjoying it more than I thought I would. In all likelihood, I won't see this stadium ever again. But I have other good memories from 1972, like standing outside the Olympic Stadium and being interviewed by *Spartacus* actor Kirk Douglas just after those Games had begun—the Germans set that up. Then after that interview, I stood in line by a bratwurst cart. And there was Kirk Douglas, buying a couple of brats. He said, "Here, you don't have to stand in line, take one of these." I said, "No, you bought them for yourself." He insisted, so I accepted his offer. Imagine, "Spartacus" just gave me one of his hot dogs. Kirk was down to earth, but I was surprised by his stature; he was smaller than he appears on the movie screen. But how good does it get—one gladiator interviewing another?

My intent in Munich in 1972 was to present a friendly image. I wasn't going to be an ugly American, putting on airs, treating people rudely. That's not me anyway. I enjoy meeting people, and I don't mind signing autographs. Some athletes insist, "I don't do autographs." Why be a stuck-up athlete or give that impression? Besides, I wanted to enjoy the total Olympic experience, beyond the competition, and that meant mingling with strangers. I'm not a recluse.

But in coming back to Munich in a new century, I was still impressed by the Olympic Stadium, which is an art piece, an architectural marvel with its spider's web covering. I haven't seen this kind of architecture anywhere else. So it wasn't at all uncomfortable, coming back after four decades. And the visit made for a lot of self-reflection. I remembered that Munich hadn't much time to build its Olympic facilities. Some other Olympic cities have failed in that regard; the stadium in Greece was a real fiasco. Not Munich. It all came together rather nicely in Munich.

What's sad, though, is that the Olympic Stadium is no longer a sport venue. Its former soccer tenants, Bayern Munich and 1860, now play at a newer stadium in Munich. Alexander Bock, a dental student who was our stadium tour guide, told me the old facility is used, occasionally, for music concerts and conventions.

Where Olympians and other great athletes excelled, rock bands like U2 now appear. So do the Jehovah's Witnesses, with their yearly convention. But whenever there's a World Cup, people still come to the Olympic Stadium to watch soccer on large TV screens. I guess it's a way to stay in touch with the past.

"The stadium's still beautiful to look at with its ionic architecture," Bock said. "You can see the flag poles where the Olympic flags once hung. You can see the cauldron, though it's very tiny, where the Olympic flame burned. The stadium's seats are colored green, the same color of the original seats, which lacked the backrests of the current seats. Only it's a different shade of green on these seats, resembling the leaves and grass you would see looking through a window. That's the concept.

"The Jewish community and the International Olympic Committee wanted to build an Israeli memorial on a hill outside the stadium. That would have meant cutting out part of the hill, so the people in the village decided that they didn't want the monument. There are two other monuments relating to the 1972 Olympics: one is on the front of Building 31, where the massacre occurred, and the second is at the Olympic Park, with the names of the slain Israelis, written in Hebrew, along with that of the German police officer who was killed.

"So," said Bock, "they looked for another hill, which was the Student Hill. The students, like myself, didn't want it there because, 'How can we party looking at that?' But the real reason why there is no monument at the original site was that kids use that hill for snowboarding and gliding in the winter, which would have meant dealing with twenty-four-hour security, a bad feeling for the neighborhood.

"I wrote a letter to the local newspaper, saying that if these same people had a chance to vote for the Olympics coming to Munich [in 1972], it never would have happened. They're against everything now. Germany always has had a problem with being reminded about its history. But the monument should be built; it's just a matter of finding the right hill."

Finally, after forty-four years, a Place of Mourning monument to honor those eleven slain Israelis was dedicated on the Munich Olympic site in August 2016. A ceremony was held, presided over by International Oympic Committee president Thomas Bach, who said that a mourning site for the eleven Israelis will be set up at every Olympic Games in the future. Attending the Munich ceremony were two widows of the Israeli athletes, Ilano Romano and Anke Spitzer.

Bock was a wonderful tour guide. Before we met up, though, I saw my name and those of my relay teammates etched in stone outside the stadium, along with those of other 1972 track gold medalists. It was a nice surprise, seeing my name on a wall in Munich, Germany, which is a long way from Pittsburg, California. That's pretty cool. Klaus Wolfermann, who won the *speerwerfen,* or javelin throw, for West Germany in '72, has his name on that same wall. He remains a national hero.

Sugar Ray Seales's name also is on the wall; he was the only American boxer to win a gold medal in 1972. The two of us met up in New York on *The Dick Cavett Show* a couple of months after those Olympics. Cavett asked me to bring my gold medal, so I did. He was very respectful, a really intelligent guy, sharp-minded and quick-witted. Once again, I didn't blame Stan Wright or any other individual. I had no proof then of who was at fault. I was able to bring Gwen with me to New York.

Borzov's name is on that wall twice, for the 100 and 200. I didn't have much contact with him in Munich. There was the obvious language barrier, though we shook hands after the U.S. took the 400-meter relay. He congratulated me on winning—our first-ever interaction—and I congratulated him on winning the 100 and 200. He took the complement graciously; we did this through hand gestures. I held up one finger, then two fingers, to signify the 100 and 200.

But in 1972 Borzov was quoted as saying that he would have won the 100 even if Rey and I had been entered in the final. Friends asked me if his statement made me mad. My answer is always the same: no. What else is he going to say? I don't begrudge him saying that. Look, if he hadn't made the 100 final for some reason, and I'd won the race, I wouldn't have said I dodged a bullet. I'd have said that his absence wouldn't have made a difference. You can't be a champion unless you believe you can be a champion, and then you should act like a champion.

At the 100 final, I showed up to watch, seated nineteen, twenty rows up, just behind the finish line. I came in support of Robert Taylor, but Robert had to have mixed emotions, knowing that both Rey and I had been disqualified. He was carrying a lot of weight, which I think affected him negatively. When you watched him in that race, that wasn't Robert Taylor. He didn't look like he was putting up an effort. He got the silver medal but thought he could have run faster. That's just me talking, but he never seemed to struggle or fight. He got into second behind Borzov at the start and just stayed there.

People have said, "How could you even watch that race?" It didn't bother me. I watched other races that day—the 400-meter run and the 120-meter high hurdles—so it wasn't such a big deal. Hurdler Tom Hill was my room-mate. Yes, I was supposed to be in that 100 final, but there was nothing strange about me watching it. This was the Olympics after all, so there wasn't anything wrong with me being an athlete and a spectator. I handled it the same way my parents would have wanted me to handle it, with dignity.

As soon as the 100 final ended, I left the stadium and walked back to the Olympic Village by myself. I just needed to be alone, to think it all through again. But I must be truthful: our disqualifications were a big story for the moment, but it's not what those Olympic Games are remembered for, back then and forever, really. Munich 1972 always will be remembered for what happened at Building 31.

But I'd like to say one more thing about our disqualifications. Stan Wright pleaded with officials to place us in another heat and was turned down. Fast-forward to Rio in 2016. Three swimmers were driven by mistake to the Olympic Stadium instead of the Olympic Aquatics Stadium, forty minutes away. The bus driver then turned around and got them to the swim facility nearly an hour later. Two medal ceremonies were moved up to allow them to compete in the 100-meter freestyle semifinals. Fran Halsall of Great Britain and Aliaksandra Herasimenia of Belarus qualified, but not Jeannette Ottesen of Denmark. Then in the finals, Herasimenia won a bronze medal, and Halsall finished fourth.

Rey Robinson and I would have appreciated the same courtesy, though I'm happy for those swimmers and other Olympians who have been ill-treated through no fault of their own but were given the second chance that was denied us in 1972.

A MASSACRE MADE EASY

A memorial is affixed next to the front door of Building 31, a symbolic tombstone at an Olympic graveyard. This tombstone bears eleven names: David Berger, Seew Friedman, Josef Gutfreund, Elieser Halfin, Josef Romano, Amizur Shapira, Kehat Shorr, Mark Slavin, Andre Spitzer, Jaakow Springer, and Mosche Weinberger (Weinberg).

This is Connollystrasse 31, where eleven Israeli athletes and coaches lived and died during the 1972 Olympic Games. The street is named after an American athlete, James B. Connolly, the first Olympic champion (triple jump) of the modern Olympics, in Athens, in 1896, and the first Olympic champion since the boxer Barasdates of Armenia in 369 A.D. But the memorial at Connollystrasse 31 also marks a mourning period that knows no end.

I'm reading those eleven names and reminding myself of the dreadfulness of September 5, 1972. I was close by when it happened, in the Olympic Village, watching the whole thing unfold on television. I remember that they had the hostages held inside Building 31, and every once in a while, an Arab came out of the building with a hood covering his face, making his demands. Then they'd bring an Israeli out, hit him, and drag him back inside.

And this was the "Cheerful Games." What got to me right away was that these Israelis had wives and children back home. That's what made it tragic to me, because family is so important to me. They don't award gold medals to widows.

Though life was taken from those eleven Israelis, life continues at Connollystrasse 31. The names of boarders are listed above the memorial: Hengl, Guttler, Rober-Roussos, Palermo, Wanzat-Fang, Fuchsreiter, Krumhoff, Jir-

The names of the Israelis killed in the 1972 Olympic massacre are listed in front of their lodgings at Connollystrasse 31. (Photo by Irmina Richter)

jahn, Make, Moser-Farbak, and Max Planck Institute. I studied their names and tried to imagine what it must be like hearing ghosts in the hallway.

I only really knew much about the Munich massacre after I had returned home. That slaughter happened between my 100-meter disqualification and the 400-meter relay. My thoughts were on my primary mission in Munich—to win gold. I still had three relay team members depending on me; I couldn't let them down. So I remained focused during the chaos.

And I was still learning about that Olympic tragedy forty-three years later, even with all that's been written and filmed about Munich 1972 in the intervening years. But I didn't fully comprehend what actually occurred inside Connollystrasse 31 until, in 2015, Dave Newhouse contacted two Israelis who had a close-up view of that gross act of violence by the Arab terrorists.

Shaul Ladany was a race walker on that Israeli team. Shlomo Levy was an interpreter for the Israelis. Both men lived inside Connollystrasse 31. From California, Newhouse phoned them in Israel.

Ladany has experienced two historic tragedies in his lifetime: He is a survivor of the Holocaust and an Olympic massacre. "No, I don't have nightmares about these events," he said from his home in Jerusalem. "I sleep properly, but I do remember those things. I spent six months at the Bergen-Belsen concentration camp. I can't forget the stench or the hunger of that camp. Those who went through it, as I went through it, will understand that no matter how much food I put on my plate now, I never leave anything on my plate.

"Even today, my family members want to know about the Holocaust. They always want to learn, even though other family members perished between 1942 and 1944. My family survived, and I just came back from a week in Germany, where I was invited to attend the seventieth anniversary of the liberation of the Bergen-Belsen concentration camp. I was there with my oldest granddaughter, who is seventeen, and it affected her, too. You see that awful scenery, you feel that hunger, and still, somehow, you are affected, even if you weren't there.

"It's the same thing," he added, "with the Olympic Games in Munich. The media has covered those Olympics so extensively that children who weren't even born in 1972 know so much about those Olympic Games. I can say that I wasn't the only survivor of the Holocaust and that I wasn't the only survivor of those 1972 Games. Six of us who escaped the terrorists lived in the same No. 2 apartment. There were two more who escaped, which makes it eight. Unfortunately, eleven didn't make it."

Just like during the Holocaust, Jews were being killed again on German soil.

Ladany participated in two Olympics, 1968 and 1972. He also set a 50-kilometer race-walking record and won the 100-kilometer race-walking world championship, making him the walking man of Israel. He earned a PhD in business administration in the United States at Columbia University before becoming a professor of industrial engineering at Ben-Gurion University in Israel.

"Some of these stories about what happened in Munich made me angry," he said. "Like reporting that I jumped from a second-story window or balcony to escape the terrorists. They made that up. I sued one magazine, and I was able to get Paramount Pictures to remove one scene from a movie. Then a year ago, a writer told me that even though he didn't have proof, still he would write that I jumped from that second-story window. Let me tell you what really happened.

"The person who told me about the terrorists' break-in was my teammate from four years before, in the 1968 Olympics in Mexico City. He was a joker, so when he told me about the terrorists, I thought he was joking. But it was too serious a thing to be a joke. I saw my roommate getting dressed, so I assumed something was happening. What I did was stand at the door and look out the entrance of my building. That's when I recognized how dangerous the situation was.

"I saw four security guards talking to someone who said, 'Jews are not human.' But I had no fear; I'm not a coward. I closed the door and went into the bathroom to urinate. Then I found my teammates fully dressed by the staircase. I asked them what had happened, and they told me that the coach [Weinberg] had been killed five minutes earlier. Then I saw Mooney's [Weinberg's] blood on the floor."

That pool of blood soon would become a bloodbath.

Shlomo Levy, who was born in Morocco, was studying in Stuttgart, Germany, when he was hired as a translator for both the Israeli and Cameroon Olympic teams. Fluent in three languages—Hebrew, French, German—and with a good grasp of English, he was given a three-month assignment during the Munich Games.

"I never could have believed that something like this could happen in an international games like the Olympics," he said of the carnage. "It was a shock, unbelievable. But I was able to put a mattress on the ground on the fourth floor and film—everything!"

Levy explained that he was initially assigned to stay in a Munich apartment away from the Olympic site. After he greeted the Israeli team at the Munich airport, the team's chief, Shmuel Lalkin, invited Levy to live at their six-apartment location at Connollystrasse 31. He accepted the offer.

"That's so I could be with the team day and night, which meant I wouldn't have to go back and forth from Munich," he said. "The coaches and athletes lived in apartments 1 through 3, the team doctor was in apartment 4, the chief, Lalkin, was in the fifth apartment, and I was in the sixth. After two days, Lalkin asked me if I wanted to move into apartment 1. Though it was his decision, I didn't move, and I was lucky I didn't, because everyone in apartment 1 was killed."

The evening before that fateful September 5 morning, the Israeli team was invited to a cocktail party hosted by Munich's Jewish community. The team returned to Connollystrasse 31 at 2 A.M., ready for sleep—a sleep that would be interrupted by murder. At 7:10 A.M., a ringing telephone in Levy's room awoke him.

"I got a call from a radio station in Israel asking if I was Jewish and did I live in Building 31. I said yes to both questions, and then they asked me to tell them what had just happened there. I was very groggy, having just been sleeping, and I told them that I know nothing. But I told them I would ask the chief, who was staying right next to me. I pushed the button to his apartment, but he didn't answer after thirty seconds, and I decided he was sleeping very well.

"I could see that the street in front of our building was empty, so I didn't think anything had happened. I went back to my apartment and told the radio station that everything was quiet, everything was OK, and I went back to sleep.

Ten minutes later, a call came from a Tel Aviv newspaper. I was asked again if I was an Israeli and living in Connollystrasse 31. I told them, 'I don't know what you want,' but I went outside for another look.

"This time," Levy said, "I saw a man in a white suit talking with a police-woman. I didn't know the man was a chief of the terrorists. He saw me at the window of the Israeli team doctor's room. The doctor told me to go back to my apartment, where I called the police in Munich, as I now believed something had happened, and I asked them if they knew anything. They said, 'We know some of your sportsmen have been captured, but stay in your apartment and don't go outside.'

"Then I took a picture of the man in the white suit from my window. He didn't have a mask or a hood, just some black coloring on his face. You see face paint at the Olympics, so it didn't look like anything different. I learned later that he wanted to talk to a policewoman, because talking to a policeman would be more difficult.

"By this time, the whole world knew what was happening with the Israeli team, more than I did. I just knew that I couldn't stay in my apartment and that I wanted to take pictures of what was happening. I was told it would be dangerous to change locations, but the street was empty, and I got away. The East German delegation let me inside their building across the way from the Israeli building. I forgot to take my camera, and the East Germans took me to a camera shop in the Olympic Village, to buy a camera with a telescopic lens. Then I started filming what was going on at Building 31."

Shaul Ladany was one of six Israelis living in apartment 2. All six escaped by walking out the sliding door of one bedroom. Another escaped from apartment 3, and a coach escaped from apartment 1. "But she was in shock," recalled Ladany, "and went into hiding for about two hours. But that made it eight who escaped.

"After we left the building, we went to police headquarters and told them they should check with collaborators who might be in the basement, because some of the Israelis were taken down there. By this time, the police already were fully aware of the break-in. After the police interrogation, I met some of my American race-walker friends. They took me to their place, and I was able to shave. Then I met with the American track-and-field coach, Bill Bowerman, whom I had first met at South Lake Tahoe, where the American Olympians trained."

Bowerman phoned the U.S. consulate in Munich. Armed military moved in on the armed and hooded terrorists, who were positioned on balconies. But

Shaul Ladany was an Israeli race walker who sneaked out of Connollystrasse 31 in 1972, saving his life. (Courtesy of Shaul Ladany)

the military kept a safe distance as the terrorists insisted that their demands be met or they would execute the hostages. The military backed off and the terrorists achieved their demands: A bus to transport the eight terrorists and their nine blindfolded and bound hostages to a helicopter pad. There they would board two helicopters to transport the seventeen passengers to the Fürstenfeldbruck airport, where, unbeknownst to the terrorists, five German police sharpshooters, or snipers, waited on a rooftop.

The snipers killed two terrorists standing by a helicopter. Bedlam ensued as the terrorists then decided to kill the hostages. The Arabs threw a fragmentation grenade under one helicopter, and its explosion turned the copter into an inferno, taking the lives of hostages Friedman, Halfin, Springer, and Berger. Another terrorist jumped into the other helicopter, and shot and killed Gutfreund, Shorr, Slavin, Shapira, and Spitzer, all of them manacled and defenseless.

Three terrorists were captured. But later that month, a Lufthansa Boeing 727 en route from Damascus, Syria, to Frankfurt was hijacked by two Black September Palestinians after the plane left a stopover in Beirut. Their demands were to free the three Arab terrorists from the Munich Olympics or they would blow up the plane and its thirteen occupants. Upon the instructions of German chancellor Willy Brandt, the three Arabs were released and flown to Libya, where they lived out their lives as heroes, without ever having been brought to justice.

"Yes, that does sicken me," said Ladany. "Going to the Munich Olympic Games, I was totally aware that there always is danger to any Israeli in any official capacity when he goes abroad. But what happened in Munich, though it was the most tragic Olympics ever, didn't affect me emotionally, because I participated in wars in Israel, like the Six-Day War. It isn't because I like wars, but because I volunteered to defend my country."

Having been to war and seeing comrades die, then, Shaul Ladany doesn't overreact in recalling the Olympic massacre.

"I was fortunate that I had no previous relationship with my teammates who were killed," he said. "The first time I met them was when I was introduced with them as members of the Olympic team. The only one I even knew was the track-and-field coach, Shapiro, but he was not my coach, and he never dealt with me. That's fortunate for me, emotionally, because what happened hasn't been haunting."

Shlomo Levy treats that blackest of black Septembers similarly. "Look, it touches me," he said. "That's because every year I go to the anniversary of that massacre, which is held in Tel Aviv. I left Munich a year and a half after what happened in 1972. I was a journalist who worked for Israeli television as a cam-

Shlomo Levy, an interpreter for the 1972
Israeli team, managed to escape from the
terrorists. (Photo courtesy of Shlomo Levy)

eraman and editor. Very much has happened to me in my work. I worked in one war in Israel, and then in 1982, I spent six months in Beirut in the Lebanon War. There was another war after that, so I've lived my life in danger." Munich was the beginning, but not the end of terrorism as it's recognized today.

There was a one-day delay of the 1972 Olympics as a memorial was held inside the Olympic Stadium to honor the eleven dead Israelis. The Games then proceeded, against the objections of Israeli president Golda Meir, who wanted to cancel the remainder of that Olympiad. Avery Brundage, president of the International Olympic Committee, insisted otherwise, and the Munich Games continued.

"For two, three days, I was very sad; it seemed like a dream," said Levy. "I stayed with the Cameroon team later on. But I knew what was going on: the German government wanted the Games to go on. And I believed they must go on, too."

"Golda Meir wanted them canceled," said Ladany, "but she was being emotional, and she wasn't an athlete. Should the athletes at those Olympic Games be punished because some terrorists killed some of our people? What of the people who have trained for years to show how good they are—should they be punished?"

Ladany and Levy are now retired, but they're still active. Ladany participated in the 2015 Jerusalem Marathon—"walking slowly, slowly"—at age seventy-nine.

The Olympic Stadium in Munich is no longer used for athletic competition. (Photo courtesy of Irmina Richter)

He's a professor emeritus, voluntarily supervising graduate work. In 2014, he wrote an academic paper titled "Optimum Sailing Policy," which was accepted for publication. Lcvy, at seventy-three, works as a translator in a judicial court, speaking in French and German. He lives on an Israeli kibbutz.

I agree with both men that the 1972 Olympics should have continued. People were using it for their own political ends, which isn't what the Olympics are supposed to be—nations setting aside political agendas and uniting as one people for two weeks. If you canceled those Munich Olympics, how would you ever be able to finish another Olympics, once that precedent had been set? Munich was a terrible tragedy, followed by a sorrowful memorial, but continuing those Games was important, not just for the athletes but for mankind in general. You can't give in to terrorists and let them dictate.

Even so, athletes in Munich were looking over their shoulders following the massacre. Some, I heard, were skittish about reentering the field of competition, picturing snipers everywhere. I'm sure there was sleep deprivation, even with security guards surrounding the Olympic Village, which then looked like a militarized zone. The Cheerful Games had devolved into the Fearful Games.

What made the massacre easy was the earlier lack of security at the Olympic Village. Virtually anybody could pass in and out of the entrance without being

Irmina Richter lives in an apartment in the Olympic Village complex that housed Eddie Hart during the 1972 Munich Games. (Photo courtesy of Irmina Richter)

challenged. I remember Olympians bringing their friends into the Village, and even into their rooms, friends who had nothing to do with the Olympics. You didn't need any kind of badge; it was a free-for-all. It was much harder to get that kind of unlimited access at other non-Olympic track meets.

With the politicized atmosphere then in the world, you would have thought the Germans would have taken some kind of precaution. Even in the Village, you had athletes from countries in serious conflict, like East and West Germany. The Germans had tried hard to put on a different face after the 1936 Olympics in Berlin, and so a police presence wasn't initially a priority. It was a huge mistake; lives were lost unnecessarily.

After visiting Connollystrasse 31, I headed for another street, Nadistrasse, to try to find where I lived during those Games. And I was having difficulty locating my residence when I bumped into Irmina Richter, who lived in the neighborhood. She remembered Munich in 1972.

"I've lived in this building since 1996," she said, "but I was twelve when the Olympics were in Munich. We lived in a small village about sixty-three kilometers south of here. My parents still live there. I only watched those Olympics on television, and when those Israeli sportsmen were killed, I was on a trip with my parents at Lake Constance. After the tragedy, the newspapers and TV were full of information. And the following years, there still were stories about the tragedy.

"And now they want to build another memorial at the Olympic Park, so not to forget the memory of 1972, but to build it on a hill, which we don't want. The memory's still here—isn't that enough? After I grew up, I worked in a bookstore here in Munich. I'm mostly retired now because I have a kidney problem. When I met you, I was coming from dialysis. It's such a surprise to meet a gold medalist."

With Irmina's help, we were able to contact Shlomo Levy in Israel. And through Mort Landsberg, a friend of Newhouse's, Dave was able to have a conversation with Shaul Ladany, because of Landsberg's relationship with Tom Dooley. Landsberg, Ladany, and Dooley all are race walkers, but only Ladany and Dooley are Olympians, both having competed at Mexico City in 1968 and Munich in 1972.

Dooley, an American, finished seventeenth in Mexico City and fifteenth in Munich in the 20-kilometer walk. Ladany finished twenty-fourth in Mexico City and nineteenth at Munich in the 50-kilometer walk. "I met Shaul at the Olympic Development Trials in 1968, when he came up to train at South Lake Tahoe," said Dooley, a San Jose State University graduate who was sixty-nine when interviewed in 2015. "Since race walkers are such a small group, we've kept in touch with each other.

"In Munich, on the day of the massacre, all the race walkers were the guests of a German race-walking champion; it was a day trip to a Munich suburb. We came back just as the helicopters were leaving for the airport. Because we were in the company of West Germans, we had no trouble getting back into the Village. That evening, we were glued to the TV, learning about the terrorists' negotiation strategy. Then there was the memorial the next day, where everyone dressed up in their Olympic parade uniforms and paid homage to the slain Olympians.

"I wanted the Games to continue, thinking that you shouldn't allow terrorism to interfere with an event that would bring athletes and cultures together. If you permit a small group to disrupt things of that importance, it will be self-fulfilling, and those things will continue to happen. Canceling the Olympics penalizes athletes who've trained for years. Look at the 1980 Olympics in Moscow, which President Jimmy Carter boycotted. The athletes get hurt the most."

All of the athletes who gathered in Munich for the Opening Ceremonies of the 1972 Summer Games, from countries scattered around the globe, couldn't have imagined that they would become a part of history, tragically as well as triumphantly.

"That would come out later," noted Dooley. "There are always back stories to an Olympic Games, some interesting, some banal. But, personally, I wasn't worried about my life being threatened when I was in Munich during the massacre. Not at all.

"I did feel horrible for Eddie Hart and Rey Robinson, and the manner in which they were disqualified. For I know the amount of sacrifice that it takes just to get to an Olympic Games. But the 1972 Olympics seemed to have so many of these stories, that by themselves, they made it bad karma, a tragic situation. Even taking the massacre out of the equation, all the other stories made it the perfect storm."

DEATH LIGHTS UP
THE SKY

As horrible as those Munich slayings were, my father witnessed something even more horrific: the bomb explosions that took the lives of 320 men, two-thirds of them African Americans, at a Port Chicago, California, naval munitions depot, during World War II. So disturbing was that explosion, it took my father another fifty years before he could even discuss it with his children.

"I was on detail to pick up the body parts of those men," he told me, finally. "I picked up a foot here, a hand there, a leg here, a head there. It was this other man and me, with a sheet between us, reaching down and picking a body part. Then the other man fell out; he couldn't take it anymore. So I kept doing it myself."

You'd have to know my father, T. J. Hart, to understand how he could even endure such a grueling detail. He was the type of person who put one foot in front of the other. He didn't deal with things in terms of how it affected him. His attitude was that if it's the right way to act, then it's the right thing to do. He once told me, "I would never want to be a mortician, but if I had to do it, I would do it."

So my father picked up those dismembered men, because somebody had to do it, and that's what he was instructed to do. At that time, a black man without an education, serving in the Navy, did basic labor. My father, with a third-grade education, did janitorial work. He also performed guard duty—and he picked up body parts. He had some other responsibilities down at the docks, though, fortunately, not loading munitions.

But my father remembered that explosion—June 17, 1944, 10:19 P.M.—like it happened yesterday.

"I was about to get into bed," he told me. "I was on my knees praying when that explosion lit up the sky. Though it was night, it felt like daytime and the sun was up. I thought the world was going to end. There were three blasts—Boom! Boom! Boom!—that blew off half the barracks I was living in, one hundred meters from the explosion. I wasn't injured, but that's the sickest I've ever been in my life without having pain in my body.

"Two ships went up in flames. Big pieces of one ship were found way up in the hills. A barrack's mate was praying by his own bed when those blasts happened. A beam came down and split open his head. He was OK, but he used to tease me about praying. With his head split, I told him, 'Now you're praying to *my* God.' Women came to the base crying, looking for their husbands. They came from everywhere."

My father, first off, was a strong Christian, same as my mother. She was a Sunday school teacher, while my father was a steward for fifty years at the church we attended. Our family was church-oriented. But that explosion can

T. J. Hart and son Eddie—stalwart men, family men. (Photo courtesy of Eddie Hart)

teach you a whole different kind of religion, especially when you're black in the white man's Navy.

"The base was nothing but black," my father said. "Four or five companies, all black." The black sailors at Port Chicago basically were stevedores, serving their country during wartime, but with little chance of making rank. The surviving black sailors were ordered to report to the docks to load more bombs being sent off to the Pacific. The majority of those men refused the order, and they were charged with mutiny.

What followed was the largest mass mutiny trial in U.S. naval history, followed by the imprisonment of those sailors who refused to load munitions. My father was neither requested to load munitions nor was he locked up in the Navy prison, the brig. "If you refused an order in the military, you could be shot," he told me. "They put [the mutineers] in prison instead. But I heard it was pretty rough in there."

Some mutineers remained in the brig until after the war, when historic progress was made, with the desegregation of the Navy. But that didn't bring back the lives of those mostly black men who loaded munitions at a pace that was too quick to be safe, and all because their white commanding officers were pushing quotas. Finally, it was made public that the deceased hadn't been properly trained to load munitions. Future U.S. Supreme Court justice Thurgood Marshall, then chief counsel for National Association for the Advancement of Colored People, was called in to investigate the mistreatment of those sailors.

"Nobody knows what happened in the explosion," my father said. "Those that knew died."

Since President Clinton pardoned those men who refused to load munitions at Port Chicago, in the 1990s, an annual memorial takes place at the site of the explosion. My father was asked to participate, and he agreed. That's when I learned, at last, of his involvement at Port Chicago.

"I was in the Navy two years, two months, three hours," he said of his service time. "I made $15 every two weeks. After my Navy duties were over for the day, I worked for Shell Oil until midnight, making $7.50 a shift. Then after the Navy, I went to work full time for Shell Oil. I stayed there forty years, from 1946 to 1986."

Like I said, you had to understand my father. Not being educated, he had to deal with adversity, having grown up in a racist environment in the Deep South. He was a sharecropper, just like his father, and his grandfather was a slave. Then my father was asked to join Uncle Sam's navy, where many blacks felt like slaves.

"When I joined up," he said, "I had to take this oath: would I pour my blood into a stream for the U.S. Navy?' I was about to say, 'Hell, no.' I was raised in

T. J. and Florence Hart with their six children. *Back, from left:* T. J., David, John, and Alfred; *middle:* Evelyn and Eddie; and *front:* Florence and Catherine. (Photo courtesy of Eddie Hart)

Alabama, where there was racism, and where I had to sit at the back of the restaurant and in the back of the bus. But I said, 'Yes' to that oath. I was sent to Great Lakes Naval Air Station in Illinois, where it was sixteen degrees below. I darn near froze to death."

In the South, my father kept his eyes low and his wits about him, or he might have been killed. There was no getting around southern racism in those times. So whatever he believed his duty was in the Navy, he did it, even though Port Chicago sometimes brought unfounded accusations, even in the barracks. "I was praying one night, and somebody accused me of something," my father said. "I took out three bunks with him, but don't be calling me no names."

You couldn't find a tougher man than my father, or a better man. He came from a humble background, so he wasn't high-minded. Regardless of his education level, there wasn't a more responsible man than my father. He became the best crane operator at Shell Oil, and that's not just me bragging on him.

The way it worked at our house, my father would bring home his paycheck. My mother would cash it, then she would buy groceries and pay bills the same day. My mother, Florence Viola Hart, was very humble as well. She went through the eleventh grade, so she could read. You'd find her awake at three or four in the morning reading the Bible. She was a strong woman. She dealt with things

Eddie Hart met his wife, Gwen, in high school, where she wowed him with her stage presence. (Photo courtesy of Eddie Hart)

that came at her without getting angry very often. I've seen situations where people go off, but my mom would respond in her own quiet way.

Even though there were six of us children, we didn't require a lot of discipline, because we didn't get into trouble. Oh, I got spanked a couple of times, but I kept my nose clean, and so did my brothers and sisters. We had so much respect for our parents that we didn't want to show disrespect for them. They were such good role models. My father showed me how to be a good husband and father.

"Eddie, a man is not a man," my father said, "if he doesn't take care of his family."

It wasn't like that with every family I knew as a kid. This one kid would take a kitchen pot alongside his father's head. That type of behavior was foreign to me, because my father was always there. My parents had a couple of disagreements in my lifetime, but my father never hit my mother. They loved each other, the same way I love Gwen and my children. The apple truly doesn't fall too far from the tree.

Speaking of trees, my parents certainly had interesting family trees. One important trait I learned from my father, as I've already stated, was to be responsive, not reactive. His example enabled me to handle my Munich disqualification in the same responsive way that he handled picking up those body parts in Port Chicago.

My father grew up in Alabama, one of eleven children. He left home as a teenager after telling his father that he didn't want to be a farmer the rest of his life. He took off for Florida, hoping for a better life. Once there, he found himself back on a farm, working even harder than he had in Alabama, and for fifty cents a day, cheap wages even for those times. My father told the man who owned the farm the same thing he had told his father—farming wasn't for him. That angered the owner, who notified the draft board that my father, a teenager, was eligible for military service. A navy recruiter came to the farm, and the next thing my father knew, he was off to California, working for Uncle Sam. My uncle J.D. followed his brother to California, and there they stayed for the rest of their lives. Uncle J.D. worked thirty-seven years on a Navy base. For my father, it was the best move yet, because farm life was gone forever, and in California, he met my mother.

"I married her," he said, laughing, "and she tied me down." For sixty-five years.

My mother was born in Louisiana but spent most of her youth in Los Angeles, moving there at age two with her pregnant mother and grandmother. Soon after the family arrived, sister June was born. My mother did domestic work as she grew up, cleaning other people's houses to help her family financially. Five years after June's birth, another sister, Pat, was born. Twin boys, Bobby and Billy, joined the growing family later on, making it five children to feed. But the men in my grandmother's life didn't treat her with much kindness; after they got her pregnant, they'd leave without giving any child support. She was working so hard, attempting to hold everything together, that she didn't have much time to nurture my mother and her siblings. Finally, it became too great a burden, and so the five children lived in a shelter for a while before being shunted off to various family members who lived in the area.

That's why my mother promised herself that if she ever had her own family, she would have a stable home life, with her children well provided and cared for. She didn't talk much about her growing up years, and I could understand why, with her sleeping in an open room with total strangers, not knowing whom to trust, and even lacking a place for her belongings. This transient life, which led to day-to-day uncertainty, at times required found money to keep going, like this one check that arrived unexpectedly just in time to keep her family from being evicted.

Though the family often was scattered, my mother managed to stay with her mother and take care of the twins. By the time she was a teenager, the twins were old enough to manage for themselves. So she moved to Port Chicago one summer to live with her aunt Jackie. That's where she met my father, who then called my mother's mother to inform her that her daughter wasn't coming back to Los Angeles. And that was that.

I learned an important lesson as a child: my parents only said something to me once, so I had better pay close attention. If I didn't get it, I might get it, if you know what I mean. It was the same way with Uncle J.D. When he spoke, it was the equivalent of my father speaking. These were black men from the South, who believed the most important thing they had going for them was their own word. So listen up, because their word was their bond. Their commitment was equally important; I can't ever remember their arriving late to work or for an appointment.

Both my dad and uncle, while lacking formal education—my dad couldn't read or write—had PhDs in common sense. I always thought Uncle J.D. had the makings of a good student, perhaps college material, if only he would have had the opportunity. Growing up as a black man in the South in the 1930s with little schooling, he wasn't able to express himself intelligently. But he was an intelligent man; he thought quickly and processed information wisely. He just lacked the vocabulary and the opportunity. If he had been given the chance, I truly believe, he would have been one of the great minds of his day.

Denied that possibility, Uncle J.D. stayed on the quiet side. Serious in nature, he didn't like anyone making fun of him, though he didn't mind a good laugh now and then. His MO, though, was that if you had something to say to him, just say it so he could deal with it. That straightforwardness made him a man you could go to for advice and counsel. The only oddity about Uncle J.D. was that he liked working in hot weather with his top collar buttoned, even when it was 100 degrees. And his occupation happened to be pouring cement and laying bricks, which he was good at, even buttoned up.

My father and uncle worked hard all their lives, though T. J. Hart loosened his collar if necessary. Both men had impressive physiques and kept themselves in shape. They each looked good in a suit and tie at church on Sundays. Uncle J.D. and my Aunt Cheetah—I'm not sure why they called her Cheetah; her given name was Annie Pearl—had no biological children. But they took in Cheetah's niece's son, Jonathan. My uncle said he regretted not having his own blood son.

One summer, when I was in college, I lived with J.D. and Aunt Cheetah. I worked with my uncle, pouring and laying cement. He gave me some sound advice, in a rather strange way. "Don't ever let a couple from Dallas come between you." That's how he spoke. He was trying to say, in his own way, that friendship is more important than money, and anyone who betrays you is not a friend. Those words of wisdom remain with me today.

Uncle J.D. was Mr. Fixit. There wasn't any handy job he couldn't do, though he was best at pouring cement. He took me along as his helper on smaller jobs, giving me the opportunity to make money, which was music to my ears. Who doesn't want to make money, even if hauling cement darn near breaks your back? When I lived at home and Uncle J.D. picked me up for work, I would have already been waiting for him for some time. My father made sure of that—punctuality was important.

"You need to be up and ready to go when he gets here," my father said. "And don't be lazy. Pay attention and work hard."

My uncle had an old, raggedy truck. After he picked me up, we stopped at a cement plant to rent a cement mixer and to purchase bags of cement and sand. After getting to the job site at 8 A.M., my uncle wasted no time. He put water in a mixer, plugged it into an electrical socket, dumped in a couple bags of cement, and started shoveling in sand. He added more cement, stuck his finger in, and watched the cement fall from his finger. "That's how you can tell if the mix is ready," he said. After getting the right consistency, every time, he was ready to go to work.

My job was to bring the cement from the front yard, where the mixer was, to the backyard, where the job was set up. I wasn't strong enough to handle a wheelbarrow, so I carried five gallons of cement to my uncle. I haven't worked harder in my entire life. Even with gloves on, the handles of those buckets dug into my hands. I knew I couldn't quit, and I didn't want to quit, because I couldn't have my uncle tell my father that I didn't finish the job. I tripped and stumbled, but I didn't drop one bucket or have any cement spill over.

My uncle and I worked hard all day long, even though I was drenched in sweat from the heat. One day, the thermometer read 106 degrees. Whenever the homeowner offered us something to drink, my uncle declined. So I did too. At the end of the day, my uncle asked me if I remembered how much he was to pay me. And I quoted the correct amount. Pulling up to my house, he paid me, and complimented me on my work.

"Tell your dad that you can do a day's work like a man," he said.

I learned a lot from Uncle J.D. about hard work and being competent. I also stayed in shape. It became clear to me that my uncle and father had worked hard their whole lives, for it was the only way they could make a living. My uncle said that of all the people he worked with, my father was the best and hardest worker he knew. That was nice for the son of T. J. Hart to know, and I tried to be that same worker bee in track and field.

Minimum wage at that time, in the late 1960s, was $1.65 an hour. Though that didn't seem like much money, I saved everything I earned and was able to buy clothes for the schoolyear. I was proud of that, but prouder that my parents didn't have to buy my clothes. Times were tough. My father purchased a little, three-bedroom home for $12,500 and had a house note of just under $100 per month. Though I never had a conversation about it with my parents, I knew they were grateful I was able to take a little bit of financial pressure off their shoulders.

Even with six children in our family, our childhood was great, though we didn't have much financially while growing up in the projects. Our friends in the projects didn't have much either, so we didn't know any difference. We didn't have a TV set at the time, so we didn't get to watch such African American role models as the Jeffersons, living in a fancy high-rise apartment, or the Cosbys, with a doctor and lawyer as parents. Still, we felt rich, with open fields to play in and living in the best of times in terms of feeling safe.

No one worried about kids being molested or kidnapped. Or getting shot. My dad went to work every day, and my mother stayed home, taking care of the family. We had plenty of food, and while it wasn't shrimp, lobster, or filet mignon, it didn't matter, because my mom was a good cook, and we appreciated her cooking. Even the desserts she prepared were better than money could buy. She kept the house clean, she took care of our needs, and while she didn't wear dresses and high heels like June of *Leave It to Beaver,* she was a great mom.

We got toys for Christmas, though they weren't bikes or some of the expensive toys that kids living outside the projects found under their Christmas trees. But we had Christmas and Thanksgiving dinners, just like everyone else. During the summer holidays, we went on picnics. We went to church on Sunday. Our parents loved us, and we knew it. That love showed every day of their lives.

My parents instructed me not to cross the street without supervision. But while we were playing one day, our ball rolled into the street, and I went after it. So did our dog, Spot, and he was hit by an oncoming car right in front of our house. Was he dead? Was he even breathing? Was I in trouble? Imagine my state of mind. I was six, maybe seven, and I was facing the first crisis in my life.

"Where do you live?" the driver of the car wanted to know. "I need to speak to your parents, to tell them what happened." The man actually was nice, and he carried Spot to where we lived. Spot was alive! The man told my mother that he tried to avoid hitting Spot, but didn't have time, yet he wasn't holding me accountable. The unexpected happens; kids do crazy things.

After my father came home, he didn't punish me. He hadn't wanted a dog in the first place, for it was another expense. But he relented after I convinced him that I would take care of Spot and clean up after him. All the time I had him, I fixed Spot a place near my bed. I'd tell him to go to sleep, but fifteen minutes later, I'd look up and he was staring at me. We'd go through this same routine two or three times, but, somehow, we'd both make it through to morning.

Our parents taught their six children to be supportive of one another. How supportive? One day when I was in elementary school, this older boy jumped on me and started hitting me. When my sister Catherine saw that I wasn't hitting him back, she jumped on him and beat him up. That was the first, and the last, time he ever hit me. Mess with me, buddy, and I'll sic my sister on you.

My father had another brother who wasn't anything like him or Uncle J.D. Uncle Thomas was stubborn, opinionated, and unyielding in his positions. He came to California later than the other two, because he had first gone to Florida with another brother. Uncle Thomas had this fighting spirit. He loved to argue, even when he was clearly wrong. He just needed to vent the fighter within him.

Well, he found the perfect outlet for his stubbornness and, sometimes, hostility: prizefighting. He stumbled into a Florida gym, liked the atmosphere, and asked the manager how to get involved. The manager handed him a pair of gloves and told him to climb into the ring. Uncle Thomas hadn't boxed before, but he showed that he loved to hit and, more impressively, didn't mind being hit. The manager told him that though he was raw, he had natural ability and could do well if he trained diligently.

Uncle Thomas was a Hart; he didn't mind hard work. So he put in the hours and began fighting for real. He won his first few fights in Florida and then moved on to Cuba, where he had an eye-opening experience. It was his first time mingling with black people who spoke no English. They were tough inside the ropes, and at first he wasn't sure if he could handle them. But he had this deep-seated desire to win, and he left Cuba still undefeated. His next stop was Panama, where his success continued. From what he told me, he trained too hard to lose.

According to Uncle Thomas, he had thirty-two fights and lost just once, on that rare occasion where he was lackadaisical in his training and paid for it in the ring. He said the decision could have gone either way, but it wasn't decided in his favor. He wasn't in boxing for the long haul anyway. During a period of serious self-evaluation, he retired from the sport and started working as a servant in wealthy folks' homes in Florida.

But boxing hadn't released, not entirely, the fighter within him. He was very angry about many things in his life, especially his lack of education. He was bitter about that in a way that my father wasn't; Uncle Thomas was embarrassed that he couldn't read or write. He explained it in baseball terms: "It's like everyone else has a bat the size of Babe Ruth's, and my bat is a toothpick." I could feel his anger and frustration. He spoke about his mistreatment as a black man, being made to sit at the back of the bus, and having to go around to the side door or back door of a restaurant to order and pick up his food.

But Uncle Thomas did have a sense of honor. He told me about his life as a servant and how the people he worked for trusted him totally, knowing he wouldn't ever steal from them. He helped them with their domestic work, and if the owner came home drunk, which happened on many an occasion, Uncle Thomas would pick him up, take him into the bedroom, get him into his pajamas, and put him to bed. By the tenderness in his voice, I could tell that Uncle Thomas really cared for the people he worked for. He really wasn't a violent man.

Sinclair Hart, the sharecropper father whom my father, Uncle J.D. and Uncle Thomas left behind, had instilled an important quality in all his eleven children. And that was, simply: "Don't return hate for hate. It will destroy you." Even Uncle Thomas, the most troublesome of the siblings, treated every man equally.

After Uncle Thomas relocated to California, he got into construction, like Uncle J.D. The work was steady, and it was good having Uncle Thomas around. He didn't have children of his own or someone else's child to bring up, like J.D, but they both treated T. J. Hart's children as their own. We loved it when Uncle Thomas came around, because he would bring hot dogs, the best hot dogs around. We'd eat them straight out of the bag or boil them with all the trimmings; he'd bring the ketchup, mustard, mayonnaise, onions, and tomatoes. Watching him put a hot dog together had a lasting influence on me: I still like to eat a hot dog with mayonnaise and onions.

Uncle Thomas also liked to barbecue. He barbecued twice as much as what was needed for the people who were there, which meant leftovers. As he got older, he started to fill out, because he loved eating his food. Years later, after my son, Eddie Jr., was born, we'd visit Uncle Thomas, and he would cook a bunch of Cornish game hens. My son was five at the time, but those hens were so good, he ate two by himself. Or Uncle Thomas, a master with the Crock-Pot, would cook a leg of lamb that was so tender, you couldn't even pick it up. It just melted in your mouth.

One Saturday, he came to Oakland, where we were living at the time, and he brought us a brand-new Crock-Pot. Did I cook a leg of lamb in it? Yes, I did. Did it taste as good as Uncle Thomas's leg of lamb? Yes, it did, I was told, proudly. The Hart family, from the Deep South to the West Coast, knew about tenderness and togetherness, whether in the kitchen or throughout the house. We didn't have riches, but we had one another, and that love of family made us rich.

I still have the Crock-Pot Uncle Thomas gave us many years ago. It's a keepsake I'll never give up, for it represents family, and I'm all about family.

GOLD MEDAL FOR CORRUPTION

I walked out of the Olympic Stadium in 2015, mentally juggling the heartbreak and happiness I had experienced there forty-three years earlier. Right next to the stadium is the swimming hall where Mark Spitz made Olympic history. I looked inside and saw bodies splashing; I wondered if these folks realized that they were swimming in the same lanes where Spitz won his seven gold medals and set seven world records.

Compared to other Olympiads, the 1972 Summer Games topped the list in terms of amazing achievements and devastating disappointments. There was Spitz, the human fish, and Olga Korbut, who won three gold medals in gymnastics, while winning millions of fans with her pixielike smile and grace. Valery Borzov won both the 100- and 200-meter dashes, and Dave Wottle captured the 800-meter run while wearing a baseball cap, a home run of sorts.

Along with those memorable milestones came shattering results: the USA men's basketball team lost the gold medal at the scorer's table, Rick DeMont lost a swimming gold medal over an allergy drug, Jim Ryun lost the 1500 meters after tripping and falling, Bob Seagren lost the pole vault over a pole controversy, Steve Prefontaine lost the 5000 meters, and, of course, Eddie Hart and Rey Robinson lost without even getting into the starting blocks. So much was lost.

But the greatest loss at those Munich Games, without a doubt, occurred in the Olympic Village, not the Olympic Stadium, with the deaths of the eleven Israeli athletes and coaches. And there was Spitz, a Jewish man from the United States, whom, I heard, was rushed out of the Village, and Munich, for fear of his life. To get to the truth, Newhouse phoned Spitz in 2015.

"I'll give you the overall view," he said from his southern California residence. "I was going home that same day anyway. The Opening Ceremony was on a Saturday. The swimming events started on Monday. I had events Monday through Thursday, no events Friday, and then I swam Saturday through Monday. Including trials and prelims, I swam fifteen times to get those seven gold medals.

"I stopped giving press interviews because there was going to be one major press conference Tuesday, about all that I had accomplished. After my last swimming event, a medley relay on Monday, I went to dinner that night with some people from *Sports Illustrated*. We got back to the Village at midnight, because I had to be up at 8:45 A.M. to get a ride to the press center, adjacent to the Village. When I got there at 9:00, Jerry Kirshenbaum and photographer Heinz Kluetmeier, two *Sports Illustrated* guys I had just had dinner with, rushed up to me and said, 'Do you know what just happened?' I said, 'Yeah, Mark Spitz just won seven gold medals. What do you mean?' They said, 'Well, we're not sure, but there has been a lockdown in the Village. They've updated security because they believe there has been some terrorist activity.' Press from all over the world wanted to know what had happened. I was their only resource, and I had no knowledge of what they were talking about. There were no questions, understandably, about my performance. The press conference lasted fifteen to twenty minutes because of the confusion. No one knew what was happening.

"What I learned eventually," Spitz continued, "was that these terrorists had gotten into this building at one or two in the morning and had shot and killed two Israelis before the sun came up. One of the bodies was kept in the room, and the other was thrown over the balcony. Everything was chaotic. Jim McKay interviewed me, and now it's close to 10:15 A.M. On a TV monitor, I saw a guy come out on a balcony wearing a Panama hat. My interview with McKay might have ended on the cutting room floor, because those Olympics had gone from a sporting event to a news event.

"Then I was taken back to the Village, and the German chancellor, Willy Brandt, was right there in my room. He said, 'We are here to protect you, and since you are leaving today, we're going to get you out a different way.' I was supposed to go to Stuttgart, pick up a Mercedes, and drive it to Frankfurt, where it was going to be put on a cargo plane and flown to Chicago. I was supposed to go back to dental school at the Indiana–Purdue School of Dentistry in Indianapolis."

Spitz didn't go to Stuttgart. He was flown instead to London.

"That's where I took the famous poster picture with my seven gold medals," he said. "At noontime, I was on a Pan Am flight to Los Angeles. No one was

This is the Munich swimming hall where Mark Spitz earned his then-record seven gold medals in 1972. (Photo courtesy of Irmina Richter)

supposed to know that I was on that flight. Then I took a PSA, now Southwest Airlines, flight from Los Angeles to San Francisco. When I got home to Sacramento, Ronald Reagan, the governor, met me at the airport. Then his escort drove me to my house.

"My parents still were in Germany. But now I'm sitting home with my two sisters, forty-eight hours after my last event, watching the memorial ceremony for the killed Israelis at the Olympic site. Jim McKay was announcing that event on TV, and there were all these reports that Mark Spitz was in Italy, or in Berlin, or in the United States. It was like 'Where's Waldo?' That, in a nutshell, is what happened."

Spitz didn't return to dental school. His life had changed forever. "I needed to figure out what was going on." Upon his return to the United States, he received lucrative corporate endorsements, and then he evolved into an entrepreneur, stockbroker, and international motivational speaker.

His incredible gold haul galvanized those Olympics, but, of course, Spitz isn't what Munich 1972 is remembered for. Yet that Olympiad's many subplots, from gymnastic jumps to pole jumps to jump shots, bear repeating.

The most astonishing finish in that entire Olympiad occurred in the basketball arena, which I walked past on a stroll through the Olympic Park in 2015. Those who played on that USA team still were in disbelief forty-three years later.

"It was so chaotic, a comedy of errors," reflected Tom McMillen in April 2015. "As you step back from it, you realize it was all part of the Cold War. We became pawns in that chess game. We didn't even need to play that game. Nixon and Brezhnev could have arm-wrestled." Without a doubt, it was the craziest end to a basketball game in the history of the sport. Nobody could have made it up: the Three-Second Controversy and Cover Up—the most controversial basketball game ever played.

The United States hadn't ever lost an Olympic basketball gold medal, let alone an Olympic basketball game, until Munich, where the USA met the USSR in the championship game. Though foreign countries were catching up to the Americans in hoops, the USA believed it had pocketed yet another gold medal when Doug Collins sank two pressure free throws for a 50–49 lead with three seconds left.

Then insanity took over. The Soviets inbounded the ball, but after two seconds, the head referee, Brazil's Renato Righetto, blew his whistle for what seemed no reason. There was a commotion at the scorer's table, so Righetto signaled for an administrative timeout. An administrative timeout; who ever heard of such a thing in a basketball game? The Soviet coach, Vladimir Kondrashkin, contended that he had called a timeout prior to Collins's first free throw. According to Olympic rules, a coach can call a timeout in such a situation and take that timeout before or after the second free throw. Kondrashkin vigorously insisted that he had asked for the latter option. With one second left on the clock, Righetto awarded Kondrashkin his timeout.

After this, the Soviets inbounded the ball but couldn't get up a shot, and the Americans rushed off the court, ready to celebrate their gold medal. But, wait! They were ordered back on the court after R. William Jones, the British secretary general of the International Amateur Basketball Federation (FIBA), had appointed himself the final authority. He added three seconds to the game clock, because that's how much time was left when Kondrashkin originally requested that timeout.

"Jones was so interested in seeing parity," said the 6-foot-11 McMillen, "and we became victims of that."

Given an unbelievable third opportunity, the Soviets made it work. An ensuing full-court pass over McMillen's head was caught by Alexander Belov, who then laid the ball into the basket for a 51–50 USSR victory, tainted or otherwise. The USA protested the outcome, but a five-person FIBA board voted down the protest, 3–2. Those three votes were from Eastern Bloc representatives, from Cuba, Poland, and Hungary, while the other two votes were from Italy and Puerto Rico. The Soviets had scored a Cold War victory.

Tom McMillen and the USA basketball team were robbed of gold at Munich and refused to accept silver medals. (Photo courtesy of Tom McMillen)

"It was a game that was almost destined to turn out this way, with the United States having such a hegemonic dominance of the sport," said McMillen. "The Soviets wanted so badly to have a victory, and this led to an East versus West outcome. It was like we were playing with one arm tied behind our back. There's never been a game where the others [outside of the game officials] lost control—a very charred outcome.

"You're going into the Olympics—the paragon of perfection, the epitome of sports—and then you get there and you find that it's fraught with all the human frailties: bad refereeing, misjudgments, miscalculations. You go over with this idealistic view, and you come home sobered by reality."

The USA team was so disgusted by that foul-smelling outcome that its players refused to accept their silver medals. Their place on the medal stand was left unoccupied. "I think that position still holds," McMillen said of the medal boycott. "Somewhere along the road, there was talk of giving us a dual gold medal, but I don't think that's going to happen. The irony of that situation is that we were truly amateurs, and all the other teams were professionals. As the result of what happened in Munich, the game of basketball opened up [toward American professionalism at the Olympics] and went forward. But those Olympics were particularly sobering because there were so many scandals and controversies."

Bob Seagren would wholeheartedly agree with that evaluation, for he was caught up in another Olympic Games controversy, one that bordered on scandalous. Seagren, the pole-vault winner in Mexico City in 1968, would have trouble defending his gold medal in Munich because of more rules confusion, this time over the pole itself.

Six weeks before the 1972 Games, the Technical Committee of the International Amateur Athletic Federation announced that it was banning the latest pole innovation, the Cata-Pole, the preference of the world's top vaulters, including Seagren. The East Germans complained that these poles contained carbon fiber, which wasn't true. But the IAAF refused to withdraw its ban because the poles "hadn't been available through normal supply channels" for at least twelve months before the Olympics. On August 27, four days before competition, the IAAF reversed itself and lifted the ban. Relieved vaulters returned to using the Cata-Poles, but three days later, it imposed the ban again. Bungling IAAF officials confiscated all those poles and brought them in for inspection. Vaulters with the forbidden poles were given new ones, which were really manufactured old models heavier than the Cata-Poles. Did the "I" in the IAAF stand for insensitive?

"I didn't know that my poles were illegal," Seagren recalled in May 2015. "I brought nine poles with my name on them that I delivered, and all nine were

The poles Bob Seagren used to win the 1968 pole vault competition in Mexico City were ruled illegal at Munich in 1972. (Photo courtesy of Bob Seagren)

determined illegal. So I asked, 'How can I be expected to pole vault without a pole?' I was told by IAAF official Adriaan Paulen, 'You can use any of those poles over there in a pile.' They were all lighter poles. If I had jumped my normal way, I would have broken the pole on my first jump. I found the strongest pole I could, lowered my hands six inches to keep from breaking the pole, and qualified the first day.

"The other Americans had to choose from the same pile, but the West and East Germans got to use their own poles. So did the Greek vaulter, Christos Papanicolaou. The only difference between the new and old poles was that the newer ones were thirty-five grams heavier. I told Paulen. 'That kind of blows your theory that the new poles are lighter.' He replied, 'We know what we're doing, and if you say one more word, we're going to throw you out of the competition.'

"It still makes no sense to me why they did what they did. According to Olympic rules, a pole can be made of any material, of any length and diameter. It doesn't have to be shared. The whole thing was mind-boggling. Everybody just bombed out. They actually had to add some vaulters, those who hadn't qualified, just to have a big enough field for the final. Steve Smith didn't even make it to qualifying, and Jan Johnson just did qualify. He took the bronze, but jumped [17 feet, 6½ inches] way below his normal height. I ended up [17 feet, 8½ inches] nearly a foot below my best. If I hadn't won a gold medal in 1968, I probably would have killed Adriaan Paulen."

The pole-vault winner in Munich, Wolfgang Nordwig of East Germany, benefitted the most from the pole ban because he hadn't adapted well to the Cata-Pole and continued to use his old model. He cleared a personal best, 18 feet, ½ inch. One more case of anti-American sentiment? Seagren, who settled for a silver medal, finished the competition by thrusting his pole in Paulen's lap.

"He didn't want to take it," said Seagren, "but I told him, 'Hey, it's not my pole. I don't know which person it belongs to, but give it back to him. Thank you for letting me use it.' I filed a protest, but it didn't do any good. Shove it up Adriaan Paulen's ass—that's what I wanted to do."

Rick DeMont considered a similar physical act, though he wasn't sure of his actual target, the U.S. Olympic Committee or the International Olympic Committee. Though the IOC punished him, the USOC victimized him, in the cruelest way imaginable.

DeMont was a swimming prodigy, a sixteen-year-old who won the 400-meter freestyle at Munich. He had asthma and was allergic to wheat, animal fur, chocolate, grasses, and pollens. He had been taking medication for these allergies since he was four years old. But a tablet, Marax, that he took contained the banned drug ephedrine. He woke up wheezing the night before the 400 final, took one tablet, and then another early in the morning. He then won the gold medal by one-hundredth of a second, the smallest margin possible, over Bradford Cooper of Australia. Then the three medalists were taken away for dope testing before heading to the medal stand for the ceremony, without any indication of a problem.

Two days later, as DeMont was about to swim a 1500-meter freestyle preliminary race, an event in which he held the world record, he was informed that he had failed the drug test following the 400 meters, which disqualified him from swimming in the 1500. Thus he became the first American since the great Jim Thorpe (decathlon and pentathlon champion at Stockholm in 1912) to have to return an Olympic gold medal.

A sad development: the stripping of DeMont's gold medal could have been prevented if the bumbling USOC had acted in proper defense of its athletes. For DeMont had filled out a standard USOC medical form, in which he listed all the medications that he took. He didn't know that Marax was forbidden; he didn't even try to hide that he was using it. If these medicines failed to meet IOC standards, all the USOC needed to do was contact the IOC and instruct DeMont that he was in violation or suggest another accepted allergy drug. The USOC did none of these three, possibly because it was too busy planning family outings in Munich.

"Rick DeMont was taking some crazy thing for asthma, and he eventually put that down [on a USOC form]," said Mark Spitz. "The [USOC] should

Rick DeMont had a gold medal stripped from him, then was banished from those same Munich Olympics for taking a prescribed medication for asthma; today he is the swimming coach at the University of Arizona. (Photo courtesy of Rick DeMont)

have looked that up and told him it wasn't OK, but he wasn't informed. So he had the 400-meter gold medal taken away. I was sitting next to Rick when they came up to him forty-five minutes before the 1500 free and told him he couldn't swim. In my opinion, he already had been penalized, but if he was clean, why shouldn't he be allowed to swim another event? They were making up the rules as they went along."

By 1976, USA swim officials approached the Montreal Olympics wisely, questioning fifty-one members of the team about their medications and discovering that sixteen were unknowingly using banned drugs. Substitutes were found, and they were allowed to compete, although this was much too late to save DeMont, who had by then disappeared from Olympic competition, during his prime swimming years.

"I was really angry, even bitter," DeMont, the current University of Arizona men's and women's swimming coach, said in February 2016. "I wasn't taking Marax to improve my performance, but to stay alive. The USOC had my information and could have told the IOC but didn't. It took me a long time to get over what happened in Munich. I heard there's been an effort to restore my gold medal, but it hasn't happened yet.

"I did everything ethically. I was sixteen years old, and I was under the care of my family doctor, who first diagnosed me with massive allergies when I was a child. I had shots for being an asthmatic almost every week. It took years to get over what happened in Munich, and there's residue still in me."

DeMont continued in swimming after Munich, "but my heart wasn't in it at all. I felt very conflicted and honestly felt that I didn't want to represent the United States. They were the ones who screwed me. That was the mind of a twenty-year-old."

He began college at the University of Washington, then after two years transferred to the University of Arizona. "I did do competitive swimming," he said of those years, "and, in 1977, I was on top of the world again. But I was affected, and I kept changing my events. In 1981, I was the fourth-fastest 50-freestyler in the world. I still had a love for the sport. I was a good swimmer, but a messed up swimmer in terms of whom I represented and why. But I've come to a place of resolution, in that I'm not forgetting what happened, but at some point you have to decide that you're not defined by it, and you're ready to move on. So I've moved on with my life."

DeMont has a renewed love of the sport, a love affair he transmits through his coaching by "communicating to my swimmers how to do it and how to succeed. It's very satisfying. Based on my own experience of being let down, it absolutely helps me in helping kids get through difficult times. And helping them has helped me."

Another American swimmer, Michael Burton, broke DeMont's world record in the 1500-meter freestyle in Munich. And because DeMont's gold medal in the 400-meter freestyle was stripped, Steve Genter moved up from bronze to silver medalist in that event behind the new gold medalist, Cooper. Genter received a second silver medal in the 200-meter freestyle and a gold medal in the 800-meter freestyle relay. He gained even greater international acclaim for his amazing courage; he had undergone surgery for a collapsed lung in Munich and was released from the hospital the day before the 200 free. He decided to swim, but the stitches came loose in the water and he started to bleed. Screaming in pain, he took off after Spitz and lost by just one second as Spitz broke his own world record.

There was a culture of drug use at those Munich Games that was more prevalent, and more illicitly beneficial, than anything Rick DeMont was taking, though not every guilty party was caught or punished. A Puerto Rican basketball player tested positive for banned substances, but he and his team were allowed to play the entire tournament, as his test results weren't confirmed until after the Olympics. But when a Dutch cycling team member tested positive for a banned drug, the entire team was stripped of its bronze medal. There wasn't any uniformity of drug oversight at Munich; DeMont became an innocent victim.

East Germany was the most successful country in the track-and-field competition at Munich, although it wasn't the only Eastern Bloc country that encouraged doping. Anabolic steroids were prevalent in Eastern Europe before making inroads into American sports. But the price those nations paid for their gold medals is a costly one: there are ghastly tales of chemically enhanced Eastern Bloc athletes reaching their middle years while suffering from cancer, heart disease, and severe depression—and one of them having a child born without arms.

Even as these controversies played out, television cameras couldn't get enough of Olga Korbut, a sparkling seventeen-year-old gymnast from Belarus. The 4-foot-11, 85-pound Korbut lit up those Games with her radiant smile, joyous nature, and even her tears in a gold-medal trifecta. She became the darling of her sport and the telegenic face of those Olympics.

And she only competed because a teammate was injured. "It was amazing," she said. "One day I was a nobody, and the next day I was a star. It was almost more than I could take in."

Jim Ryun, another American, experienced the opposite result. The great miler was appearing in his third Olympics, still looking for a gold medal. Only he tripped on the heel of Uganda's Vitus Ashaba in the 1500-meter final, sprawled on the track, and failed to medal, thereby having to settle for the silver medal he had received at Mexico City in 1968. "All I know," Ryun said, "is that everything was going well, and I felt good, and the next thing I knew, I was trying to figure out what happened." That was his final international act. He entered politics and became a congressman from Kansas.

Then there was the sad case of Steve Prefontaine, an iconic Oregon distance runner favored to win the 5000-meter run in Munich, who boldly predicted he would run the final mile under four minutes. But he faded badly toward the end, finishing fourth. Later, in May 1975, he lost control of his sports car and was killed on an Oregon highway. He was twenty-four. Years later, two movies on his life were released at the same time.

Then there's my story, and that of Rey Robinson, which led to considerable conjecture as to who really was at fault. Some of this conjecture is just that, but that hasn't stopped those who believe they truly know what happened to Rey and me from conjecturing, including Mark Spitz.

"I can relate to that by what we knew in swimming," said Spitz. "We knew what event, what time of day, when we were to compete. I would get to each of my events two hours early. Here is the bottom line: in one sense, it's the coach's responsibility. In another sense, it's the track-and-field federation's responsibility. These things are very precisely done. Eddie may not have known what quarter-final he was in, but he had to know what time the quarterfinals were, and he should have had his butt there at the stadium well in advance to warm up.

"Eddie had been in numerous competitions, including internationally, so he knew exactly the drill that was going to happen. When does it become the responsibility of the athlete to take things into his own hands? I couldn't rely on a coach. Why would [Stan Wright] have to ask when the quarterfinals were? He had the master schedule. So unless it was a rain delay, why would [Wright] have to ask when the race was going off? That's just my opinion."

One man's opinion isn't necessarily correct, but the man can always speculate.

"I don't know the real story," Spitz confessed. "But in talking with Edwin Moses, who's a good friend of mine, plus Sebastian Coe and Jim Ryun, I've learned that track and field is pretty similar to swimming when it comes to schedules. Why was it just Eddie's event that was affected, and not the other track-and-field events? I feel sorry for Eddie. I feel sorry for the coach. But they aren't alone when it comes to disqualifications. At the 1968 Olympics, Luis Nicolao [of Argentina], who was the world record holder in the 100-meter butterfly, missed his event when the shuttle he was riding from the Olympic Village to the swimming hall got stuck in traffic. Eddie could have walked from the Village to where we competed; it was just twenty minutes.

"On another note, at the time we were competing, we didn't know how important those Olympics would be, historically. The dynamics of what was happening—Eddie's disqualification, my performance, Rick DeMont—it all just seemed like another day at the office compared to the massacre and, in a smaller way, the basketball controversy. The American coach, [Hank] Iba, should have taken his team off the court so that they couldn't redo the final three seconds."

In retrospect, Tom McMillen might agree. After graduating from the University of Maryland, he studied in England as a Rhodes Scholar, then played eleven seasons in the NBA before becoming, like Jim Ryun, a congressman (from Maryland). At 6-foot-11, McMillen is the tallest congressman ever. He founded the National Foundation of Fitness, Sports, and Nutrition, he was cochair of the President's Council on Sports and Fitness under President Clinton, and he's the author of *Out of Bounds*.

Out of Bounds is a perfect description of what happened to the USA basketball team in Munich. "It seems so outlandish to have had time added on the clock," said McMillen. "Then when the Olympic massacre occurred, my initial reaction was that they should call off the Games. The world, at that time, was not used to the concept of terrorism, which I didn't understand myself. I was just a kid from Pennsylvania. As Rudy Giuliani said, Munich was the start of modern terrorism. The spectacle of that event galvanized the world. Even though those Olympic Games were besmirched, I know now that it would have been a mistake to cancel them, because that would have meant succumbing to the terrorists. And that event had an impact on security at succeeding Olympic Games."

Bob Seagren also noticed, from the very beginning of the 1972 Olympic Games, "that security was pretty lax. My roommate was Buddy Williamson, a pole-vaulter who wasn't in the competition. Buddy and everyone else could walk into the Village without a pass. One night Buddy and I were playing Foosball in the rec room with an Israeli coach and an Israeli wrestler. The next morning, I learned that those two Israelis walked in on the terrorists."

Eleven Israelis died at the hands of those eight Black September terrorists. And Olympic officials shepherded Mark Spitz out of the Village as fast as they could. I saw him looking out the car window as they drove him away.

Those Olympics set the stage for further politicking at other Olympics. The Americans boycotted Russia in 1980. Eastern Bloc countries boycotted Los Angeles in 1984. And Olympic athletes now compete for countries fighting around the world, fighting one another: the Arabs, Israelis, Afghanis, Iraqis, Iranians, Americans, et cetera. So we need to exercise caution, to make sure that the bloodshed of Munich doesn't occur again at an Olympics, for they continue to remain a political platform.

There can be no conjecture about that.

SCHOOL DAYS

Riding the tram in Munich late at night, which my son and I did several times, gave us a chance to really see the city and to discuss not only what we were experiencing on my first trip back to Germany since 1972, plus Eddie Jr.'s first trip over here ever. On one such midnight ride, the discussion shifted to my childhood, which made me think about Mrs. Nanette Mercurio.

Mrs. Mercurio was my fifth-grade teacher at Village Elementary in Pittsburg, and an important person in my life. I told my son about my March 2015 visit with her at the Concord, California, apartment she shares with her husband. I surprised her by showing up like that, but I told her I was looking for the kid I was as a ten-year-old in 1959, and I needed Mrs. Mercurio to fill in the blanks.

Fifty-six years later, she was eighty, and nine months retired from a fifty-two-year career in education, spent entirely in Pittsburg. I hadn't seen her since the 1970s, but she still had her youthful energy, her command of the room, and quite a remarkable memory.

"Eddie, I remember you exactly as a boy," she said with a smile. "I was doing yard duty during recess, and I noticed, consistently, that you were the first person to run all the way to the back fence, which was a distance longer than a football field. I thought, 'Wow!' Of all the fifth- and sixth-graders, you were always the fastest. 'Someday,' I told myself, 'this is going to pay off for this child.' You were going to be a good football player, though you weren't a large boy, but you would be something, because you were very interested in sports."

Reluctantly, I brought up my classroom habits, as I wasn't as fast with the books.

"You were an average student," she said, "but you never gave me any trouble. You never talked back. You were very calm. I don't know if the running toned you down, but you did pretty much as you were told. You weren't loud or boisterous in terms of fighting, like hitting the person in front of you, or tripping someone, which little kids will do. You were responsive. You liked me, and you knew I liked you. So we hit it off."

Mrs. Mercurio mentioned that she had two families: her family at home and her classroom family. She's been married for fifty-seven years to Ben Mercurio, eighty-three in 2015, whom she met when she was thirteen. He owned a clothing store, Mercurio's, in nearby Antioch for years. They have two children and four grandchildren.

Mrs. Mercurio's classroom family encompassed thirty-eight years of teaching (after which she was an adult school night counselor for fourteen years), with tremendous diversity among her students, as Pittsburg truly epitomizes a rainbow coalition.

On this diversity, she recalled: "Someone once asked, 'How many black children are in your classroom?' I replied, 'I don't see them as black children. Children are children.' I had a classroom. Some people were smart, some people were mediocre, and some people really needed help. Were they black, white, Italian, Puerto Rican, or Mexican? It really didn't matter. You accepted these children, like you do your own children. Most of my students lived in my neighborhood. They walked home. I walked home. They knew I knew their parents and grandparents. I had no trouble getting hold of a parent, if necessary. I'm Italian myself. My maiden name was Smario; I married a Mercurio. So I could relate to different nationalities."

Mrs. Mercurio remembered when Pittsburg had one elementary school, one middle school, one junior high, and one high school. Then Village Elementary was built, but it was torn down to build another high school, because high school enrollment in town jumped from four hundred to two thousand. Three new middle schools then followed. Pittsburg's population was growing; if it added an *h* like that town in Pennsylvania, the additional letter would have stood for housing.

"I had a big wall outside my classroom door, and I would post anything I could find on local kids making good," she said. "Pittsburg has produced some wonderful athletic people, like John Henry Johnson, an extremely nice man; I enjoyed watching him play football and basketball. I kept track of you, Eddie, by hearing your name publicized. We need incentives for young kids, to see that there is a reward for being consistent, and for following through. So buckle down and be the best you can be, whether you're on the football team or in the band or you're the head cheerleader.

"In the '70s, we honored you, Eddie, at the high school. Then you spoke at the adult school graduation. In my fourteen years there, I heard all the graduation speakers, and you did the very best job by far. It just thrilled me to see you not as an athlete but as a man who represented his community. We had an audience of five hundred, and you could hear a pin drop when you spoke. Afterward, you approached me and said, 'You know, Mrs. Mercurio, if it wasn't for you, I wouldn't be who I am today.' And I said, 'Nooooo. I appreciate the compliment, but along the way, people helped you. You married quite the lady, too, and she helped you.'"

Mrs. Mercurio brought up my disqualification in Munich. "Wasn't your [sprint] group late for the Olympics? Knowing Pittsburg kids, there is tardiness every day. I'm used to people being tardy. Then the truth came out: Eddie Hart wasn't late; his coach got the wrong starting time."

I tried to explain that there was more to that story, but Mrs. Mercurio began talking, instead, about the car accident that kept her away from our classroom for two months. All of us kids in the class really missed her reading to us every day.

"What happened was that my hat visor came down, and when I went to put it back up, my car went into a person's tree," she said. "The man who lived in the house—I knew him—was so scared that he didn't leave his porch, knowing that it was me. Another man, who was working across the street, came down from the roof and called the paramedics, who took me to the hospital. I had to replace some teeth."

I told Mrs. Mercurio, "We were upset, because we had this off-the-wall substitute, and we liked hanging out with you."

"I knew that hanging out with me was better, for some kids, than being in an empty house," she said. "Some of my students, like Johnny Constanza and Betty Lou Harris, would come over to my house on Saturday and do whatever needed to be done, whether it was polishing silver, mowing the lawn, washing my car."

"All the boys in the class had a crush on you, even me," I told her. "We were all competing for your attention, though it wasn't anything you were trying to do or make happen."

"Well, I'm not that kind of person, first of all, and I wasn't aware of that. This lady who did my hair at the beauty shop said, 'You never noticed how the kids in the hallway parted to let you go by? They'd see you come down the hall with those high heels clicking.' That's why I'm crippled today, twenty years of wearing high heels."

"Even though I wasn't focused at that point, academically," I told her, "you always made me feel like I could do better. That I counted, and you really cared."

"Good. I watched you run, like lightning, and look where it got you, Eddie. There was a reason for that. You went on and improved your life, going to a fine school, Cal Berkeley, and then going on the get your master's degree at Cal State, Hayward. So you must have had it upstairs, because they don't let just anyone into Cal, or to get your master's. It's building up confidence, because life is what you make of it.

"You know as a teacher which ones you can help, and you go at it. You know which kids get it and which kids don't, and you spend more time with those kids who don't. They're the people who really need you. You get them on the right path. I loved my students."

"As you know, Mrs. Mercurio, I was a teacher myself. And what you just said became a big part of my coaching, taking a kid with potential and working with him to raise that potential. I had a lot of success with that. I really prided myself that 85 percent of those track kids whom I coached at the junior college level went on to a four-year college."

"Kids need respect, Eddie. That's so important. In your case, you were always a good person, and that is more important. People with good common sense and compassion benefit from these qualities as they get older, whether or not they got As in the classroom. With boys, you have to wait a while; they don't develop, academically, as fast as girls do. With you, Eddie, it just had to come out. And I'm so glad you dropped by today. I love my old students getting in touch with me."

Nearly a month after seeing Mrs. Mercurio, Eddie Jr. and I rode the Munich tram through the night. We passed by a four-story Mercedes-Benz dealership, and we could see brand-new Mercedes gleaming in the building's interior lighting. Then I shifted the story from Mrs. Mercurio to Rodell Johnson, the man who had come back from the dead. Eddie Jr. needed to hear that one.

Rodell was my friend when we were kids at Village Elementary. Our friendship really grew at Central Junior High School. After Pittsburg High, Rodell moved to southern California. I didn't see him for forty years, for a very good reason: someone told me he had passed on. I was really saddened to hear that. Then in 2012, I got a call that Rodell Johnson was in town, and would I like to see him? I said, "Rodell Johnson is dead." The person said, "He's at his sister's house." Man, I drove over there right away.

We got together then and later on when I hosted my annual Eddie Hart All In One Foundation's "Working Together Saving Youth" benefit/recognition dinner at the Pittsburg Yacht Club. Yachts in Pittsburg? You bet.

Nanette Mercurio was Eddie Hart's grade school teacher who recognized his potential as an athlete and a person. (Photo courtesy of Nanette Mercurio)

"I've never found a friend like Eddie, even after forty years," Johnson said that night. "Eddie was always someone I could trust. I could talk to him about anything. We were closer than I was with my four brothers. He's still the same Eddie today as he was back then, just older and wiser."

"We had each other's backs," I reminded him. "We cared about each other. We did things together, explored together. My brother, Alfred, said that of all my friends, Rodell was the friendliest. Even my mother liked you. Life for us was a little bit freer and safer back then. You can't be like that anymore."

"Whenever I got upset," Rodell said, "Eddie would say, 'Let's be cool about this. Let's see what's going on.' I would listen to Eddie and calm myself down. He was the calming factor."

"That was from my parents," I said. "I had goals, and it's very easy to upset the apple cart. One wrong decision can ruin things. But I had some pretty strong goals, like running in the Olympics. My parents taught me how to think and act, and my getting into trouble wasn't something they were looking forward to hearing about. I was just an average student, getting Cs, but I knew how to take care of things.

"The two of us kids, Rodell and me, we stayed together, and we stayed out of trouble, except for one experience, which took some honesty to keep us straight. Remember the fruit trees, Rodell?"

Rodell Johnson was Eddie Hart's running pal as a boy, now "back from the dead." (Photo courtesy of Rodell Johnson)

"Those trees were so big," he said, "that they'd be hanging over the fences. Whenever we wanted food, we'd cross the tracks and head for those fruit trees. The fruit was free—apricots, peaches, and plums."

"We didn't bother to ask the people who owned those trees if we could have some fruit," I said. "Well, this one day, we did ask. So we're eating the fruit, and a policeman came by. "Did you ask?" he said. We said yes we did, but any other time, we'd have been in trouble."

I cherish my renewed relationship with Rodell, because I don't have a lot of friends from way back. There's Rodell, Cliff West, Rey Brown, and Larry Winston. Gwen and I don't have a lot of house parties.

"I remember when Eddie met Gwen," Rodell said. "We were seniors at Pittsburg High when she was a sophomore. She was always real quiet, seemed shy, stayed to herself, but she was someone you could talk to. I told Eddie, 'Gwen is a keeper. Don't be bothering with all these other girls.' They were made for each other.

"Eddie was more like a brother to me. We'd stay over at each other's houses. Every time you saw Eddie, you saw me. Every time you saw me, you saw Eddie. We'd sit by the bay at night, and I would sing. I was in the school chorus. Eddie couldn't sing. Sometimes we would walk up in the hills and watch the cows. We didn't bother them. We'd sit there and talk about what was going on in school. Or we'd catch a bus to Oakland, walk around, and visit Jack London Square.

"You know, Eddie, I have one true friend in Los Angeles. People down there want to get into your business, so I keep to myself. Here in Pittsburg, everyone knows one another. They speak to you. Down there, you say hello to somebody, and they think you've lost your mind."

"Here's the thing about Pittsburg that is unique," I said. "There was no town around like Pittsburg when we were growing up. All kinds of people got along and interacted. We had some racial differences, but we were exposed to a diverse culture, so we didn't have the racial problems that other cities had. They wouldn't even serve blacks in Antioch in the 1960s. So Pittsburg was unique.

"When we were kids, we had this Pop Warner football team called the Mallards. Remember, Rodell? The Mallards had players who were black, white, Hispanic, Island kids. They went undefeated in 1963, and there were negative yards gained against them. They played a championship game in Philadelphia and won. Some towns wouldn't play them because it was a mixed team. But what held Pittsburg together was sports; sports are big in Pittsburg."

"When we played flag football," Rodell said, "Eddie was so fast, nobody could catch him. When we were together, we'd sprint a block, walk a block, sprint a block, every day. And Eddie would have me pop his back, because one of his legs was shorter than the other."

Imagine, a shorter leg for a sprinter who tied the world record in the 100 meters and won an Olympic gold medal! Rodell spilled the beans, I guess, though it wasn't a big secret. My right leg is a quarter-inch shorter than my left leg. I was fourteen or fifteen when I discovered the difference. Rodell was my personal trainer. He would stretch me and align my ankles. That way, it kept me running.

"I had to be there before every race," Rodell said. "I had to be there for Eddie, and he won a lot of races as a teenager. But he wound up third when competing against Dave Masters and Mel Gray. Eddie hadn't yet reached full maturity as a sprinter, but he and Dave Masters got real close, and we'd go visit Dave at his family's home in the El Cerrito hills. It was a really nice home with a view; Dave's father was a doctor. Eddie's dad started letting him use the car, and we'd drive over to Dave's house.

"That was forty years ago, before I moved down south and went to work for Shell Oil, just like Eddie's dad. Then I got into security work and started my own security business. I'm now designing Christian T-shirts. Eddie said he would help me out. I'm thinking of moving back to Pittsburg."

We'll see how that goes, but we're two old best friends, Rodell and I, still building on our friendship. Now that he's no longer dead.

THE BAVARIAN
PERSPECTIVE

There were two important people I needed to contact for my book upon my return to Munich. One man was a surprise 1972 gold medalist, while the second man covered those Olympic Games as a journalist. Both men were from the west side of a divided country.

Klaus Wolfermann won the javelin competition in Munich by the narrowest of margins, and Michael Gernandt wrote about it for the *Süddeutsche Zeitung,* Munich's leading newspaper and one of Germany's most prominent.

Gernandt didn't only know track and field from research: he was a German junior sprint champion before the country became West and East. In 1958, at nineteen, he was timed at 10.4 seconds in the 100-meter dash; injuries prevented him from competing in the 1960 German Olympic Trials. Athletic prowess runs in his family: his wife, Erika, threw the javelin at the Rome Olympics in '60, before shifting to the high jump and then basketball, leading Germany's women hoopsters in scoring.

Gernandt joined the *Süddeutsche Zeitung* in 1961, and before retiring as sports editor in 2002, he covered eight Olympics, winter and summer, starting in 1964. But the massacre of 1972 still lingers in his mind.

"Directly after the attack, people were shocked," he said, "shocked like the police, who made so many mistakes. Before the shooting of the terrorists at Fürstenfeldbruck, the terrorists were allowed to go to the airport by bus. Everything went wrong: the terrorists, the hostages and a policeman, all shot down. The whole case was full of mistakes, by the police and by the Bavarian government, which was unprepared on the security end. They had no experience with such attacks.

Germany's Klaus Wolfermann won the 1972 Olympic javelin throw in his native land by the narrowest of margins. (Photo courtesy of Klaus Wolfermann)

"When the public learned about these mistakes, they were even more furious. Even today, you can read about them. There are TV movies about these mistakes, and when these movies come out, it's full in the newspaper. And we had a very good Olympics until the attack, a brilliant Olympics, showing strangers that there was a new Germany. The Second World War was behind us; we had learned our lesson from Hitler and the Nazi regime. The Germany of today is liberal and free."

Then disaster struck. Even the divided Germany of 1972, in the thinking of that misguided Munich Olympic Committee, was too liberal and too free with an Olympic Village that didn't protect its athletes from armed invaders.

Wolfermann's English isn't as polished as Gernandt's, but the javelin gold medalist has an able interpreter in his wife, Friederike. The Wolfermanns still are troubled by the slayings.

"We knew some of the people," said Friederike.

"Two, three people," added Klaus. "They were often here at a training camp in Germany. The weightlifter, Romano. The coach, I can't remember his name [Weinberg]. It's been too long, but the tragedy was crazy, the first type of terrorism in sport. My competition was two days before the attack, on September 3. If my competition had been two days later, I don't know how it would have turned out."

"You see TV," said Friederike, "and it's always Munich, Munich, Munich, and the Olympic Games. They tried, in 1972, to make the Olympics friendly, for the area and the people."

"There was music inside the stadium," Klaus noted, "and on the outside in the Olympic Village."

"At that time, security wasn't necessary," said his wife. "You didn't need it. You can't forget what happened, but life goes on." Munich didn't need security until it found out it was too late to have it.

The Wolfermanns brought their twelve-year-old granddaughter, Katherina, along with them to our meeting. What does a young girl know about Munich 1972? "German history comes later in school, in high school," said Friederike.

"It's important that you tell people the truth about Munich," Klaus said in general, "so that they will understand what happened. I don't forget it."

"They will speak about it in school," his wife said. "They don't try to hide it. I remember after the tragedy, one sprinter went home. I can't remember his name, or his country, but he didn't want to compete. I think it was right that they continued the Games. If you break, all those other terrorists, it's a license to kill. You can always find a reason to protest, but the Olympics are not supposed to be political."

"Sports and politics," contradicted Klaus. "It's normal."

Munich did have reason to smile in 1972, partly because of Klaus Wolfermann's gold medal, which came as a shock to the Germans, the rest of the world, and Wolfermann himself. "As for my story," he said, "my chances of winning the gold medal did not seem real before the Olympics. I was just trying to make a good place for myself. Bronze medal, silver medal. . . . Hallelujah! But a gold medal? That is sport. You see the favorite as your teacher, and then you're better than your teacher. That is sport. Yeah, yeah . . . an upset. Very surprising for me."

Wolfermann's teacher, or main challenge, was Janis Lusis of Latvia, the bronze medalist at Tokyo in 1964, and the gold medalist at Mexico City in 1968. On his fifth throw, Wolfermann achieved a lifetime best of 296 feet, 10 inches. Lusis had a sixth, and final, chance and uncorked a throw of 296 feet, 9 inches. Wolfermann had won gold by the narrowest of margins, two and a half centimeters. "When I won the gold medal," Klaus recalled, "the whole stadium was going, 'Wolfermann! Wolfermann! Wolfermann!' Am I still a hero today? Yes, yes, sure."

Triumphs like this aside, one wonders, after the Berlin Olympics in 1936, and the reign of Nazism, and following the Munich Olympics in 1972 and the terrible tragedy, will Germany ever host another Olympics? Will Munich? "I hope so," said Friederike. "We tried for the Winter Olympics in 2018. Klaus was like a delegate, representing Germany.

"Hamburg is trying to get the Summer Olympics in 2024," said Klaus. In the spring of 2015, Hamburg was among four cities, along with Paris, Rome and Boston, seeking the 2024 Olympics. Then Boston removed itself, replaced by Los Angeles, which hosted the 1932 and 1984 Olympics. Hamburg's bid, at last, represents all of Germany. Mexico City in 1968 was the first Summer Olympics during which Germany was divided. Then after the Berlin Wall came down, Germany competed as a united country again at the Summer Olympics in Barcelona in 1992. The decision regarding the 2024 host will be made in 2017.

"Perhaps Germany will get those Games in Hamburg and show that the Germans are able to manage the Olympics," Michael Gernandt hopes. "The Germans have good relations with Israel today, and, in terms of security, Munich became an object lesson for Olympic Games that came later. London had to pay $1 billion for security in 2012. Compared to that, security in 1972 was laughable."

Yes, security at the Munich Olympics was laughable, in one sense, but also tragic, and the tears haven't dried yet.

"However, as for Munich's chances of getting another Olympics, I don't think so," Gernandt noted. "If Hamburg gets the 2024 Olympics, Germany would have to wait another thirty years for another Olympics. And there's really no need to have another Olympics, because Germany failed in its bid to host the 2018 and 2022 Winter Games."

Gernandt shed further positive light on the 1972 Olympics: West German high jumper Ulrike Meyfarth, who, at sixteen, won the gold medal with a leap of 6 feet, 3½ inches, a nearly three-inch improvement over her personal best. Remarkably, twelve years later, she won again, with a mark of 6 feet, 7½ inches in Los Angeles. "She is a hero today in Germany," said Gernandt, "even bigger than Heidi Rosendahl," a West German who won the long jump in Munich at 23 feet, 3 inches. Meyfarth is a bigger Olympic hero in Germany than even Klaus Wolfermann."

Another reason Gernandt can't imagine Munich hosting another Summer Olympics is that the Olympic Stadium isn't used for sports anymore. "German people are upset by this," he said, "because the memories of that stadium are so big. Its soccer teams, Bayern Munich and 1860, no longer play there, and there's no more track and field either. It's such a big decline. Now they're having a difficult time placing the [Israeli] memorial. They all want the memorial—they just can't find a place. And this would be a great memorial, like a museum."

Further shades of 1972: I asked Wolfermann and Gernandt how much they remembered about what happened to Rey Robinson and me at those Olympic Games.

"There was a big fuss about your coming here to Munich," said Wolfermann. "Eddie Hart's here! There were big sprinters in Munich, and I remember your story. It was forty-three years ago, but it seems like yesterday."

"We were surprised," Gernandt said. "We couldn't see any reason why you weren't running. But in the evening, we learned what happened. Then the public was laughing. How could this happen? Did you have the wrong schedule? You got it from your coach, Stan Wright? I know this name. All we knew was that something was wrong.

"Then in the morning, we learned what happened. It was a joke for us. A big, organized team like the United States could make such a mistake. We thought of the poor boys who had to run, you and Rey Robinson. Only Robert Taylor made the final, but he had no chance against Valery Borzov. I think you two, you and Rey Robinson, had no chance against Borzov. But every Olympics since 1972, we are joking about this incident. It's still a story, because we never had such a case."

I started to explain what happened to the four of us: Rey Robinson, Robert Taylor, Stan Wright and myself. But Gernandt, ever the reporter, began interviewing me.

"Eddie, when you learned you were wrong, did you rush to the stadium?"

"I was in my room," I answered, "very confident that I would win my next race. I was looking through some literature when I discovered—"

"Was this correct story written in the American newspapers, in *Track and Field News?*" Gernandt interrupted.

"I don't think so," I said. "Stan Wright put out a book, and he talked about it. But the only challenge for the three of us Americans was the final. No one in the world was running 9.9 seconds, 10 flat at that time. Borzov wasn't running that fast, and Rey and I tied the world record of 9.9 seconds at the Olympic Trials."

Now I played the reporter. Didn't Gernandt think it odd that only Stan Wright, of all the sprint coaches at the Olympics, was given the wrong time schedule?

"It's mysterious, I don't know," he replied. "All other sprinters were punctual at their races. Only the Americans weren't. Do you think there's a secret about your case? I heard this question for the first time [now]."

That situation, plus the weird outcome of the men's basketball gold medal game between the USA and USSR—it all seemed so strange. Then in the 400-meter relay final, and in the 200-meter final with Larry Black representing the United States, we were both in lane one, the worst lane around the curve, despite our very fast times. Stranger still. Did Gernandt ever consider that there was some possible political collusion against the United States?

"No, never," he said. "I heard this problem for the first time now, but did you know the name of the official that gave Stan Wright the wrong schedule? It's too long ago to have those details. We had only West German and international officials, but no officials from Russia and East Germany.

"The basketball final, it was a surprise result. The Americans lost by their own fault, I think. The last fifty seconds, they made mistakes. The Russians, very clever in their heads, used that situation to make their victory. The officials at the [score table] weren't Germans; they were international officials. Germans had no experience with basketball at this time."

And Gernandt made it clear, once again, that he didn't believe Robinson and I had any chance against Borzov, regardless of our disqualifications. "At this stage," he said, "he was unbeatable during the Olympic Games. That's my opinion."

I liked playing the journalist, me, Eddie Hart, against a journalist. And so I asked, "Why was Borzov so unbeatable?"

Gernandt looked uncomfortable. "Should I speak the truth?" he said.

Of course.

He put a finger in his mouth.

"We called him a sprinter out of the laboratory," he said. "He was the first European sprinter with good experience with doping. The Russians had always known everything about doping, since thirty years before. Russia and East Germany exchanged information. Borzov was accompanied by science—by scientists."

"I would support your statement," I said to Gernandt. "At that time, the

Michael Gernandt, a retired Munich sports journalist, has documented proof that Eastern Bloc athletes abused drugs. (Courtesy of Michael Gernandt)

Russians and East Germans were ahead of everyone in terms of the science that they employed with their athletes."

"Borzov's from the Ukraine," Gernandt pointed out, "and the Ukrainians have so much scientific information about doping and technical circumstances. Sergei Bubka [the first pole vaulter to clear nineteen feet] is also from the Ukraine. He and Borzov are now both sports ministers in the Ukraine. I saw Borzov some time ago, and he is fat. You wouldn't recognize him."

I wondered how Gernandt knew so much about those Ukrainian and Eastern Bloc athletes who doped. "I have a stack of papers this high," he said, raising his hand a foot off the table.

He then excused himself to catch a Bayern Munich soccer game on television; his passion for sports hasn't abated with retirement. He wore Bayern Munich–supporting clothing to our meeting, showing his fierce loyalty. And his visit offered clarity about Munich in 1972, assuring me that my suppositions about Borzov weren't misguided.

Eastern Bloc athletes, scientifically enhanced? That's common knowledge. You can look at certain athletes and tell. In Munich, Hungary won thirty-five medals, Bulgaria twenty-one, and Romania sixteen. In Rio 2016, Hungary won fifteen medals, Romania five, and Bulgaria three. In Munich, East Germany won sixty-six medals. In Rio, a unified Germany won forty-two medals. Draw your own conclusions.

But my thing was the race itself, not Borzov, not chemicals. My mentality was that if I ran my best race, it didn't matter who else was in the race, or what he was ingesting. Like I said, I don't begrudge Borzov his gold medals. I'm only saying that in the 100-meter finals at the 1972 Olympic Trials, I ran the best race I had ever run, and that was the fastest anyone in the world had run in that particular year.

But I didn't get to run against Borzov in the 1972 Olympics 100-meter final. Let's just leave it at that for now. Perhaps I have another 100 meters to run in Munich.

LEARNING TO SPRINT

I was six years old when I became a sprinter. I don't know what Jesse Owens, Bobby Morrow, Bob Hayes, and Usain Bolt were doing at age six, but that's when I had my first competitive sprint. And I felt pressure right away, because my family was watching little Eddie Hart toe the mark at the starting line.

My first race was at the annual Shell Oil Company picnic for employees of the Martinez Refinery. One of those employees was my father, T. J. Hart. I wanted to make him proud, especially in front of his colleagues. And I did just that, easily running away from the field in the 50-yard dash. A sprinter was born that day.

Every year as a kid, I ran that 50-yard dash at the Shell picnic, and every year I won against kids my own age. It felt good to be fast, but it felt even better to be undefeated. And I received more recognition for sprinting, I discovered, than I would later for hitting home runs.

My father would have preferred my continuing to hit home runs, because he loved baseball. I was born two years after Jackie Robinson integrated baseball, and I grew up when Willie Mays and Hank Aaron were becoming major-league stars. I'm not sure if my father thought I would break Babe Ruth's record, but I did lead the youth midget league one year with thirteen home runs. I had good hand-eye coordination, and I also developed defensive skills at third base. I was showing early promise as a ballplayer.

My dad was an assistant coach, which made it tougher on me, because I couldn't fool around. I was asked to pitch, which I hated, because it was too much work. I threw the ball OK; I just didn't like it when I walked a batter or the other team got a bunch of hits. I didn't look like the next Bob Gibson, but

I'd be at the park every day in the summer, playing ball all day long. I guess I was too committed to the game, because when I returned to school in the fall, the nurse weighed me, and I had lost sixteen pounds. She weighed me three times to make sure the scales were right.

Well, you didn't have to weigh much to be a sprinter. And for winning those races at the Shell picnic, plus other races I won in elementary school, I received trophies, medals, and ribbons. We won our Little League division in baseball, but we didn't get any awards, just a trip to the A&W Root Beer stand. That didn't beat the awards I got for running, and I always got sick from drinking too much root beer.

I loved showing off those awards to family and friends. One Sunday in church, the pastor announced that I had won my race, with my whole family listening in the pews. If that made them proud, it made me even prouder. I didn't miss hitting home runs; I had found my true calling. Sorry, Willie Mays, I had other footsteps to follow in.

God gave me the ability to run fast, whether running around the bases or running down the track. Speed even worked in kickball or playing hide and seek. I ran all the time, down the street, or around the schoolyard. I ran or raced any time I had the opportunity, even when I wasn't in a hurry. When I wasn't beating kids even older than me, I'd imagine being in races, stumbling out of the blocks, and coming from behind to win at the tape. Running had possessed me.

I needed that validation because, as I've said, I wasn't a good student at that age. My brother John was the smart one. When he was five years old, our church gave him a Christmas speech, about Joseph and Mary and the birth of Jesus, to read. It lasted ten minutes, and he read it perfectly. Every time someone came to our house, my parents had John recite that same speech. I had a speech, too, a very short poem: "What are you looking at me for, I didn't come to stay, I just came to tell you today is Christmas Day." Then I went and sat down. Quickly.

I wasn't jealous of John, even when he was student-body president of Pittsburg High School. The two of us, actually, were very close. I'd tell people how proud I was of John's academic achievements, and he'd tell people how proud he was of my track accomplishments. And we both meant it.

But after my positive fifth-grade experience with Mrs. Mercurio, everything crashed in the sixth grade under Mrs. Martha Ascherl, though it wasn't her fault. It was the first troublesome time of my young life, and I can't explain why. I began feeling sad, like I wanted to cry all the time. I don't know what caused it, but it felt like a net was cast over me, and I couldn't get out. I now believe it was depression, which then became so severe that I didn't even want to play sports. I felt weak, lacking energy. I grew quieter, so no one really knew what was going on inside of me. I walked alone to school and back. It was a scary time for me. I was eleven.

One recess period, I spent the whole time crying. I didn't want to go back to class. A friend, I can't remember who, confronted me and asked what was wrong. I didn't have the courage to tell him what I was feeling, because I didn't think he'd understand anyway. Things were getting worse, and I didn't know what to do. I felt so helpless, like I was isolated on some island.

Finally, I worked up the courage to talk with Mrs. Ascherl. I wasn't very articulate, but I tried my best to explain what was going on inside me, even though I was crying. Like Mrs. Mercurio, she really cared. When I finished talking, she offered words of encouragement. I'm sure this was something new to her, but she was there for me, and that helped. She asked if I had told my parents, and I said no. She asked if I wanted her to speak with them for me, and I said no again. But the conversation between us was soothing, and it was the beginning of my recovery.

After a few weeks, I was back playing with my friends, even hanging out with them, walking to school with them. I was back to being my old self. Who can explain why these things come and go? But it passed. I have a feeling Mrs. Ascherl might have said something to my mother—not because of anything my mom said; it's just a feeling. Reuniting with Mrs. Mercurio in 2015, I told her about my depression in the sixth grade, and how Mrs. Ascherl guided me through it. Mrs. Mercurio's reply surprised me.

"Eddie, she was my sixth-grade teacher."

How could that be? My sixth-grade teacher taught my fifth-grade teacher.

"I didn't know that," I replied. "Mrs. Ascherl saw my tears, which made it serious for her. She talked to me about it, and it made our relationship closer."

"She saw you in a different light, Eddie. She was a very experienced teacher, one of those old-time teachers. I learned so much from her. She was a lady. You didn't say 'boo' to her, but she knew her business. She knew I was a good student, and she encouraged me to go higher, to raise the bar. I tried to become a teacher just like her."

Both those teachers were instrumental in my life, and I tried to become a teacher just like Mrs. Mercurio and Mrs. Ascherl, helping kids whenever and wherever I could. For kids remain our best investment, and teachers need to make that investment pay off with big dividends.

Though I received more compliments for my track sprinting than for my baseball slugging, which made me turn to sprinting full-time, I wasn't going to stay undefeated forever, and all because of Collins Meyers.

One day, the top sprinters from the three classrooms of sixth graders at Village Elementary School were matched in a 50-yard race, and Collins nipped me at the wire. That was the one time he beat me, and only because I ran in oversized, floppy shoes. We became good friends after that. Unfortunately, he died in 2014.

But winning or losing, there's always another race to run. Life goes on.

BLACK AND WHITE

How many memories can a visit to your past reawaken? Walking into that Olympic Stadium for the first time in four decades stirred my memory in many different ways, especially in terms of controversy—podiums and protests, images and insinuations, perceptions and reality.

Besides what happened to me and Rey Robinson, I thought about the cases of Tommie Smith and John Carlos and of Vince Matthews and Wayne Collett, and their separate Olympic medal stand protests four years apart.

All four men became my friends. And I'm not condemning their actions. Each man must make his own choices, but I wouldn't make my point, if I had a point to make, in the manner they chose, for the entire world to see. That's not who I am.

Smith and Carlos, who finished first and third in the 200-meter sprint at the Mexico City Games in 1968, are remembered mainly for their humanitarian salutes on the medal stand. That image led to a slew of accusations and death threats, and all they did was stand up for their ethnicity, which isn't a crime.

Matthews and Collett finished first and second in the 400-meter dash at the Munich Games in 1972 and then challenged Olympic protocol with their podium behavior. First, Matthews pulled Collett up with him on the victory stand. Collett was barefoot and in shorts. Matthews left his jacket open, and both men casually looked around and chatted while "The Star-Spangled Banner" was played. Matthews fiddled with his goatee. Collett had some old shoes hanging around his neck. Upon leaving the stand, Matthews twirled his gold medal around a finger, and Collett gave a Black Power salute. But winning Olympic medals doesn't translate into jail time.

Nonetheless, Smith, Carlos, Matthews, and Collett paid for their demonstrations. They were banished from their respective Olympic Games on the spot and were told that their Olympic days were over. That's reality, but perception is another story. Maybe the best way, sometimes, to respond to certain perceptions is to ignore them, or to offer a comparative perception, like Dave Wottle's story.

Wottle won the 800-meter dash at Munich while wearing his familiar baseball cap. The courteous thing to do when "The Star-Spangled Banner" is played is to remove your cap. Well, the whole world saw that Wottle didn't take his off during the anthem's playing, but that was the beginning and the end of it. He wasn't kicked out of those Olympics or banned from further Olympics.

Wottle is an American, just like Smith, Carlos, Matthews, and Collett. But Wottle is white, while the other four are black. Wottle apologized later for his gaffe, while the other four didn't. Yet disrespect is disrespect, and as applied to black and white people, there is a different set of standards.

Look, I've never been a member of a protest group, and I don't mean to pick on Dave Wottle. He got caught up in the moment and forgot to take off his hat. I get that. And I'm not suggesting that he should have been banned from the Olympics. But he wasn't, and why do you think that is? Because he's white, that's why.

Smith and Carlos planned their last-minute protest, but Wottle didn't plan his show of disrespect, and Matthews and Collett didn't plan theirs, either, from everything I know. It wasn't some racially motivated gesture, just two guys hanging out on the victory stand. So, what's the big deal? Well, it became a very big deal in several ways. With Matthews and Collett suddenly banned from the Munich Olympics, and John Smith having torn a hamstring in the 400-meter final, America couldn't field four runners for the 1600-meter relay, and thus was disqualified, my least favorite word.

The color of Wottle's skin and the color of Smith's, Carlos's, Matthews's, and Collett's had everything to do with the punishment meted out. It's hard for a black man to get away from the color of his skin. All over the world, we're not looked at as people; we're looked at as black people. That's something we can't get away from. No white person can get a handle on what it's like to be black. That isn't perception; that's just reality.

I'm African American, or black, whichever you choose. And like other African Americans, or blacks, I've heard the N word a lot, and in a lot of different contexts. I'm so glad I grew up with the parents I had, because I didn't grow up with hatred. They taught me to treat everyone fairly. That allowed me to be open to all people. For example, take the relationship I have with Dave

John Carlos, the controversial 200-meter bronze medalist at Mexico City, admired Eddie Hart's toughness as a sprinter. (Photo courtesy of Eddie Hart)

Maggard, my track coach at Cal. He knows I love him, and I know he loves me. Dave's played a very special and significant role in my life. He's white, I'm black, but I talk to him all the time. I've spoken with him since I arrived in Munich on this trip. He helped me deal with my disqualification in Munich. He was there. I wouldn't have made it without him.

I have no hatred toward whites, though I know black people who've lived with this weight, this bear on their backs, and all because of the hatred that they carry around inside them. They can't even have a life because they're imprisoned by their own hatred. Words can't describe how grateful I am to my parents for teaching me to give all races and ethnicities the same chance, because we're all people. But hatred is reciprocal, and there are whites just as hateful as blacks, using more hateful language.

I know not just whites use the hateful *N* word. African Americans use it, too, when speaking to one another, although not in a hateful manner. It's a term of affection, used to laugh off its racist connotation. In an amicable relationship, you'll hear blacks calling whites the *N* word, and whites calling blacks the *N* word, quenching a brush fire with humor.

From what my father told me, "black" once had the same connotation as the *N* word. There was a time when my father said, "I don't want to be called black," because of how that word was used when he was younger. James Brown had a great deal to do with changing that perception. When he appeared on *The Merv Griffin Show,* Griffin called him "colored." Brown stopped him: "Colored is out, and black is in." We're all black people, and we refer to one another that way. It's OK, it's accepted. President Obama is a black man to the universe, and everyone's cool with it, except some dissidents, who see him as half white. So it's not always about the word; it's about perception, and who's saying it.

There are white people who say, "I'm not a racist." Yet racism still is a problem in this country. It's not a black problem or a white problem but a people problem. You have people who have sworn to uphold the laws of the Constitution, and they don't. These are laws that guide us, inalienable rights that have been around for two-hundred-plus years. There are people in important government positions who should not be in power. People who run on racial tickets, like George Wallace.

My father never looked at himself as African American. He saw himself as an American. One undeniable truth that came out of 9/11 is that we all have red blood. We all live; we all die. All of us have more similarities than differences, but we focus on our differences. We each have one heart, two eyes, two ears, a nose, a mouth, two kidneys, and two lungs. We all have skin, just different shades.

But back to Tommie Smith and John Carlos: I had the same opportunity they did, to stand on the podium and raise my fist. But that isn't my method of dealing with racial subjects. I'd rather talk it out than protest. Dr. Martin Luther King Jr., and Malcolm X took dissimilar routes on this same journey. I'm not saying who's right and who's wrong, but both were talking about race. Look, President Kennedy, who was white, forced other whites to let black kids go to school in Alabama, where George Wallace was a racist governor. Separatism and apartheid, these aren't secrets. To change racist policies, people must speak their opinions at the tops of their voices. I speak softly, but I believe my voice carries the same force.

Do I consider myself a patriot? I have a very specific way of answering that question. I was born and raised in the United States. I am a U.S. citizen, but I'm also black. So wherever I've gone as an athlete, or even now as a retired athlete, I am a citizen and I am a black person. I don't have a problem with being either. But I believe I'm entitled to all that goes along with that privilege of being born in this country, though it hasn't always worked out that way for me, my parents, or their parents.

There's just a big difference, sometimes insurmountable, in being black. Look, most Jews, Russians, and Irish folks can hide their ethnicities, because they're predominantly white. It's harder for blacks to hide their heritage. We know we're going to be treated a certain way, depending on which part of the country we're living in, but always based on our color. We'll be treated with greater contempt in the Deep South, where we were not always allowed to enter certain places. The South, remember, is the birthplace of the Ku Klux Klan. But the North isn't always hospitable to blacks either.

In 1976, when I was a Cal assistant coach, the NCAA Championships were in Philadelphia. Julian Lucas, a friend of mine, and I went to visit Cornel West in Cambridge, Massachusetts. It was the night after white people had beaten up an African American man at Harvard Square. As I drove our rental car near a bridge, Cornel said, "That's South Boston. No black people can go in there." I said, "Nonsense," and drove right on. Right away, white people started pointing and calling us the *N* word. I turned around and got out of there quickly.

That reception was clearly racist, but it's part of the African American's life. I've tried to live my life like most African Americans, respectfully. My faith addresses this issue better than politics does. Growing up, I heard that you were either part of the problem or part of the solution. I never tackled that issue by joining certain political groups at Cal, though various activists urged me not to compete in track and not to get on the team bus. That seemed part of the problem, not the solution.

Here in Munich, I've had this same conversation with Eddie Jr. while riding the tram at night. He has his own family now; in this generation, though, does he ever hear the *N* word?

"For sure," he told me. "But if I can speak for my generation, words are just words, unless we get into certain problems. Words can't hurt you unless there's a connotation behind them. It's how the *N* word is used that will decide how I deal with it. Words only have the power that we choose to give them. You and Mom didn't tell me how to deal with that word, but I was given examples. You can read body language and know that it's time to get away. Or it's time to deal with it. It's all about being aware.

"But I'm fearless. I'm not afraid of much, like getting beat up, bombed, or killed. And I'm not afraid of differences. I could walk down the street, and an elderly lady could fear me because of what she might have heard about me. She'd pull in her purse and move farther away from me. It's the fear of differences that creates our problems. It's not just 'You're black' or 'You're white.' It's just fear. When blacks were freed from slavery, whites feared that blacks would harm them, just like whites had harmed blacks. But the blacks only wanted to live their own lives.

"It's all about differences. I have a thing about people with glasses, like how do they see the world? When I was in high school, people used to think I was making fun of them when I asked to look through their glasses. I just wanted to know how they saw things. I'd ask them what it was like being near-sighted, or far-sighted, to understand what that meant, because I had 20/20 vision. I was just trying to embrace difference, but difference makes people nervous. Or, like I said, fearful."

Fear is part of racism, and people feared—or intensely disliked—Tommie Smith and John Carlos in 1968. The death threats they were sent after Mexico City included bullets in envelopes. Smith's mother also found dead animals on her doorstep. The two men paid a steep price for exercising their rights of free speech.

"It was a freedom of speech that was dishonored, and that went on for the better part of twenty-five years," Carlos said in June 2015. "Today, Tommy and I aren't seen as heroes or villains but as legends. It just depends which side of the mountain you look at. Forty-seven years later, a lot of people want to take my picture, both of me and of my fist in the air."

Olympic banishment to camera ops—who would have thought? So who showed up at Munich in 1972, but Carlos, as a representative for Puma footwear, passing out athletic apparel to the Olympians. He was there when the terrorist attack occurred.

"It struck me," Carlos said of the massacre, "that four years before, Tommy and I tried to make a statement in terms of humanity on the medal stand in trying to deal with issues. And then these individuals (in Munich) were fighting for issues that they thought were of great concern, and violence occurred and lives were taken. I don't know who's the good guy and who's the bad guy." It all comes down to perception, though Carlos doesn't condone violence. The Arabs and Israelis are still harming each other nearly a half century after Munich, with no end in sight.

How did Carlos think Matthews's and Collett's 1972 medal stand actions compared with his and Smith's protest in 1968? "They appeared with more of a sarcastic attitude toward the American echelon, which hadn't made it easy for these guys in terms of training facilities. They had a little bit of arrogance on the victory stand, but I don't think they were being disrespectful. Despite everything, they were there, and they succeeded. I'm sure they endured some hardships afterwards, but they weren't the same hardships that Tommie and I faced. We've had our own disagreements between the two of us, but now we have a better understanding."

Harry Edwards, a retired University of California, Berkeley, professor of sociology, planned the Olympic Project for Human Rights, the proposed boycott of the 1968 Olympics that petered out. Edwards elected not to travel to Mexico City, leaving Smith and Carlos on their own. They decided just prior to the 200-meter final to give Black Power salutes. But did they feel abandoned by Edwards?

"I have no problem with Harry," said Carlos. "I'm on good terms with him."

Carlos was protesting long before Mexico City. As a youngster in Harlem, in a bold move to improve his school cafeteria's food, he told the principal, "You've got forty-eight hours." He didn't explain his ultimatum, but the principal caved in when Carlos wouldn't back down. Carlos later set fire to trees infested with caterpillars so that his mother, a nurse's aide, could sit down in a courtyard during her hospital breaks. Thus, his actions in Mexico City were no surprise.

"I would not take away anything, man," said Carlos, reflecting on 1968. "It would have to be the same today as it was back then. I'm very much at peace when you stand for what's right."

Like Smith and Carlos, Nat Turner and Malcolm X were feared, too. Some people are afraid of other people because of their clout, as if they're going to destroy your world and your values. Remember the question from back in the day: what does the black man want? It's simple: the same things anyone wants—to buy milk, to feed his children, and to get them into college, and to make it day to day.

Blacks don't have any hidden agendas; we just need to appreciate the differences in one another. Differences make the world go round. Just ask my son.

"Differences and uniqueness, dad," Eddie Jr. said. "Differences are what make us great. But what came from you, my parents, was the importance of being an individual. I never drink. I never smoke. My peers said I needed to do these things to fit in. But I never wanted to fit in, because I was OK with being different. Does that make me unique? I can't say, but now that I'm a father, I want my children to be able to make decisions. And the best way for them to do that is by being themselves and not being afraid to look in the mirror. Yes, I want them to be brilliant, but it all starts with being themselves and being happy with themselves."

Tommie Smith and John Carlos were being themselves in 1968, just as Vince Matthews, Wayne Collett, and, yes, Dave Wottle were being themselves in 1972. Vince and Wayne, whose actions were unrehearsed, ended up getting banned, just like Tommie and John, unrehearsed, delivered Black Power salutes and got banned. Dave Wottle wasn't banned. He didn't receive death threats, bullets in envelopes, or dead animals on his doorstep. Different strokes for black folks? Must be so.

THE EAGLE FLIES

It's early morning in Munich, and I'm running through the city's streets. I've been running all of my life, and I can't stop now, even in my mid-sixties. Running, like tram riding, gives me time to think. Since I'm getting little sleep on this trip, excited about renewing an old relationship after a long separation, I've done lots of thinking.

It's cold this early spring morning, like it's been every day since we've arrived. I'm dodging automobiles and buses to get in my daily four-mile run. But despite the thirty-degree weather, I'm thinking about a turning point in my life that really influenced my track career, and that thought gives me a warm feeling in spite of the frosty air.

Bert Bonanno is on my mind, because without his influence, I wouldn't have won an Olympic gold medal. I was thirteen when we met in Pittsburg, California. I was an eighth grader, and he was the new track coach of the Central Junior High School Eagles. He wanted me to join the team. I rejected him twice before he tricked me.

He followed me into the boys' bathroom. He had picked up a cigarette butt in the teacher's lounge, and he dropped it on the bathroom floor. There was just the two of us. He said, "Mr. Hart, there's a cigarette on the floor." And I said, "Coach, I don't smoke." And he said, "I'm going to cut a deal with you. I'm not going to send you to the dean, who's a nasty guy. You come out for track and we'll forget the whole situation." So I went out for track, a better alternative than facing that nasty dean.

As I could see, Coach Bonanno was the new sheriff in town, and he wasn't blowing smoke as far as his intentions, which were to build a strong track

Bert Bonanno discovered Eddie Hart in junior high school, but he had to coax him to come out for track. (Photo courtesy of Bert Bonanno)

program at our junior high. And he did it first class, ordering brand-new uniforms with "Eagles" on the back, along with brand-new running spikes. Coach Bonanno got what he wanted, including me, which meant that I had to, first, run cross-country if I wanted to be a sprinter. Huh?

That didn't sound too logical, but he had all of his runners—sprinters and dash men—running long distance. I'm not the cross-country type, and I couldn't keep up with those who were, but when the track-and-field season began in the spring, I was in the best shape of my life, having acquired new stamina that improved my sprinting. Coach Bonanno was the first coach who showed me what it takes to win.

He knew how to train athletes and how to prepare them for competition. He pushed us to the limit, and then he pushed us even harder. He understood the mechanics of good running and sprinting techniques. He was my first coach to emphasize relaxation, high knees, and the proper use of your arms in order to spur you on when fatigue takes over your body.

"Relax, relax," he yelled over and over. "Loose jaws; your face is grimacing. Pump your arms." In the spring, he had us running these 330-yard distances, which I hated. I never argued with him, because it wouldn't have done any good anyway. It was his way, period. And I'm glad it was, because we all got into great shape, and we destroyed our competition, which consisted of four junior high schools.

Then he entered us in the Martinez Relays, where we performed well, followed by the El Cerrito Relays, where we did extremely well, winning the 440- and the 880-yard relays. In the latter, I ran anchor, and when I got the baton, I was a couple of steps behind. When I crossed the finish line, I was at least ten yards ahead, and I had plenty left, thanks to Coach Bonanno.

The Central Junior High Eagles were flying high, and I felt like I was flying the highest. By the end of the season, we had established ourselves as a dominant force, winning the conference championship and the North Coast title. Coach Bonanno gave me the confidence to shoot even higher. At thirteen, I decided to become the World's Fastest Human. I wanted that title. I dreamed of that title. I even saw my name in lights: "Eddie Hart, the World's Fastest Human." This meant becoming the 100-meter champion in the Olympic Games. I wasn't sure in which Olympics that would be, but I envisioned standing on the podium, hearing our national anthem playing, and having that gold medal placed around my neck.

When I told Coach Bonanno, he said, simply, "Eddie, you're capable."

Coach Bonanno had a mission, too, which he told me about years later. "My dream, Eddie, was to come back to Pittsburg, where I was born and raised, to train distance runners," he said. "At that time, very few African Americans were distance runners. So I had this testing program, where a nurse would be involved, also a counselor, and there would be strict rules for academics.

"We didn't have a track at Central, but we had this stretch of lawn, 380 yards. Every time we tested, the African Americans were really ahead of the others. You, Eddie, were in that group, along with Donald Ray Pierce, who was the first American to high-jump seven feet in high school competition. Your speed during those tests was phenomenal. But you were shy, extremely shy, and that's why I had to convince you to try out, because we had, potentially, the best freshman group in the country."

(Opposite) Eddie Hart's track potential blossomed at Pittsburg High School. (Photo courtesy of Eddie Hart)

What exactly did Bonanno see in me, at thirteen, that even hinted of my becoming world-class one day? "Besides your speed, your ability to lift your body when fatigued was very unusual," he told me years later. "You had a very economic running form—chin down, arms in the correct position, loose jaw, et cetera."

We were the Eagles, so proud to be wearing those brand-spanking-new red-and-white uniforms, and those brand-spanking-new spikes with red trim. They felt a lot better than those old Jesse Owens spikes—that's what we called them—which felt like boots, and made me wonder how Owens won four gold medals in the 1936 Olympics, wearing those clodhoppers.

Coach Bonanno had ordered those new uniforms without the approval of our principal, Warren Waite, because he wanted us to look good on the track. His motivation was to make us look good and to perform well, and he believed the two went hand in hand. "These are your school colors, and the Eagle is your school mascot," he told us. "When you put this uniform on, you're not just representing yourself, but your school and your community. And you must do it with pride and self-esteem."

Cardinal and white, of course, are the colors of Stanford University, Cal's longtime rival. I wouldn't be caught dead wearing those colors, but when I was in junior high, I was hardly a candidate for admission into Cal. Thus, blue and gold weren't yet my favorite colors. I hope all Cal alums—Old Blues—will understand.

Every time Central Junior High traveled to a track meet, there would be a school counselor on the bus, motivating us, talking about our potential for winning. Coach Bonanno believed success had many components, and he wanted all of them covered. A Central alum himself, perhaps he saw in us the teenager he once was.

We certainly were ripe for learning, some of us more than others. While training near some old coalmines in the hills, one of my teammates came running up to Coach Bonanno, shouting, "I just saw a deer." Only it wasn't a deer—it was a cow. Coach Bonanno told me much later, "See what I was dealing with?"

The first sign of Central Junior High's having a special track bunch occurred at the King City Relays. Donald Ray won the high jump, and I won the 100 in the high school competition. But the key to my later success, Coach Bonanno believes, was the day I had a runoff with a Berkeley High School sprinter at Miramonte High in Orinda in order to qualify for the North Coast section meet. "Eddie was a good-looking kid even then," Coach Bonanno told Dave Newhouse. "And he was looking me straight in the eye when I told him, 'You are so much better than that sprinter. I want you to act like this is a workout, not a race. And when the gun goes off, I want you to think about going home.' Eddie then destroyed that kid."

Coach Bonanno had taken a step back in his career to return to Central Junior High. He had been an assistant track coach at San Jose State under his mentor, Bud Winter, who had developed Tommie Smith and Lee Evans. Coach Bonanno believed he needed experience in running his own program, so he returned home to Pittsburg. And he started off with a bang, organizing school rallies at the junior high level. He was imaginative on and off the track.

How imaginative? Well, there was this one situation at Central where the female cheerleaders were chosen, with not one African American girl among them. So African American students put pressure on the African American boys on the track team not to compete in a meet. Facing a potential boycott, what did coach do? He pulled the bus right up to the gym door. The African American boys boarded and got down on the floor. When the bus drove off, only the Caucasian kids were visible, sitting in their seats. After the meet, Coach Bonanno convinced the local paper, the *Pittsburg Post-Dispatch,* not to print the meet results. So it was like we hadn't even competed.

Coach Bonanno had another obstacle: "T. J. Hart," he said. "Eddie kept getting home late from track practice, and his father thought he might be up to something other than sports. So he told Eddie not to come home late, or else. Eddie explained his situation to me. I drove over to the Hart home to tell his father that Eddie was telling the truth. The father never said another word about tardiness.

"Another time, I drove Eddie home and there were all these African American kids standing on the corner. Well, I'm Caucasian, so Eddie rolled down the window and told the kids, 'He's white, but he's all right.' Eddie and I have had a kinship all these years; we're connected at the hip. We're very close." Coach Bonanno and I have maintained a lifetime friendship, even though we don't see each other all that often. But the mutual respect is immense.

"You have to treat sprinters and quarter-milers differently from others," he said, "because those races happen so quickly. But even up to six hundred yards in training runs, Eddie would blow by people. With his innate ability, Eddie would have been a great quarter-miler, even a half-miler. He had an unbelievable reservoir of stamina."

Thanks to all those cross-country runs.

"I really believe Eddie's initial reluctance to come out for track was shyness," said Coach Bonanno. "He was very shy, even in the classroom. It was hard to make eye contact with him. My thinking was that he didn't have high self-esteem; track and field helped him so much in this regard. Then he enjoyed beating the tar out of older sprinters. Eddie had this special smile when he won. His eyes got big.

"When he got to Contra Costa [Junior] College, the coach there, Jack Albiani, did a real good job with Eddie, with vitamins and weight training. That's where Eddie began running some of the best times in the nation and around the world."

Coach Bonanno spent three years at Central Junior High before becoming the national track-and-field coach of Mexico, a four-year stay that included the 1968 Olympic Games in Mexico City, where he helped American athletes prepare for the altitude adjustment and a second hazard, the drinking water.

"My father would send the *Pittsburg Post-Dispatch* to me in Mexico, so I could keep up with Eddie," said Coach Bonanno. "The sports editor there, Charlie Zeno, wrote a lot about Eddie, who went on to Cal. Then I was in Munich with Eddie when I was the national coach of Peru. I remember the massacre like it was yesterday. One of my San Jose City College athletes, Reinhart Voltshoft, had grandparents who owned the land where the Olympic Stadium was built in Munich. Germany wanted to erase the stigma of World War II. How do you murder 10 million people? Then security became a definite problem in Munich.

"My Peruvian team got there early. I lost my identification information, so they gave me a second ID. Security was that loose. With all the people coming through the gate into the Olympic Village, security didn't really check everybody out. So the terrorists had no difficulty attacking the [Israeli] delegation. The next thing I know, I see a tank with its turret going back and forth. And the Germans had Julie Menendez of San Jose State, the U.S. assistant soccer coach, backed against a tree with a submachine gun in his face, while Julie tried to explain that he was an American. You could have cut through the tension in the Village with a bolo knife."

And just like Central Junior High, after my disqualification in Munich, Coach Bonanno was right there, looking after me, though even he couldn't understand how I had missed my race.

"When I was at the 1968 Olympics," Coach Bonanno said, "the Mexicans were very concerned about their reputation for being late and for doing things tomorrow, not today. Don't worry about it, that kind of thing. And so every country, when it arrived, including the U.S. delegation, was given a schedule for their events. That schedule was posted, and if there was a change, the Mexicans actually came to the head coach, who was Payton Jordan of U.S. Track and Field, and notified him.

"They did not do that in Germany. Stan Wright had the original schedule; he did not have the changed one. I'm not blaming Stan, like Howard Cosell did, but Eddie was devastated. I called the *Pittsburg Post-Dispatch* and told them that it wasn't Eddie's fault. I also called Dan Hruby of the *San Jose Mercury-News* with the same story.

"But Eddie was a mess. It was a mess. Dave Maggard was there for Eddie, so he was well taken care of. At the same time, the terrorists were holding the [Israeli] people in that compound. I later told Eddie, 'You can't let this later haunt you for the rest of your life. You have an opportunity to erase part of it in the relay. You need to blow Valery Borzov away.' And that's exactly what Eddie did; it looked like he was shot out of a cannon. I was so proud of Eddie that I started crying."

Coach Bonanno told me that he flew out of Munich after those Olympics with an indelible memory. "I don't want to say security was lax at the Village, just not as strong as it should have been," he said. "When we got to the airport, it was just the opposite. We kept changing gates to catch our plane. You'd look out on the tarmac and there were tanks and all these soldiers. It looked like there was a war going on."

How could I have known as a seventh and eighth grader what the world would be like in ten years, a war zone at the Olympics? Back then, I was just beginning to visualize myself as an Olympian, receiving inspiration from Jesse Owens, one of the greatest Olympians. Watching TV one day, I saw a documentary of Owens winning his four gold medals at the Berlin Olympics in 1936. That hadn't been done previously, one athlete winning four gold medals, and Owens captured my imagination. When he was called the World's Fastest Human, I got emotional in front of the TV. I decided right then that I would do everything I could to one day achieve that same recognition.

I truly believe you must visualize a goal to attain it. Long after my track career was over, I saw another documentary, this one about Shaquille O'Neal, who commented that he had seen himself playing in the NBA many years before he did so. He said, "If you don't see yourself in a dream, you don't have a dream. You must see it, feel it, taste it and, most of all, you must want it more than anything else." He was exactly right. That's the same way I felt at thirteen.

Only I was still learning about life at that age, and also beginning to learn about death. I had a homeroom teacher named Mr. Quido my first year at Central Junior High. He was from a foreign country, like somewhere in the Middle East, so he spoke with an accent. He mumbled a lot, though he was funny and made us laugh all the time. We didn't make him laugh, however. Rather, we got under his skin.

Mr. Quido had all of us students reading out loud. He'd call out a student's name, and the student would say something like, 'Who, me?' And Mr. Quido would say, "I'm not accusing you of anything; I'm just asking you to read." Sometimes, he would simply pass a person by and go on to the next person, which was all right by me, because I didn't want to read in class. Mr. Quido was a little overweight, he wore glasses, and he was fidgety, acting nervous all the time. I don't think we intimidated him; I just don't think he understood us.

Well, one day the vice principal came into our room and said Mr. Quido wouldn't be returning to our class. I thought he had gotten into some kind of accident. His teaching replacement was totally different: he told us, right off, that we had to be on our best behavior at all times, which meant no more laughing at the teacher, and no more getting out of reading to the class. The party was over.

We learned later why Mr. Quido was replaced: he had a heart attack and died. I felt bad because I was one of the kids who gave him a hard time. I don't know if he was married and had children, but he couldn't have been more than forty. I wondered if our attitude toward him endangered his health. I didn't intentionally mean to hurt him; I just wanted to laugh and have fun. But I regretted my behavior, and decided I needed to treat people better. Life is short, I learned. I wanted to apologize to Mr. Quido, but it was too late.

I wasn't good at sharing my feelings, anyway. I was introspective in those days, rather quiet and thinking all the time, unlike some of my friends, who talked about anything and everything. I channeled much of my energy into sports. I really liked gym class, because it gave me an opportunity to exhibit my physical skills. We played all kinds of sports—baseball, basketball, volleyball, dodge ball—and, of course, we ran. And I still was the fastest kid in my class.

Seventh grade was the first year I participated in an organized, or so I thought, track program. Unfortunately, the track coach was in it strictly for the stipend. He was stuck with us because the school couldn't find anyone better to run the program. His idea of a workout was those 50-yard races, but we weren't in good enough shape even for something as short as the 50. We were disorganized and mediocre, and neither the team nor I performed very well. The kids I competed against from other schools received much better training and discipline.

Therefore, I wasn't interested in running track a year later, until Coach Bonanno came along and changed my whole attitude. He taught both academic and physical education classes, though he didn't look like your typical athlete. He had a medium build, was pudgy, had a round face, and he liked to laugh, although Coach Bonanno could be serious. Very serious. He changed us from mediocre into magnificent.

He later changed San Jose City College into an Olympic-style training center.

Olympic decathlon champion Bruce Jenner (1976) worked out there, as did weight men Mac Wilkins, John Powell, Al Feuerbach, and Ed Burke from the USA and athletes from Germany, Finland, Iceland, and other countries.

Coach Bonanno spent thirty-three years at San Jose City College before retiring in 2003. Turning eighty in 2015, he spoke about how disheartened he was by the devaluation of track and field at the junior high school and high school levels.

"It's embarrassing," he said. "Seventy-five percent of the [high school] track coaches in the state of California are part-time people. So they don't know what these kids are going through, because those coaches don't arrive on campus until 3:00 p.m. Old uniforms, rag-tag, it's gone from something special to nothing."

But with Coach Bonanno, it was a special time.

"First off," he told Newhouse, "Eddie Hart was a young man from Pittsburg, California, where I'm from. It was so gratifying to see someone like Eddie come through the way he did. He was a visionary in the way he made something of himself. Eddie didn't get down emotionally. He was always positive, very independent, and didn't let anything get in his way. And he was fortunate to have key people help him.

"Also, he's a natural leader. Kids just rallied around him naturally. When he would speak, which wasn't often, they would really listen. He has some innate abilities that a lot of people aren't blessed with. He put things in the right order. And I don't think Eddie is capable of swearing, maybe a 'Gosh' once in a while.

"This same young man from Pittsburg, California, graduated from Cal. In his wildest dreams, who would have thought that? Then he went on and got his master's degree. I've thought about what made Eddie the man he is, and so I wrote these things down: Rare. Bold. Curious. Fearless. Intuitive. Undaunted. Daring. Dynamic. Strong. Unwavering. Genuine. Visionary. Legendary. Dreamer."

Legendary?

"Eddie set the standard for kids coming from Pittsburg, California," Coach Bonanno explained. "All I know is that I was at the right place at the right time. If I did anything right for Eddie, I must tell you this: I love him."

POST-OLYMPIC STRESS FACTOR

What psychological help was there for the Olympians after we returned to America following the worst massacre in Olympic history? What counseling and therapy were made available to us? Marilyn King, an American pentathlete, still was upset by the lack of help forty-three years later.

"After the terrorist attack," she said, "there were no psychological services available. Looking back on that, from my perspective, it was like PTSD [Post-Traumatic Stress Disorder]. I came home very confused on a number of different levels. I didn't know what was going on inside of me. I also was injured and severely disappointed and not properly cared for by the coaching staff.

"Following the Black September hostage-taking and murders of the Israelis, it was like the Games must go on, without help to shift from that tragedy or the Olympic Village lockdown that followed. We were trained as athletes to focus and to compete, and this was the most important part of our careers, but how do you compete at a time like this? Then you're shipped home, and there was no debriefing whatsoever regarding the terrorist attack that took place right there in the Olympic Village, the same Village in which we were living! I'm just an Olympic athlete; I'm not psychologically sophisticated. I don't have much emotional intelligence. And I don't know why I can hardly function. I was deeply and severely depressed."

But if Marilyn, like other Olympians in 1972, was depressed by the massacre that cost the lives of eleven Israeli athletes and coaches, what about my mental state? I had to deal with a double shock: those brutal killings and my own disqualification. That got me thinking how I might have been guided through this dual crisis. Sometimes, therapy can help you by putting things in perspective. I had a pretty good handle on things after Munich, but I did go through an adjustment period of several months. I didn't just jump back into life. I didn't get right back to school. I hung around the house a lot, I hung out with Gwen, and I didn't mingle with others.

And I was dealing with the pain of other people as a result of what happened to me—my mother, for example, who wasn't as concerned about me missing the race as she was about the pain I was going through. I was seeing my disqualification through the eyes of other people rather than through my own. And I was grieving for the families of those Israelis. Family is family.

But looking back, somebody helpful would've been a neutral person, somebody I didn't know, just to have somebody to talk to about things: missing the race and the Israeli incident. This hurts, that hurts; I'm dealing with this, I'm struggling with that. I felt bad that I had brought so much pain to people around me. Hanging out with Gwen helped because she didn't care about all this other stuff. She cared about me.

Somebody approached me after I returned home: "Let's put something together, I can write this book for you." Huh? "No way," I said. "I wouldn't touch that with a ten-foot pole." I can finally talk about it now, but it took forty-three years.

What Marilyn said about PTSD, or whatever it was, makes complete sense. I needed friends to tell me what they thought about my situation, but they were putting on a front for me. I mean, everybody! I talked to my friend and Cal

teammate, Cliff West, and even he held back. But I was also putting on a front. I was feeling so much hurt. If anybody did bring up Munich, it wasn't about me. They'd mention Stan Wright and how he messed up my life. I'd tell them, "That's how you feel, but that's not how I feel. Stan Wright is a friend." Munich didn't change that and wouldn't change that.

Marilyn King was a two-time Olympian: Munich in 1972 and Montreal in 1976. We're good friends and

Marilyn King never competed in the 1972 Olympic pentathlon, as she was injured upon arriving in Munich. (Photo courtesy of Marilyn King)

practically neighbors. I live in Pittsburg, she lives a half hour away in Oakland. One thing about Marilyn, she makes perfect sense. "Munich was the most tragic of Olympic Games," she said. "But what was crazy for me was a hallucination I had walking into the Olympic Stadium for the first time, putting my gym bag down by the long jump pit, and seeing Heidi Rosendahl at the start of the runway. I couldn't believe the awesome athlete I saw; I looked like Twiggy next to her. She was a woman athlete like I hadn't seen before. She started down the runway, and she was like a locomotive—the strength, power, and speed as she accelerated. And when she hit the takeoff board, it was like she exploded into the air. Oh, Lord! I was sunk."

Rosendahl had that same effect on all the long jumpers, winning a gold medal for West Germany in Munich, while also taking the silver medal in the pentathlon. But the long jump pit proved Marilyn's ruination. She twisted an ankle and strained her Achilles tendon while landing on a practice jump, and so she was knocked out of the pentathlon competition even before it started. She could have used some physical and emotional therapy right then, but it wasn't coming from the USA team coaches and staff.

"If that injury wasn't bad enough," she recalled, "it took the Americans a half hour to get an ambulance. And during that time, I was begging to get the foot wrapped in ice, but the Americans took charge and insisted on getting me to the medical facility to ice it there. I had chipped an anklebone and needed to plunge it in ice, but the ambulance gets lost, and it took them more than an hour to get me to the medical facility, and all this time my ankle was swelling without ice.

"Over the next few days, before my competition was scheduled to start, I'm on crutches trying to get taken care of in the American facility. I'm there at the same time as Mark Spitz, who's got fifteen people around him as he's getting a massage, while I'm getting zero attention. So I went to the German doctors, and they took exquisite care of me, even though I couldn't stand on the ball of my foot.

"The finishing part of an injury situation like this is that the coach must declare within twenty-four hours if one of his or her athletes can't compete. Nell Jackson, the USA's head women's track coach, had not contacted me or even seen me before, during, or after my injury. I know you have to declare an injury, but she was nowhere to be seen. So I decided to go see her in her room, on crutches, to inform her that I couldn't stand properly on my injured foot. She opens the door, this little tiny crack, and said, 'What do you want?' I told her of my injury, and that she had to declare I was out of the competition. She said, 'Oh, just show up tomorrow, and it will be all right.' And she shut the door. Really?

"So there was a string of about fifteen things that happened to me in Munich," Marilyn said. "By the time I got home, to finish up my college degree at Cal State, Hayward, I was a basket case. I would drive around, very depressed. It wasn't 'poor me' or the need to bash people, but there was an incompetence in Munich that was appalling and needed to be addressed.

"Beyond the personal events, there was the terrorist attack. I did go to one counselor at Cal State, Hayward. What took place in that one-hour session was so bizarre that I never went back. So I was basically on my own. I've since done a lot of work to get through the tragic stuff. What worked best for me was realizing that to be a true Olympian, I would have to go again and compete against the best in the world, to see just how high, how far, how fast, and how good I could really be. And try not to think about what had occurred in Munich, the terrible tragedy and my own unfortunate situation. That set me on a new course, although I couldn't forget that when I returned from Munich, there was no reception for me, and not even one newspaper article describing what I had gone through.

"Back then, people would say, 'Oh, are you an Olympian?' I'd tell them I am, and they'd say, 'Did you medal?' And I'd answer, 'Well, no.' Then they'd say, 'Oh, we're going to the mall. Want to come along?' In other words, if you didn't medal, there was nothing of value to talk about. Maybe you don't completely heal from something like Munich. Fast-forwarding many years later, when I heard that Nell Jackson was to receive some distinguished coaching award, my stomach turned and I chose to bite my tongue."

Before the Israeli tragedy, Marilyn and I enjoyed life within the Village, looking around and seeing, from Marilyn's memory, "seven-foot-tall Japanese basketball players and seventy-two-pound Romanian gymnasts, people from every country, every race, every religion. And we're all walking around with respect for one another. In the discotheque, you're dancing with someone, and you don't even have to speak the person's language, because we're speaking the language of music and dance, looking in one another's eyes, and busting moves on one another. That was before I was injured.

"From that part of my first Olympic experience, I felt like we could live in peace," Marilyn said. "Here you get the most highly competitive people on the planet. How could people whose countries are at war, and whose political philosophies are different, and whose religions clash with one another, live in peace inside this fence? My experience was that we all had respect for one another and we had curiosity about one another. So I live even now with the reality that we could create a Global Olympic Village, adopting those two Olympic values: respect and curiosity."

Marilyn and I, both in our mid-sixties, still feel that immense pride in being Olympians. I had one individual event, but Marilyn had five events in the pentathlon: Hurdles, shot put, high jump, long jump, 800 meters. When she was healthy in Montreal, she finished sixteenth. An automobile accident prevented her from training physically for the 1980 Olympics in Moscow. Thus, she was forced, to rely on mental training. While she thought it was a temporary injury, for seven months she couldn't train at all on the track. So she used her brain, solely, and remarkably finished second in the U.S. Trials. But it was for naught. President Jimmy Carter declared the U.S. would boycott the Moscow Games.

So Marilyn didn't officially become a three-time Olympian, but through that process she came to the conclusion that "ordinary people sometimes do extraordinary things, and there is an Olympian in each and every one of us." She embarked on a thirty-year career creating Way beyond Sports, a consulting business instructing international corporate leadership teams and educators on how to align the same three traits common among all high achievers. Those are always present, innate, and can be identified and developed in everyone: exceptional human performance, being always passion-powered; vision, guided by Olympian thinking; action-oriented, aligning a game plan with daily practice both mental and physical.

Thus hurdling on the track and groovin' in the disco at the Olympic Village evolved into a career for Marilyn. But she blames the 1972 Olympics for changing the whole dynamic of the Olympic movement, though not necessarily because of the terrorists' attack.

"When the USA basketball team lost to the Russians," she said, "whether you think it was right or not to have time put back on the clock, the U.S. Olympic Committee became upset that we could actually lose a basketball game. From that moment forward, the push was on to allow professionals [to replace American amateurs], which had a cascading effect. Most of the athletes at an Olympic Games are still not professional; many you will never see struggle just to be there. But we now have multimillionaires in basketball competing against athletes from countries like Zimbabwe, which almost cannot afford to come to the Olympics, while our basketball players are playing golf before rushing back to play Zimbabwe, with [Charles] Barkley throwing an elbow at one of their players for no apparent reason. Is that what the Olympic Games are meant to be?

"I believe the advent, and the shift, from amateurs to professionals has changed the Olympics. I'm not naïve, realizing that Eastern Bloc athletes are employees of the police and fire departments in their countries. They're paid full-time without having to fight crime or fires. I'm not saying there weren't abuses before the pros. Many American men were on college scholarships and rarely went to class. But it's not right to open the floodgates for multimillionaires to play small countries; it is a very different game, and not one in agreement with the true Olympic spirit."

Marilyn further emphasized: "Because we have an aging population, we no longer have a situation where everyone is watching or talking about the Olympics. Ask kids in school, 'Who is Michael Phelps?' And they'll say, 'Isn't that the guy with the bong?' They're not interested; they're watching the X Games, [with its] skateboards and motorcycles. The professionals have changed the landscape, and the younger generation is playing video games or watching those X Games."

Marilyn then sounded a warning that should ring across the planet. "The Olympic movement has strayed far from its original purpose and is in very big trouble. Drugs and professionals with all their sponsor conflicts, it's all found troubling by young people. It is all market driven. Money has taken over and left in its wake the focus of educating youth to create a better and more peaceful world. In trying to address these problems, the Olympic movement now includes sports like the X Games sports, created to attract younger viewers. What has evolved is the 'Youth Olympics,' a movement I find defeating in purpose.

"It's sad to me that the Olympic movement is in trouble and older Olympians are dying off and the younger people aren't that interested. The Olympics once was the biggest game in town; it's not anymore. The concept of the modern Olympiad [1896], as created by its founder, Baron Pierre de Coubertin of France, was to 'educate youth through sport to create a better and more peaceful world.' If you look at the modern Olympic Committee, it has moved that purpose to, like, tenth position, and the first nine articles are all about self-perpetuation.

"This is just Marilyn King talking in April 2015, but if you look at the soccer corruption going on in FIFA, its No. 1 guy, Sepp Blatter, who was just forced to resign, also happened to be on the International Olympic Committee. It's one big incestuous corrupt system, with very little to do with the baron's idea to 'educate youth through sport to create a better and more peaceful world.'

"It is gross, and many Olympians whom I respect, and who have been involved with the International Olympic Committee, are disgusted."

Marilyn King is highly intelligent, and highly perceptive. But while I agree with many of her criticisms of the Olympic movement, perhaps I should offer a counterbalance to her viewpoints. When I competed, the Olympics were an amateur sport. I got a $2 per diem, which you could hardly live off of. There was no professionalism to it; you did it for fun until you were ready to go off and do something else in your life. You couldn't make a living off track and field. And I wanted to get married and have a family, so I had to retire from competition.

There's some truth to the supposition that the controversial outcome of that gold-medal basketball game eventually led to the USA sending its NBA players to compete in the Olympics, to face countries whose players were already being compensated. So it was pros versus pros, though it became a "let's show 'em" philosophy in the United States, because no other country, even those with paid athletes, can compete against us in basketball if we aren't an amateur team.

Look at Teofilo Stevenson of Cuba, who won three Olympic gold medals in boxing as an "amateur." Fidel Castro himself bestowed favors on Stevenson, so we can't say he was a true amateur. He was a superb heavyweight, and a superhero in his country. Should we have sent some amateur to fight him, or Muhammad Ali?

Marilyn said the Olympics are no longer marketable; however, that may not be the entire world's perspective. Track and field is a stepchild in this country. The Fresno Relays, the California Relays at Modesto, the Kennedy Games—those were once standing-room-only events. They're all gone, and you'd have to pay athletes to come to a U.S. track meet. That's not the case globally.

But I'd listen to Marilyn's views on just about anything, because she makes perfect sense—even her defense of me and what might have happened in Munich had I not been disqualified in the 100-meter dash. "Anyone who says that Eddie Hart could not have beaten Valery Borzov because Valery was chemically enhanced should remember that there are athletes who did not take steroids who beat steroid-enhanced athletes," she pointed out. "Eddie [and Rey Robinson] had the fastest time[s] going into Munich, including anything that Valery had run all year.

"I lived in the era in which steroids were pretty prevalent for the men, some sports in particular. I trained with a lot of male athletes, shot and discus throwers in our country, who were steroid-enhanced and competed against weight men from other countries who were steroid-enhanced. There were jokes in the weight room, and steroids were just beginning to drift even among the women, from Europe to the United States. But there were few female U.S. athletes taking steroids in 1972.

"I knew I would be competing against women who were taking steroids. I just wanted to know how good I could be. If I was someone who was gold-medal caliber, competing against steroid-enhanced athletes, my inclination was, 'Well, that [using steroids] is not who I am, and that's not why I'm here.' So I never had to make that decision."

But, setting aside for the moment the need for psychological counseling for athletes traumatized by the Munich massacre, Marilyn refuses to give the Germans a failing grade for their second Summer Games: "Everyone has criticisms because of the terrorist attack. But from my perspective, in so many areas, they did a fabulous job. The competition facilities were fabulous. Transportation for athletes was fabulous. The Olympic Village itself—the food, the accommodations, the opportunities—it was really well done."

Unfortunately, it's hard to look past the Olympic Village tragedy.

THE TURNING POINT

How does a sprinter who's clocking 9.7 seconds in the 100-yard dash and who's hardly considered gold-medal caliber, slash that time down to 9.2 seconds and suddenly look like a world-beater? And his postrace urine drug test is clean.

Sound improbable? Well, I was that sprinter who reduced my 100 time by a half second in the remarkably short span of a single track and field season. Honestly. I blossomed suddenly, in 1969, as a sophomore at Contra Costa College in San Pablo, California, a junior college on the eastern side of San Francisco Bay. I emerged as the hottest sprinter in the state among the two-year schools.

I hadn't been a state champion at Pittsburg High School, but I became a two-time state champion that year at Contra Costa, winning the 100 and 220, back when yards were run instead of meters during non-Olympic years. I remember my coach, Jack Albiani, giving me a great big hug after my double victory at the state meet.

"I think Eddie's body was maturing and getting stronger," Coach Albiani told Dave Newhouse in 2015. "He was just a late bloomer, cutting his 100 time down from 9.7 to 9.4 early on. His big competition that year was Warren Edmondson at Merritt Junior College in Oakland. The big question was: when are those two guys finally going to meet? Well, that happened at the Camino Norte Relays, and Warren won. He just kept getting better and better and better.

"How did that actually happen? Well, let me tell you a story. We didn't have a track at Contra Costa College. Our 'home' meets were at a local high school. We did have a grass field, so I had a groundskeeper mow a 330-yard patch of that grass down real low. That's where we worked out, on that grass field, which meant we didn't have any pulled leg muscles or Achilles injuries.

"You know, I was at Contra Costa three years before leaving in 1969 to become the coach at Modesto Junior College, where I stayed until I retired in 1997. Here it is, 2015, and I'm now eighty-four. But before I left Contra Costa, I designed the track at the school, even though I never got to use it."

Coach Albiani was a good coach. I improved a lot under his leadership, and I liked him a lot. He wasn't overbearing, but he commanded respect. I learned that about him the hard way. I decided to catch a ride with a friend to school on the same day we had a track meet. Well, wouldn't you know it, we had car trouble—and I could see another kind of trouble coming when I got to school.

This was the 1960s, so there were no cell phones. We weren't near one of those roadside phones, so there wasn't a family member or friend to come pick us up. We had to wait for a mechanic. The time it took to correct the problem made me late getting to school, possibly too late to catch the team bus to our meet. I was really anxious. But when I got to the gym, the bus was still there. I felt a sense of relief; then Coach Albiani said he wanted to see me in his office. He tore into me, letting me know that I was a central figure on the team, so there was no excuse for my holding up the whole team. He had told the bus driver to wait for a late passenger. That would be me, the sprinter who was in deep, deep trouble.

If it ever happened again, Coach Albiani warned, he would leave me behind, no matter how important I was to the team's success. He really let me have it, the toughest coach-athlete conference I ever experienced. I wanted to tell him

that I wasn't a prima donna, that I had made an honest mistake, and I was sorry for the whole incident. But I didn't say a word, and I felt even smaller when I climbed on the bus, wanting to apologize to my teammates. Instead, I sat there with my head down.

The only way to make it up to Coach Albiani and the team was to have a good meet. I was so focused

Jack Albiani coached Eddie Hart at the junior college level. (Photo courtesy of Jack Albiani)

With one shoe on, one shoe off, Eddie Hart poses at Contra Costa College, where he began running international times in the 100. (Photo courtesy of Eddie Hart)

when I got off the bus that I felt like I could have won the Olympics. I won every race I was entered in that day, and I would have competed in the long jump if Coach Albiani needed me. He didn't, and we won the meet. The coach, the team, and especially this chastised sprinter were happy with the outcome on the ride home. I wasn't ever late again. You can bet on that.

However, I had another, er, issue that really affected my performance at Contra Costa. It was the Northern California Trials, and my stomach was acting up. I tried lying down for a few minutes to see if the feeling would go away, but it didn't. I couldn't figure out the problem—then I realized it was Mother Nature making a house call. A 220-yard heat was coming up, I had just won the 100, and the nearest facilities were in a parking lot across a big, wide field.

I couldn't run this way, so I asked the starter if I had time to make a bathroom run. He said yes, but he added that I was cutting it close, and if I didn't make it back in time, the race would go off without me. What choice did I have; I decided to stay and run. The gun went off, and I ran like a freight train. Somehow, I managed to qualify, but in one of my slowest times ever. Coach Albiani came over to ask if anything was wrong, perhaps a pulled leg muscle or a sprained ankle. No, coach, it was Mother Nature. He started laughing and said, "He wouldn't let you go to the john?" He said it again and laughed some more. Then I took off for the john.

At the Northern California Finals, life returned to normal. I won the 100 and looked to repeat in the state meet. I now was considered a favorite at the state level. This wasn't ever the case at Pittsburg High, where I dealt with two big distractions.

The first was the drowning of my good friend Thomas Siegler. He was thirteen, I was a year older, and we went swimming with some other kids in the San Joaquin River. Thomas had a piece of candy in his throat, and he might have choked on it, because he went underneath. I jumped in and grabbed his thigh, he came up, but he went under again, and he was gone. The river was so muddy that you couldn't see a foot below the surface. They found his body four, five hours later.

Thomas and I had walked to school and back every day. My dream was going to the Olympics, while Thomas's dream was to go into the Marines. He talked about it a lot. Going to his funeral was painful. They asked me to be a pallbearer, but I couldn't do it. I stood at the back of the church, and after the service, I just left.

I probably could have used some help then, because I couldn't talk to anyone about Thomas's death. It bothered me throughout high school, though meeting Gwen helped some. But I would talk to Thomas in my head, tell him what I was doing. I could lean on him. I kept thinking about our relationship, not that I thought he would be coming back to life. Still, he was on my mind.

Fifty years later, I still think about him every now and then. He was four, five inches taller than me at the time. He had this trench coat he liked, and he wore it even in hot weather, maybe to hide his skinniness. He'd come watch me at track meets, and then he wasn't there anymore. I missed him, a cool dude.

My second distraction started with a hamstring pull in my right leg, which led to lower back pain. That's when I discovered that one leg was slightly shorter than the other leg, when I started junior high school. Before I learned that, I was getting up early in the morning, training to, I thought, make my body stronger. That's the worst thing I could have done, for it exacerbated the situation. It took a while to correct it, and then I was fine, as long as my friend Rodell Johnson stretched me out.

But going from junior high to high school, you're like at the bottom of the barrel again, starting over. I was the fourth-fastest 100 sprinter in school my first year at Pittsburg High; the other three 100 men were seniors. I was faster than one junior, but the coach took him, not me, on the sprint relay team to the state meet. I didn't quite understand that decision, because track and field is based on who jumps the highest, throws the farthest, and runs the fastest. So I didn't think I was being treated fairly. I guess I had to run even faster.

My junior year, I did just that, winning the 100 and 220, plus the long jump, and running on the victorious sprint relay team at the Diablo Valley Athletic League championships. I had beaten Dave Masters of El Cerrito High School as a ninth grader, but Dave and Mel Gray of Montgomery High in Santa Rosa, who was in our same class, were bigger and stronger than me as upperclassmen. I don't think I weighed 150 back then. I qualified for the state meet but not the finals. Mel ran a 9.4, Dave a 9.5, while I ran 9.7. At that stage, they were looking more like Olympians.

Another thing that happened my senior year: half the track meets were rained out; it was one of the rainiest years in local history. Pittsburg High ran on a dirt track, so you can see the problem. Thus at the end of my high school career, I still was a work in progress. But track played a huge role in keeping me eligible for sports. That's how I kept up a C average in my schoolwork.

When Coach Albiani recruited me for Contra Costa College, I caught a break. "Before Contra Costa," Coach Albiani recalled, "I was Piedmont High School's track coach for seven years. Eddie graduated from Pittsburg High in 1967. I went to the North Coast Section meet that year at Miramonte High in Orinda. I had just been hired at Contra Costa, and I was looking for athletes, because the track team I inherited wasn't very good.

"After the section meet ended, I walked back to my car, and I saw an athlete sitting on the curb. I said, 'How did you do today?' He said, 'Ah, not too well.' And I said, 'You're Eddie Hart, aren't you? Where are you going to school next year?' He said, 'I'm not sure.' I introduced myself and invited him to come to Contra Costa. He said, 'Oh, that sounds good.' I called his high school coach, Ray Kring, and he agreed that Contra Costa would be a good fit for Eddie.

"Well, lo and behold, I discovered, Eddie not only came to Contra Costa, but he brought along some friends: Howard Carter, who was a 1:55.0 880 guy, and the brother of Eddie's future wife, and Roy Finks, who was a 49-flat quarter-miler. I got a good package deal out of recruiting Eddie.

"We had a good team Eddie's freshman year, with one outstanding athlete, Marion Anderson, whose 24-foot, 9-inch long jump took second at the 1968 state meet. Eddie, that first year, ran a 9.8 or 9.7 in the 100. He also did OK in the 220, at 21.3 or 21.4. But I could see that he was a dedicated, hard-working individual."

Coach Albiani was impressed that Howard, Roy, and I would drive twenty miles from Pittsburg to San Pablo every day, without missing a day of track practice. We helped Contra Costa win the Golden Gate Conference dual-meet championship that year, finishing with a 10–0 record. At the conference championships, I won the 100- and 200-meter dashes and anchored our winning 400-meter relay team.

"Any time I asked you, Eddie, to enter the long jump or to run the 400 or to run on the 1600-meter relay team, you would do it," Coach Albiani reminded me years later. "You were always a team man, first."

The next year, 1969, Contra Costa College shifted to the Camino Norte Conference, and we repeated our 10–0 dual meet record. The same kids who were freshmen my first year at Contra Costa were much improved as sophomores. And we won the conference meet as I stood out in the 100, 220, the two relays, plus the long jump.

The state meet for junior colleges back then was held in conjunction with the California Relays at Modesto, which had been run for a half century by Tom Moore, who tied the world record in the 120-yard high hurdles, at 14.2 seconds, as a Cal student and who was the U.S. 440-yard hurdles champion in 1935. The annual Modesto meet drew amateurs from around the world. It's not like that now. International stars stay home because European track promoters pay astronomical appearance fees, which killed off most of America's relay meets, including Fresno and Modesto.

But in 1969, Modesto was the place to be for track and field enthusiasts. My normal routine before a meet was to eat a light meal early if my competition was scheduled for the afternoon or later on or to not eat at all, if my competition was that morning. At the California Relays, I had toast and orange juice that morning; I wasn't running until early evening. By the time my race occurred, my stomach was empty and I was hungry, just the way I liked it, because it made me feel light and fast. And I was feeling fast—faster than ever.

I won the 100-yard dash in 9.3, my best time yet, but it was wind-aided, thus denying me a share of the national junior college record set by Travis Williams, a Contra Costa College alumnus who later played for the Green Bay Packers. I wasn't going to let some asterisk rob me of my sense of accomplishment, though. Then in the 220, I won again, with a time of 21.1, slower than I had run that season, but still satisfactory because I really saw myself as a 100 man. I didn't like the 220 much, but because I was an excellent turn runner, I usually got to the tape first. Teammate Clarence Taylor won the 440.

Topping off my performance as a double champion, I was named the outstanding athlete of that state meet. Though I was in Modesto, I felt on top of the world, even after we lost the sprint relay. Running anchor, I was eight yards behind when I got the baton, too much distance to make up in a short amount of time. I gained on everyone, but we finished fourth. Well, you can't have everything all the time.

A popular song back then was "Oh Happy Day." I couldn't have been happier after Modesto. Because of my performance, I was arguably the biggest junior college recruit in the country. Every major college in the West contacted me. Oh happy day, indeed. I had worked extra hard on the track and in the classroom at Contra Costa, making sure that I could transfer and be eligible to compete immediately. I wanted that college degree, which meant as much to me as an Olympic gold medal.

I knew Cal was interested in me, and I liked that idea, because Cal usually is rated as the nation's No. 1 public university. So I accepted Cal's scholarship offer from Coach Dave Maggard, and I moved to Berkeley, a half-hour ride from Pittsburg. I was asked to run in the Pacific AAU Championships at Hughes Stadium in Sacramento, the state capital. This was a step up in competition, although it was an unusual meet format. There would be several races in some events, and even if you won your race, if someone had a faster time in another race, you might not be declared the winner.

I didn't recognize the other 100-yard entrants, because they were from out of state. I was in the fourth, and final, heat, and I hit the tape with my familiar lean in what was a blanket finish. I thought I had won, but I was given second place. It was my most jubilant runner-up position ever, for I ran a legal 9.2, the fastest time run by a junior college athlete. But it wasn't a junior college record,

I learned, because I ran it after the junior college season was completed, even though I wouldn't enroll at Cal until the fall. But a 9.2 is a 9.2. I also won the 220 in 20.9, a good day's work.

So how was I able to reduce my time from 9.5 the previous year to 9.2? Well, I had gained five pounds, pure muscle, during my junior college years. I was a lot stronger, and I was really focused. I now saw myself as world class. Those factors played into cutting my 100 time by a half second. And I wasn't done cutting.

Coach Albiani knew Dave Maggard from before, when Dave competed as a weight man at Modesto Junior College before transferring to Cal, where he developed into an Olympian who took sixth place in the shot put at Mexico City in 1968. Dave was more than a coach; he was a good man, someone I felt totally comfortable with. And our relationship evolved into a strong lifetime friendship.

Dave put me to work; he didn't waste any time. I became a global traveler that summer even before entering Cal. Following the Pacific AAU meet, he had me join the Athens Athletic Club in Oakland, for the primary purpose of competing in the National AAU Championships that year in Florida. I was wary about making that leap, not because I feared the competition, but because I feared flying. A cross-country flight was my idea of a nauseous stomach waiting to happen. But if I wanted to run in Munich in 1972, I'd better start learning to fly to distant places in 1969.

Dave picked me up the morning of the flight and drove me to the San Francisco Airport. Though he wasn't going with me, I saw then how much he cared about his athletes. He had taken care of the reservation, but he wanted to make sure there was no foul-up. Well, there was one: my name wasn't on the passenger list. Dave explained to the lady behind the desk that he had phoned the night before and had been told that my name would be on the list. He then looked at him and said, "If he doesn't get on the plane, there's going to be some crap." Dave is one of the friendliest, kindest people you'll ever meet and not one to usually lose his temper. But he is intimidating in size. The next thing I knew, the man printed out my ticket.

Feeling confident that Dave would take care of me at Cal, I surprised myself by sleeping most of the flight. We landed in 80-degree heat, the same temperature as the Bay Area, but with the humidity factor. When I stepped down from the plane, it was like walking into a sauna. Perspiring at once, I asked the guy in baggage: "How do you stay dry around here?" He said, "You don't." Leaving the airport, I noticed that all the skycaps were white. In the

Bay Area, they're mostly black. Track and field was offering me an education that I didn't always get in the classroom.

I got to the hotel where we would be staying for a week. I had a light snack before going to bed. Checking the 100 entrant sheets the next morning, I saw I was the only junior college athlete in the field; the others were college or track club entrants. They seemed like nice guys when we met; they didn't make me feel like a stranger.

My goal was to make the 100 finals, and I was able to do that without winning any of my heats. Then as the starter called us to a set position for the final, the crowd roared just as he fired the gun. Most of us got off to a good start, but John Carlos didn't hear the gun. He got a late start but managed to pass everyone except Ivory Crockett, the winner. I finished a disappointing sixth; I wanted to finish better than fourth. In all fairness to Carlos, the starter should have re-called the field.

I now experienced the loneliness of track and field travel. I had three or four days before I would run again, in the 220. I called my father's brother, who lived in Florida; my dad had given me his number. It was an awkward conversation with an uncle I hadn't ever met and just as awkward a conversation with his son. Thus, it was a short phone call, the first and last time we would ever speak to one another.

The 220-yard dash wasn't my favorite race, but after my sixth-place finish, I was eager to get back on the track, even with the humidity factor. Once again, I made it to the finals, where Carlos blew away the field. I wound up fourth and was happy to fly home to see Gwen and my family.

Dave Maggard got me a job at Cal, watering parts of the campus. I didn't play gardener all that long, for he had other travel plans for me. Two weeks after getting back from Florida, I was on a plane to Sweden, competing in six meets in two weeks. There was no time for sightseeing. The Swedes were really into track and field; there were thirty-five thousand in attendance at one meet. I won all six 100-meter races, clocking 10.2 in one meet, to tie the national record. Following the race, people poured out of the stands, wanting my autograph. I swear the line was fifty meters long, or half a sprint. For a college kid, I felt like a world-class celebrity. And I have to admit that it was a great feeling, something you don't experience in America.

Coach Jack Albiani groomed me for this opportunity to become a Cal Golden Bear and, inadvertently, a world traveler. I can't thank him enough for both gifts.

"I can say this about Eddie," Albiani said in 2015, "he was a team leader. Everyone looked up to him, even though he didn't say a lot. He was a pretty quiet kid, and shy, but he had great character and he showed what he could do on the track. Even in practice, he led the way. I coached for thirty-nine years all together, and I didn't get too many special guys like Eddie. He was my only gold medalist."

Coach Albiani believes Contra Costa College was "the turning point" in my track and field career. He is correct. He also was familiar with track coaches up and down the West Coast, and he had known my eventual Olympic coach, Stan Wright, at Sacramento State.

"Stan was a good coach who entered kids at the Modesto Relays when I was at Modesto JC," Coach Albiani said. "But paperwork wasn't really his forte. Evidently, what happened in Munich, with the mix-up of the time schedule, that's something you've really got to be on, and it's unfortunate what happened.

"If Eddie had run that 100-meter final, he would have won. I really feel that. Obviously, it was Stan Wright's fault. Like I said, it's unfortunate. Whom do you blame? Do you blame the official [at the track]? Do you blame the coach? I don't know. I wasn't there. It's what I've heard, what I've read in the newspaper."

But what's said or what's read isn't necessarily the truth.

I LOVE PARIS

My wife, Gwen, sensed it before I did: something was different about our first child, Paris. She wasn't yet two years old, and she seemed to have a hearing deficiency, for she didn't respond immediately to sound. Then we discovered the painful truth—it wasn't her hearing. Paris had a developmental disability, which meant that she would live with us the rest of our lives, under our permanent care.

Gwen and I realized that we would need to be more patient, and more protective, in terms of Paris's personal growth. But I never looked at this as a problem, and I can't say that I'm saddened by it. I just accepted that Paris would not compete on the same level playing field with the rest of the kids her age. She would always need special attention, with special classes, and she wouldn't be going off to college.

But Paris has taught us a lot about ourselves, and our fortitude, which has helped us grow as parents. Others tried to help us with her situation, but they've never been in this situation. Some people even talked to us about putting her in an institution. Because they were well meaning, I wasn't offended. Paris is a unique person. She just exudes love. She doesn't know a stranger. And she has endless patience. She works on the computer, sitting there for hours until she gets what she needs. She likes old sitcoms, old music, and Richard Nixon.

That's right, Tricky Dick. I took her to the Nixon museum, and she really enjoyed it. We went inside the helicopter where Nixon gave the peace sign following his presidential resignation in 1974. We took family vacations for twenty years, sometimes three trips a year, traveling to Disneyland every summer with our two kids. (Eddie Jr. is three years younger than Paris.) We became a real family in that sense, going to the parks, the fairs, and the carnivals. We cherished those times.

Paris, who's now in her early forties, knows she is an important part of our family. She's treated very well—when we go to church, they all love her. She is a total extrovert; just don't give her the microphone. She can get overexcited and get into people, so we have to watch that side of her carefully. Gwen watches over her constantly.

Does that responsibility wear on Gwen? I think about that all the time. Paris is always well groomed. She eats well; that's evident. Gwen does yeoman's duty with Paris, because she's still a girl, really, even in her forties. Gwen doesn't tend to Paris begrudgingly; my wife is very loving. Our faith plays a significant role with our family; we believe God is in control; Paris is in His hands.

Gwen is like a gift from God. Let me explain that from several different perspectives. I grew up in a home where my mother and father worked as a team; their example played significantly into how Gwen and I work together. In forty-plus years of marriage, we've seldom argued. I heard my parents argue once or twice in the whole sixty-five years of their marriage, which lasted until my father's death. They had a clear delineation of roles and responsibilities, just like Gwen and me.

As for bringing up our children, I believe Gwen and I have done well. Eddie Jr. went to Cal and got his degree. He and I have bonded, a strong father-son relationship. Gwen is especially close to Paris. When I look at other mother-daughter relationships, I've noticed that as the daughter grows older, their

Eddie Hart and his wife Gwen, pictured with daughter Paris and son Eddie Jr. (Photo courtesy of Eddie Hart)

relationship flourishes. They do a variety of things together. They go to lunch, go shopping, or just converse about girlie-like stuff.

Paris is special to Gwen, though they don't have the usual mother-daughter relationship. Gwen has to be more the caregiver; she takes care of Paris's clothing, grooming, and all of her needs. She is excellent at doing all that. I couldn't ask for a better wife in that regard, or a better wife, period. We've worked things out, once again, partly because of our faith.

The reason we've succeeded this way with Paris? Gwen and I both come from solid family foundations. Her parents, Sherman and Lottie Carter, were married fifty-nine years before Sherman passed away. Virtually all of our friends are divorced, but I've never thought of divorce as an option. For me, Gwen is the best, the very best. It's a matter of working things out, seeing things through, focusing on the family unit, and staying strong together. How did I get so blessed to have Gwen as a mate?

She was perfect for me from the very start. It was how she looked, but, equally, she had the right style—the way she carried herself, the way she spoke. She was shy when I met her, but she always acted in a dignified way, different from most girls, and that appealed to me. She wasn't ever profane, and she is very talented; she very easily could have been in the entertainment field. She dances, she sings, she writes. And she does a great James Brown impersonation.

The first time I saw Gwen was at the Creative Arts building on the Pittsburg High School campus. There was a talent show in the auditorium, which has two thousand seats. Gwen impersonated James Brown, "the hardest working man in show business." She had her work cut out for her, but there she was, complete with long pants, a long-sleeved shirt, and necktie. When the music started, she jumped into her routine, doing James Brown's most famous dance, "The Skate." She was smooth and graceful, doing all of his gestures, with his head and hand movements down to a T.

Right then, she struck me as a perfectionist, not missing one step during the whole performance. She was so tiny, with perfect body control, but she morphed into this star entertainer, like she had been doing it her whole life. She really owned the stage. She finished her routine by sticking out her tongue, though not at the audience, which loved her act; the tongue was sort of a nervous habit. Then she turned back into the shy little girl. I thought to myself how pretty she was.

A couple of years passed, though, before we actually met. She was the little sister of Howard and Sherman Carter, my teammates in high school. Howard and I were in the same class, with Sherman one class ahead of us, and Gwen

Eddie Hart Jr. poses with his parents on the day he graduated from the University of California, Berkeley, just like his father had. (Photo courtesy of Eddie Hart Sr.)

two classes behind me. During the summer, Ray Kring, my high school coach, held a track meet, and I got a trophy for winning the 100. I'm not sure how the conversation started, but I began talking with Gwen. It was kind of jerky, but pleasant, and I gave her my trophy. Then she left without the two of us making any future plans.

I thought, "How am I going to see her again?" It was the middle of the summer, and school wouldn't start for two months. Then I vaguely remembered saying something to her about getting the trophy back. So I showed up at her door. She was surprised to see me and just as surprised to hear that I wanted the trophy back. She seemed a little hurt, at first, but we had an enjoyable conversation.

I liked everything about her; she was beautiful. But I had to be careful because I didn't want her thinking I was staring at her. Like my father said of my mother, "she is the woman for me." That was it with Gwen. Though she was shy, she exuded an element of confidence. She was smooth without being showy. Her clothing was immaculate, not a spot anywhere. All those characteristics appealed to me. Some girls leave the house sort of careless about their appearance, but when Gwen came out, she was ready to be seen.

She was athletic, too. She played basketball, and she won the 220-yard dash in a girls' track meet. Later on, after we were married, I taught and coached at the College of Alameda. Gwen would come over and play badminton. We'd be on different teams, but she was very active, and she was always in great shape. I later taught at Laney Community College.

Was there love from the start? Well, we were no secret to each other. We'd known each other since high school, when we started dating. Whatever that word "love" means to me, I've always loved Gwen. I never took another girl to a dance or party, and I didn't date girls overseas. I was true blue. Did Gwen and I talk about marriage? By the 1972 Olympics, that was pretty much a foregone conclusion. We dated eight, nine years. A year after those Olympics, we got married. Gwen wanted children, and I did, too.

We've had difficult times since, but we've always gotten through them. It's more than just a family commitment; we believe God will take care of us. If I didn't feel that way, I would worry myself sick about problems. And that wouldn't help me, Gwen, Eddie Jr., or Paris. If Gwen and I predeceased Paris, we wouldn't be worried about her. For Eddie Jr. is very protective of her, and she minds him. He has three children, but he watches out for Paris. He takes her places. His wife, Tara, is good with Paris. Tara's a blessing. I'm positive she and Eddie Jr. would look after Paris.

I love Paris. Gwen loves Paris. We all love Paris. I even gave Paris her name. I was thinking of some names, and Paris, France, was one of the places where I competed. So I mentioned "Paris," and Gwen liked it. Plus it's unisex. We were at an amusement park, and I yelled "Paris." This guy kept looking at me strangely, then he told me that his name is Paris. Our Paris's middle name is Rochelle, Gwen's pick.

I've never looked at Paris as a daily responsibility; I see her as a timeless joy. She's a treat. She's easy, too. In this world of sex and violence, we don't worry about any of that stuff with Paris. She's always right there with us. I have other worries. During my career involvement with youth, some of my track kids have actually OD'd. One of my students came up to me and said, "I'm a changed man." Then he opened up his shirt to show me nine bullet holes. I couldn't believe he was still alive. I told him, "You should walk the straightest of straights." He should be that blessed.

We don't have that parental concern where, perhaps, Paris is out late: where is she, and is she being mistreated? We still worry about her getting sick, but not about her being alone and helpless. If Gwen and I want to go out for dinner, Paris isn't totally dependent. She can be at the house by herself for a few hours at a time. She can use the microwave, and she can feed herself. She can shower and dress herself. She's not an invalid. She has the computer, radio, and television.

Paris will do chores. She makes her bed, cleans her room, and washes the dishes. We prefer she doesn't cook on the stove, being around fire; we don't want to take that chance. We've invited her to go out and have dinner with us, but she'll usually say no. She has this world she's created; she's very happy and comfortable in it, and she can't enjoy it with people hovering over her. Yet when she does go out in public, she's fully into the world of people around her. She loves all the nostalgia stuff—the music of the '70s and '80s, and, of course, Richard Nixon.

I've heard of developmentally disabled people who've dated, but that's not in the cards for Paris. That idea, in fact, would be offensive to Gwen. Paris is happy; she's enjoying her life. I look at Paris and sometimes think, "I wish I was enjoying my life like Paris, and I was as happy as she is." She approaches life as "What's in store for me today?" Every day is an adventure. She's in her room creating. Or she's singing, she's dancing, and she's talking. She entertains herself. She watches *Judge Joe Brown* and *Judge Judy*, or old sitcoms like *All in the Family* and *Sanford and Son*. Then she'll take a nap, and she recharges.

Gwen deserves all the credit for Paris; she takes care of her so well, and people do notice, complimenting Gwen for Paris's grooming. We see other families where the children look so neglected in their appearance, wearing rumpled clothing and scuffed shoes. Even the way those children act—I don't understand how any parent can overlook their children with such disregard.

Gwen and I have kept a strong marriage in spite of life's challenges. Eddie Jr. went through a divorce with his first wife after bringing a son, Eddie III, into the world. Eddie III was affected by the divorce; he was three or four when that happened, so it confused him. He is close to Gwen's heart, and Gwen and I trusted our faith in this matter. Eddie Jr. and his first wife were of different family backgrounds and values, though I'm no marriage counselor. Eddie Jr. and I spend a lot of time together. He's happily remarried to Tara, who was his teenage girlfriend. They've had two children together. We feel blessed by their marriage.

Family's everything. I grew up in a poor family, but watching how my parents worked through issues was reassuring. To me, marriage—bonding, children, the good times, the bad times—it's all been worth it. I have no regrets. Gwen and I keep growing closer together, even though we're less than ten years from our golden anniversary. Issues continue, but we're better at working through them.

And our daughter loves the role of Aunt Paris. She'll tell Eddie Jr.'s kids, "You can't touch that, you might break it." Or, "Get over here." She'll say things that amaze me. She's conscientious; she pays attention to things. She's such a good aunt that she tickles me.

Eddie Hart and Eddie Jr., dressed to the nines at a formal function. (Photo courtesy of Eddie Hart)

On one of our midnight Munich tram rides, Eddie Jr. addressed having "Hart" as his surname. After graduating from Cal, he became a federal investigator with the U.S. Department of Labor, which enforces wage and labor laws in companies over which the department has jurisdiction. Eddie Jr. looks out for the common man; it takes plenty of heart to be a Hart.

"As I've gotten older," he told me, "I've realized the importance of what our name means. I've been able to experience those men on our family tree—real men—through their handshakes, and by what their word stands for. Whatever they said they were going to do, that's exactly what they did. You didn't have to figure it out. I've loved being named after you, Dad, and giving my son the same name. There is no greater testimonial. My son, Eddie III, loves to call you 'Poppy.' And he understands that Poppy was an Olympian.

"You and Mom have treated me the same way as Paris, up to her disability, of course. But if she did something wrong, she got into trouble. If I did something wrong, I got into trouble. There was no separation in that sense. I knew early on that Paris was different. I enjoyed that from this perspective: she has taught me a lot about life, and how not to be afraid of difference but to embrace it. I've learned a lot from Paris, including the art of patience.

"Paris and I went to different schools, all the way up through high school. She graduated from her school at twenty-two, and since she's three years older, we graduated together. You and Mom bought her a better computer, because she doesn't like to leave the confines of the house. She couldn't have grown up in a better family, because our family is extremely close. We took all those summer trips to Disneyland, Magic Mountain, Knott's Berry Farm, and Universal Studios. We did that every summer, and now I want to do the same thing with my children. Mom is a Disneyland fanatic, so we might go there twice on the same trip. We also went to fairs and zoos as a family. You and Mom weren't into separate vacations. Our family is so tight that all of us talk just about every day. That means a lot, it's a big part of who I am. I strive to be the best family man because of how I see you and Mom."

Eddie Jr. had more to say about family in talking with Newhouse back at our Munich hotel, while I stayed in the room, which my son and I shared.

"If you want to know how I was shaped as a child, it was my dad's presence," he said. "It's the same exact way that my father talks about his father. I love being around my dad. Before I started kindergarten, I'd go to work with him at his junior college campus. When it came to discipline, he did take a belt to me, but he stopped doing that early, compared to some of my friends' fathers. He would just talk to me instead. I was highly excitable as a kid. I wondered how I came from such quiet parents.

"My dad's experiences, I'd have to say, shaped me the most. What I learned from my mom is love. She's not very affectionate, hugging you and saying 'I love you' all the time. But when I was two years old, I still smelled like a newborn baby. She would have three or four sets of clothes there every day for my sister and I when we went off to stay with our grandmother. That's how my mom showed us love.

"I'm a Cal man, just like my dad, and I've been able to take care of my family, just like my dad and his dad took care of their families. My paternal

Eddie Hart is as wonderful a father to son Eddie Jr. as T. J. Hart was to his son Eddie Sr. (Photo courtesy of Eddie Hart)

grandfather had the reputation of being the best crane operator Shell Oil ever had. A bus turned over in the 1960s, and my granddad was called off vacation with his crane, because he was the only man who could do the job. My great-great-grandfather was a slave, so every generation of that family represents progression. That was very powerful for me. My father was 'Fast Eddie' in Pittsburg, but he was just my dad. He would talk about his travels in track, where he went to, what he ate. He wouldn't brag about his exploits, but his friends would tell me about my father, the great sprinter. I enjoyed that.

"My mom and dad's relationship showed me what love was. I could see how much they loved each other. They would hug and play around. I'd be in the back seat of the car, and I'd see them holding hands. I do that with my wife."

That Creative Arts building, where I saw Gwen impersonate James Brown, fell into disrepair after fifty years. I joined a group of concerned Pittsburg citizens, and we raised more than $700,000 to replace all of the seating and carpeting inside that auditorium. Our group also laid the groundwork for another project that totally refurbished the building. As James Brown might say, the grandfatherly building "got a whole new bag."

When I think of what happened to me in Munich, I understand that Gwen and my children, especially Eddie Jr., have to live with that legacy, too. He gets asked questions about me, about my disqualification. It doesn't just die away. But Gwen, once again, has only cared about me. Always. She attended all my local track meets, and I could hear her voice above the crowd, cheering for me. She loved me if I won, lost, or was disqualified. But my disqualification happened in front of the whole world, and so I wanted Eddie Jr. to understand my full perspective on that whole situation. His traveling with me to Munich, to see it all for himself, helped him understand.

I also wanted this book to be inspirational. Paris's story can be encouraging and uplifting to other families in similar situations. It's been a wonderful, enjoyable, fantastic experience having Paris as a daughter. I couldn't ask God for anything more. I have a wonderful son, a wonderful daughter, and a wonderful wife. We have a great family.

Some people may look at our situation negatively, pitying Gwen and me for having to raise a very special daughter who will have this struggle and that struggle all her life. But it doesn't have to be like that. I've learned, instead, from Paris that she is capable of handling this challenge. Through her, I've also learned about sharing, about giving, and that I can allow people to be who they are without putting them in some kind of box. So I, myself, have gained.

It hasn't always been easy, granted. I could have felt sorry or sad for myself and for Gwen. But when I look at the total picture, that won't ever happen. I'm happy, and I'm happy with Paris. She's not out to hurt anybody, or to pull one over on anybody. She's not worried about having to make all sorts of money. She's just happy doing her own thing. What the world may be looking for, she already has in abundance.

While other forty-year-olds are getting facelifts, Paris doesn't look older than eighteen. She has no wrinkles. Life hasn't worn on her, because she doesn't deal with life the same way we do, with all that pressure and stress. She has no grudges or ill feelings, like other people have. She's always looking for a hug, always with a smile. That's a good way to be, the best way, really. We could all take lessons from Paris.

Like Gwen said, God gave us a very special child.

13

THE FOG

My chief competitor, I learned at a very early age, wasn't some sprinter on the track, but an enemy in my own mind. I had depression.

This foglike cloud descended on me out of the blue. I had no way to explain it and nobody to explain it for me; I dealt with it on my own by not telling anyone. I couldn't see through that dense fog when it hit me. But I had to find my way through it, hoping it would lift and that life would clear up again.

The first time it hit, I thought it was a freaky thing. I was in the sixth grade when I started crying one day for no particular reason. Then I isolated myself from classmates. I was confused and felt like I needed to be alone. I did, finally, speak with my teacher, Mrs. Ascherl, but only after she caught me, deep in my funk. She tried to be helpful, and she was, and then the fog lifted after a few weeks—for good, I thought.

I was wrong. There would be four more instances—a total of five times in ten years—the last when I was twenty-two, when the fog returned. Like an unwelcome guest, it would just show up and then leave when it felt like it, always after a short stay. And each time, I went through it alone.

The second time it happened, I was fourteen and playing basketball in James McGee's backyard. His father and mine worked at Shell Oil together. They were visiting inside while James and I were outside shooting hoops. All of a sudden, out of nowhere, this thick fog came over me. Pow! I started crying, and I couldn't tell you, if my life depended on it, why this was happening. I just stopped playing, like I was frozen. James could see instantly that something was wrong.

He said, "Eddie, what's the matter?"

"I don't know. This feeling just hit me."

The next thing I knew, I was sweating, trembling, hyperventilating—all that kind of bad stuff. James put a hand on me, to calm me. He was very concerned.

"Eddie, has this ever happened to you before?"

"Yeah, two, three years ago."

"Does your father know about it? Have you told anybody else?"

"No, I haven't told anyone."

James got me to sit down on the ground. He tried to calm me, to stabilize me. He got me to discuss the first time the fog happened. By talking about it, the load lightened a little bit. Just talking to him, I started feeling better. I answered his questions, but his concern for me really came across. In fact, I didn't want to leave him; he was that calming. James was four years older, sort of an authority figure, so it felt good to let him take control. But it took an hour to make the fog subside.

"Eddie, should we tell your father?"

"No, James, not right now. Let me work it out."

I never told my father. I never told my parents about any of these bouts of depression. I was bewildered, but I toughed it out. So I told no one. But that was the way we did things inside the Hart home. My father and my uncle lived through hard times with no sour grapes. Their attitude: when things go wrong, you just worked it out, and you went forward. You internalized it, or whatever, but you didn't complain to others. They had their own problems.

But did this second fog scare me? Sure, although once again, I couldn't explain what was going on inside my mind and body. I felt helpless, wondering if this was the last time it would happen or how much longer this fog would blanket my life. Still, I faced it by myself rather than seek professional help.

The third time the fog appeared, one year later, I was asleep in bed. I woke up and, oh, man, was I breathing hard. I was so frightened that I got down on my knees and started praying. I even thought I was going to die because of this intense feeling I was having—short, shallow breathing, and I was hyperventilating all over again.

Those minutes felt like hours. But I managed to calm myself down, thinking that if I were going to die, I'd be dead by now. If that sounds crazy, remember I was just a kid, trying to figure out what life was about. I didn't understand what was going on with me, so I was rationalizing things. Because I saw no rational explanation for any of this, I tried to fit the whole puzzle together. This was my third bout, but I learned to suppress and repress a lot.

The one tactic I used effectively to lift the fog was the Olympics. So I focused on that long-term goal. But talk to someone? Get help? I was the same Eddie

Hart; I internalized it all. I'm a man, not a boy, so just tough it out, I told myself. There was no crying towel. In my family, you didn't cry. You might cry in your room, but when you came out, you regained your composure. I just pushed the fog out of my mind. And right after that episode, Gwen and I began dating, so life started looking a lot better. But, like everyone else, I never told her about the depression either, not until I started writing this book.

The fog was not done with me yet. The fourth time it happened was six years after the third episode. I was attending Cal, and I became depressed after my performances at the NCAA and AAU championships in 1971. I was moping around the house, upset that I didn't make the '71 national team after having done so the year before. The Olympics were a year away, and the '71 USA-Russian meet was going to be held at Cal. Here it was, right there on my own track, and not being in that meet just tore me up. So it was almost like I had induced this latest depression. I was in my room, crying, totally distraught. The fog hit me like a ton of bricks.

It stayed like that for a couple of hours. I stayed in my room, hiding from view, until I realized that this feeling was different from the others. I could see the cause of this fog—my own personal failure—where as the previous ones had just descended on me out of the blue. Depression is one thing, but nothing scared me more than not making it to the Olympics, which was the most significant part of my existence. I'm sure Gwen will understand.

That was my fourth bout of depression, though there was another period during the Munich Olympics when the fog hit me like split-pea soup after my disqualification. But I had a more successful way of dealing with it this fifth time, by winning a relay gold medal, which evaporated the fog forever.

No longer was it hard to see where I was, and where I was going. Having Gwen in my life helped me immensely. Getting my degree from Cal, and then my master's degree from Cal State, Hayward, brought more positives into my life. Having children made me feel even more accomplished. I never even saw Paris's medical situation as a negative. She is a loving daughter, and I love being her dad.

James McGee's no longer with us; he's passed. But his attempt to help me through my second bout with depression influenced me later on when I tried to help a second childhood friend—let's call him Charles—through a difficult situation. I was in my late fifties or early sixties when Charles lost his wife, who was twenty years younger. Her death was more than he could handle. Five or six years later, he still was dealing with it, really suffering. He was depressed, refusing to seek therapy, just sucking it up and trying to go forward. One of

There is a plaque in Eddie Hart's honor on the Cal campus, saluting his character. (Photo courtesy of Eddie Hart)

Charles's exes tried to forge a new relationship, but he was just not there yet. I had James McGee and Mrs. Ascherl to counsel me, and I tried to counsel Charles, just by being his friend. However, he won't seek therapy; he's just going to tough it out his way. I'm not the only stubborn one.

My bouts with depression, though, have added value to my life by making me stronger, and healthier, like giving me a mental polio shot. And I can now help others in similar situations by sharing my own experiences, listening to them, and being there for them as a friend. That way, it becomes easier for them to open up about what's troubling them. When Gwen's feeling low, she'll open up and talk to me. It works both ways.

But I needed to know for sure if my own condition would be diagnosed as depression or possibly anxiety or panic attacks. So I reached out to a friend, a psychologist, and I explained what I had been feeling. He agreed that it was, indeed, depression.

"The reason that it's depression, Eddie, is that you lost all interest in doing things, a common sign of a depressed individual," he said. "Young kids don't have anxiety and panic attacks, especially if they are athletes like yourself. Anxiety and panic attacks affect sleep, and you said your sleep wasn't affected. Depression can come and go; it doesn't have to be extended over months, years, or a lifetime."

I have thought a lot about what caused my depression so many years ago. I was somewhat insecure as a boy. I worried how I looked and whether my clothes were nice enough. None of us in our neighborhood was rich or had a leg up on someone. Most of us did have a mom and a dad, so there was love at home.

But my most traumatic experience was fighting dyslexia; I was very insecure in the classroom. I dreaded the teacher calling on me. I mean, take a gun and shoot me first! So I struggled with school. My homework wasn't always done. School was always traumatic, except for sports. School probably was the primary reason for my depression. Winning the gold medal, as I said, enhanced my life. No longer do I worry, like I did in school, about getting up before a group and speaking, In fact, I love it. I'm a different person since Munich.

So if the fog hovers over me again, I've got sunlight to burn it off. The truth is, I didn't even know I had dyslexia until after graduating from Cal. I used to fight it by burning the midnight oil. There's always a solution, I figured, if you work hard enough. Training for the Olympics, I wasn't going to let anything, depression or dyslexia, stop me. Success strengthens us as individuals. It gives us self-esteem. And self-esteem is a wonderful deterrent to what troubles us.

This fog would come over me and I allowed it to hang there by not seeking advice. I'm sure others who are fighting depression see themselves as victims, out of control. That's not always true; we do have control, by seeking therapy. That's so important, because in some instances depression becomes so severe that people commit suicide.

Suicide is never the only way out. No one can lift a five-hundred-pound weight alone. That's the message. The night that I thought I was going to die, it would have been so much smarter to seek another voice. I was too bullheaded, believing I could beat depression on my own. I'm a man of faith, and I could have reached out to God, but I didn't. Instead, I let depression dominate me.

I should have found out earlier how I could have benefitted from depression, how I could have used it to strengthen myself as a human being. Only sharing brings healing; I could have dissipated the fog of my youth by seeking professional help. Having done so, finally, made life clearer.

VIEW FROM OLYMPUS

Two important events I'm involved with every year represent the gold standard of Olympic greatness. If there were a combined medal stand for both events, the top step would need to be five meters wide to accommodate all the gold medalists.

The first is the Willie Davenport Track and Field Clinic in Union City, California, named after the late 1968 Olympic 110-meter hurdles gold medalist. The second is the Eddie Hart All In One Foundation Track and Field Clinic and Dinner in Pittsburg, California, named after a certain 1972 Olympic 400-meter relay gold medalist.

The combined gold-medal list includes Tommie Smith, Jimmy Hines, Lee Evans, Dick Fosbury, Randy Williams, Barbara Ferrell, Gerald Tinker, Mac Wilkins, Kevin Young, Mel Pender, Edith McGuire, Millard Hampton, and Stephanie Brown Trafton. All are committed to developing future Olympians.

While showing youngsters how to run faster, jump higher, and throw farther, these Olympians engage in Olympic chatter. For the purpose of this book, their conversations dealt with my Olympic misfortune. But these athletes also shared their own Olympic experiences and, in some cases, misfortunes.

Before he was the fastest 200-meter sprinter in the world, Tommie Smith tasted disappointment at the 1964 Olympic Trials, which were divided, oddly, into two stages: the semifinals at Randall Island in New York and the finals in Los Angeles. This meant two steps to qualify for the Olympic Games in Tokyo.

He trained for those Olympics in the 400 meters while he was a freshman at San Jose State. The Santa Clara Youth Village Track Club he ran for, when school was out, didn't have the money to send him back east. So his hometown of Lemoore, California, raised the money, and he went by himself. He qualified in one race, but before the next, he went up on a hill and fell asleep under a tree. There was nobody to wake him up. Realizing what he had done, he jumped up, but the race already had started. He could see the smoke of the starter's gun. It was too late to do anything about it; he was disqualified, something I know only too much about.

Smith won an Olympic gold medal four years later—in the 200, the same race in which San Jose State teammate John Carlos took the bronze. Carlos also knows what being left out feels like. "At San Jose State, we had such great sprinters," he said. "The way that we looked at the 1968 Olympics, Tommie would win the 200, Lee Evans would win the 400, and I would win the 100. That was our methodology. But Stan Wright had Jimmy Hines [at Texas Southern], and Stan had his own hidden agenda. I had run the 100 in all the trials, but when it came time for the final trials at South Lake Tahoe, I was told that I wasn't allowed to run it.

"I understood it: every coach wants his athlete to excel. Stan Wright had Hines, and Payton Jordan had Larry Questad [at Stanford]. So I didn't have any misgivings about their hidden agendas. I accomplished what I wanted to do in the Olympic Games. We had to do what we had to do. I'm happy that Jimmy Hines got his gold medal and that Stan Wright got the recognition for being his coach. They got theirs, and I got mine. No big deal. There's always tomorrow, but there is no doubt about politics when it comes to the Olympics."

Lee Evans, among those "Speed City" Olympic medalists at San Jose State, knows about disqualifications, too. He lived through his own in 1972. "We didn't get to run the 1600-meter relay at Munich because Wayne Collett had his trousers thrown over his shoulders and Vince Matthews didn't even wear his trousers at the medal ceremony, plus they slouched on the medal stand," Evans said of Matthews's and Collett's controversial one-two finish in the 400-meter run. "So they were kicked off the team. John Smith was hurt in the 400 final and didn't finish the race. I was just there to run the relay, but with three guys gone, we couldn't run the relay. We were disqualified, when who was going to beat us? Nobody. I've won three Olympic gold medals, but I couldn't talk about that relay issue for four years."

Other Olympians at the two Bay Area track clinics, men and women who sacrificed their young lives to achieving their Olympic goals, but weren't disqualified, discussed that concept as it related to Rey Robinson and me. "It would have been the most devastating thing in my life," Jimmy Hines told Dave Newhouse. "Eddie Hart had the same thing going for him in 1972 that I had in 1968. When you don't get a chance to prove yourself in front of a

Through suspensions and injury, Lee Evans, 1968 Olympic 400-meter champion, was left without a 1600-meter relay team in Munich. (Photo courtesy of Eddie Hart)

half-million people, you can't replace it, because it's your chance to be No. 1 in the world—not in your state, not in your country, but in the entire world. And if you know that you're the best, being disqualified will stay in your mind forever. As long as you're breathing, you're going to feel it. For Rey Robinson, that was his last memory as an athlete. I've known Eddie all these years, and even though he doesn't come out and say it, he's thought about it. It probably crosses his mind once a day. But he's cool, calm, and collected. A lot of athletes might not have been able to handle it like he did."

Stephanie Brown Trafton won the gold medal for discus in Beijing in 2008, the first American woman to win that Olympic event since Lillian Copeland in Los Angeles in 1932. Trafton has an interesting perspective on disqualifications. "I've never been in that situation," she said, "but at the same time, there's always a letdown any time you're done with competition—either you didn't make the final, you didn't medal, or you're disqualified. There's this kind of finality in competition. Even when I won the gold medal, I still had the feeling of 'That was it, really?' So no matter if you hit the top or crash and burn at the bottom, that's the end of your opportunity, or the end of the season, whichever comes first. The only difference is the repercussions afterward, whether you get invited to meets or not. Eddie had tied the world record, so he still would have been invited to competitions, if he wanted that in his life.

"But there's an emotional wall that every athlete hits when the competition is over, whether you get a medal or you don't. It's the navigation of the ups and downs, and trying to smooth out those peaks and valleys that are going to give you a long career. I still competed after Beijing because I'd never won a national championship, and the American record still was out there to be broken. I succeeded in both endeavors. Now it's 2015, I'm thirty-five, married with a sixteen-month-old child. And I'm a three-time Olympian who's trying to make next year's Olympics in Brazil. [Editor's note: she didn't qualify.]

"A final thought on disqualification," she continued: "I've had an athlete-coach relationship for about twenty years with Robert Budke. If he had made an honest mistake about an event time, and I didn't verify it, then it was my fault. I am the one who should have all my t's crossed and all of my i's dotted, because it's up to me. Ultimately, Robert isn't the one in the discus ring. The coach is there to assist you, but I am the team manager. I have my physical therapy assistants, my massage therapist, sports psychologist, and training partners, coaches, and nutritionists. These people are a part of my team, but I'm the one who has to put it all together."

Barbara Ferrell won a gold and silver at Mexico City—a gold in the 400-meter relay and a silver behind Wyomia Tyus in the 100-meter dash. But she didn't get to compete in 1972, having become injured in Munich. Her

Jimmy Hines was the 1968 Olympic 100-meter champ; he saw Eddie Hart as the perfect sprinter. (Photo courtesy of Eddie Hart)

husband, Warren Edmondson, finished fifth in the 100 at the '72 Olympic Trials, narrowly missing a relay berth. Barbara said, "So it got to Warren, because that near miss epitomized the whole year. With the massacre and everything, 1972 was a mess."

One big mess, and Rey Robinson and I would know that more than anybody else. I had raced against Warren Edmondson in junior college and college—I was at Cal, he was at UCLA—so I can see where Barbara's coming from. I guess it's a matter of how you handle the mess. I handled it by choosing not to asign blame for what had happened.

John Carlos's view: "Eddie was an arch competitor for anyone. His main competitor was Warren Edmondson. They came up together, had pretty much the same talent, so it was a tug-of-war as to which one of them was going to win. Warren was a little more outspoken than Eddie, but when it came down to the starting line, I don't think any sprinter was more competitive than Eddie Hart."

Jimmy Hines offered another perspective, regarding the aftereffects of disqualification. "Eddie wasn't given the chance to run in Munich when he clearly was the best sprinter in the world," Hines said. "Eddie mentioned that I was his role model. I was the first man to break the 10-second barrier in the 100-meter dash, clocking 9.95 seconds in Mexico City. My Olympic record stood for twenty years because Eddie didn't get a chance to run in that 1972 final in Munich. If he had, he would have broken my record for sure.

"Before you can compete, any athlete must believe in himself, especially when it comes to sprinting, because it's so quick, and it's an individual sport. You can't get anything from a teammate in the 100. There are no substitutes. If you win, it's your victory. If you lose, it's your defeat. Eddie believed in himself, that he couldn't lose."

Gold medalist or disqualified, Carlos believes it all comes down to character. "The biggest thing about Eddie wasn't the distance he had to run or who he had to catch in the relay," he said. "The biggest thing was Eddie's heart, saying to himself that whatever the challenge was before him, he was up for it. That was his greatest asset: 'I'm a fighter.' Everyone has their own character in how they deal with issues. The object of every athlete is to go to the Olympics and win a gold medal. And if not a gold medal, then a medal. Eddie missed his race, but he got a second chance. He accomplished his goal: he got a gold medal. He's Eddie Hart: gold-medal winner. He had a complicated situation, not to mention all the turmoil that was taking place in Munich. He got a chance in the relay, and he got his rewards.

"Eddie Hart and Stan Wright had parallels, because Stan was a humble man, just like Eddie. Stan expressed himself in a very articulate way, in terms of a workout form, or in terms of a mind-set. Stan was the producer of Jimmy Hines. Stan has taken a lot of heat because he missed the call for the start of the 100 quarterfinal in Munich. But you have to put some onus on the athletes themselves. It's very difficult for me to think that Tommie Smith would go to the Olympic Games and rely on any one individual to tell him what he's supposed to do. Tommie Smith knows what time the race is going on."

Whenever he's awake, of course.

"The onus would have to be on me as well, because we're adults and not some sixteen- or seventeen-year-old," Carlos continued. "Eddie is aware of

Stephanie Brown Trafton won the women's Olympic discus in London in 2012 but just missed qualifying for Rio in 2016. (Photo courtesy of Stephanie Brown Trafton)

that, and that's why he doesn't have any ill feelings toward Stan Wright. And Stan didn't have any ill feelings toward Eddie. They both might have felt guilty about what happened. That's a heavy load for both of them to accept. Eddie didn't point at Stan, and Stan didn't point at Eddie. But there still was the court of public opinion."

Evans extolled Wright as "a great guy. He always took us to the stadium. If you had a race, Stan would wait downstairs. That was his way, to not watch. He always made sure you were there for your race. If you missed it, then everybody missed it. Stan took what happened in Munich very hard; it was a big mistake. He didn't teach me to run faster, but he was very organized. He showed you love. He not only cared about you as a runner, he cared about you as a person. He was a very serious guy, respected by everyone. Howard Cosell raked him over the coals and made him look bad."

Wright played a significant role in Hines's development as a gold medalist. "He was my coach at Texas Southern until my senior year, when he left to coach at Western Illinois University. He was the greatest coach you could have," said Hines. "He understood his athletes. He was a sprint coach, but he was a total coach. What they pulled on him, and what they pulled on Eddie in Munich, showed that the Olympics are high-stakes politics. Nobody likes the United States of America; they'll do everything to break our back. There's a history of that, but Stan Wright is a very honorable man.

"I felt bad for Stan because millions of people put the blame on him. But those millions don't understand that the Olympics are the biggest political sport in the world. I kept up with Stan after he moved out to Sacramento, and I know what happened in Munich had an effect on ending Stan's life early. I can truthfully say that, because I was like a son to Stan Wright. He knew Eddie was the best sprinter in the world in 1972, and when he couldn't run in Munich, it broke Stan's heart."

Gerald Tinker said on the matter: "What happened to Eddie and Rey wasn't Stan Wright's fault; that information should have been passed on to Stan early. But that [disqualification] wouldn't ever have happened to me. When it was time for Eddie, Rey and Robert [Taylor] to run, I already was sitting up in the stands waiting for them. But, once again, it was not Stan's fault. He had an impeccable way of making sure that everything was done correctly. It was upper management's fault, for hobnobbing and having a great time with family members, and not doing its job. So the Olympics became secondary.

"Stan wasn't only impeccably honest, he was forthright, and he had a great heart. He also was a very nice man. I think he looked at that Munich event as just some misfortune that happened. He took it as another day, another time, and now let's look forward to tomorrow. I don't think the rest of his life was affected by what happened in Munich. I hope not."

Smith and Carlos would receive honorary doctorates from San Jose State University, plus permanent commemoration of their Olympic power salutes—two statues located there in the heart of their old campus. They now, in their honorary dotage, refer to each other as Dr. Smith and Dr. Carlos.

"I look back on Eddie Hart as a youngster who wouldn't say ten words in ten years," said Carlos. "He was very low-key in expressing himself verbally. Then he crossed over the bridge. He's very talkative now, like a public relations person for track and field. There aren't many guys in any sport who can be perceived as greater than the sport itself. That's where Dr. Smith and myself are, and Eddie Hart is entering that realm himself.

"Eddie's crossed that bridge into immortality. He's truly one of the legends of the sport now, like Dr. Smith and myself. You can't mention track and field and not have Eddie Hart's name pop up."

I've heard comments about the possibility of my receiving an honorary doctorate from my alma mater, UC Berkeley. That would be nice, although I'm not sure if I could take Dr. Smith and Dr. Carlos calling me Dr. Hart.

THE BERKELEY MAN

Dave Maggard and I are joined at the heart. It's as simple as that. I love him, and he knows it. He loves me, and I know it. We love each other's families, and they know it, too. Some coach-athlete relationships turn out great, and some turn out just the opposite. Dave and I had the perfect relationship, and we still do, a lifetime bond.

Dave recruited me to run track for him, and it was an easy recruitment. Cal is a great university, ranked tops in the world among public institutions. And though I had unlimited choices of four-year schools, Dave was someone I liked immediately and felt very comfortable around, even though he didn't know it.

"I started recruiting Eddie at Contra Costa College his sophomore year, in 1969," Maggard recalled in June 2015. "I called his JC coach, Jack Albiani, an old friend, and asked about Eddie. 'He's the best,' Jack said. I told Jack that I wanted someone who can come in here and develop in track and field, and who will also graduate. 'He has all those capabilities,' Jack replied. So I offered Eddie a scholarship, and he said, 'I'm coming to Cal.' But, then, he didn't sign the scholarship offer right away.

"My feeling is that you build a strong track program around the sprints; there are a lot of points in the sprints. Cal had the reputation of having great sprinters who went there and never panned out. They either flunked out of school, like Leamon King, or they became injured, like Forrest Beaty. I wanted to change that image, and what I needed was a real hammer, a sprinter like Eddie Hart.

"So I began to recruit Eddie. I knew he had pressure to go to San Jose State and be part of their 'Speed City' program. They told him: 'This is where it's

Eddie Hart stayed home to go to college, and Cal was the benefactor. (Photo courtesy of Eddie Hart)

happening.' Eddie told me later what people said to him: 'If you go to Cal, it will end your career.' But Eddie kept saying: 'I'm coming to Cal.' I learned an important thing about Eddie: he keeps his word. Whatever he says he's going to do, he's going to do it. And that led to the great resurgence of sprinters at Cal: Eddie and Isaac Curtis."

Isaac became a standout wide receiver for the Cincinnati Bengals, playing twelve seasons in the NFL. But he was recruited to play football at Cal as a running back under the name of Bobby Curtis. Cal unretired the number (36) of its great halfback from the 1940s, Jackie Jensen, as a recruiting enticement to Isaac. But there were three issues: Isaac had no moves as a running back, he didn't know who Jackie Jensen was, and Maggard had talked him into coming out for track as a hurdler.

Well, Isaac kept knocking down hurdles, and he was ready to quit track. Assistant Coach Al Ragan told Dave Maggard that Isaac was quitting. Dave convinced him to stick around as a sprinter, someone who could run, at least, on the relay. He agreed to stay, and he wound up doing much more than passing the baton.

Dave Maggard and I were size opposites. Dave was huge, 6-foot-4, 280, and an Olympian shot-putter in 1968. I was 5-foot-10, 150. Despite our size disparity, we both had big appetites. "Eddie, do you remember the cake?" Maggard reminded me in 2015 during a conference call with Dave Newhouse. "Eddie brought his girlfriend, Gwen, who is the salt of the earth, to dinner at our house. The cake went quickly, and Eddie became a part of our family. Even to this day, my two kids will ask, 'Have you heard from Eddie?' They only ask about Eddie and Randy Matson, who won the shot put at Mexico City.

"Eddie comes in with a quiet demeanor, and yet great confidence. Looking at Eddie, you might think he's soft. He's a nice guy who didn't talk a lot back then. But he's as competitive as anybody I've ever known. He really has the fire in his belly. One night, I dropped by his place, just visiting. Cliff West, his roommate, said, 'My dad was a good sprinter. Without working out, he ran 10 flat over 100 yards.' Eddie said, 'You don't have to work out to run 10 seconds.' He cracked me up. Eddie's always had a sense of humor.

"Let me tell you a story about Eddie from 1972. We were in Oslo, Norway, at an Olympic training center. Al Buehler, the Duke coach who was one of Bill Bowerman's assistants, told me: 'We're really going to have a problem with Eddie Hart, with his Afro and goatee.' Now Al's a good guy, and he isn't racist. But I told him, 'Al, you may have a problem with some guys, but it won't be Eddie Hart. With everybody in this entire camp, Eddie Hart is sterling.' People were very sensitive in those times. I told all my athletes, 'I don't care if you have long hair, a mustache or goatee. You've got to put out; we're just going to judge you on results.'

"Eddie was very quiet. So as a consequence, people didn't know what he was about. Eddie's background, coming from Pittsburg, isn't as affluent as some other Bay Area cities, like Piedmont and Atherton. That threw some people off. But Eddie's always been absolutely straight. Whatever Eddie wanted to do, he wanted to do it the right way. Not only to be a track champion, but he's a champion as a person."

My first track season at Cal was 1970. Dave's vision about the utmost importance of having fast sprinters on the team really took shape the day Isaac Curtis was given a 100-yard-dash time trial on the dirt track at Edwards Stadium. One of the managers timed Isaac, and when he showed the time to Dave, he said, "You did that wrong." Dave was in disbelief, but it was the right time—super fast!

Then Isaac beat me in every dual meet. That hurt, because Isaac was a surprise. I was the one on a track scholarship; he was on a football scholarship. But with Dave's encouragement and expertise, I kept working hard. What I got most from Dave wasn't training or technique; it was the psychological aspect of competition. His strategies made me mentally tougher, and that strengthened the bond between us. I always wanted to do well in competition, especially at Cal, because Dave had done everything possible to help me. I wanted to reciprocate, and I felt bad when I didn't win my events.

Isaac needed approval from the football coaches to keep running track during spring football practice. It's a good thing the coaches agreed, because we were having trouble on the relay. We had the right foursome, but we were making mistakes, and we kept losing. Isaac ran the second leg, and I ran anchor, but a bad baton pass or something else always kept us from achieving our full potential.

When the Pac-8 Conference meet arrived, I was loose and mentally relaxed, feeling more prepared than I had been all season. We finished one-two in the 100-yard final, my first victory over Isaac that year. I took second in the 220-yard dash, and our sprint relay team also managed a second; I got the baton too far back to make up the difference.

Then I had a conversation with an old-timer who was a dishwasher at a local Veterans Administration hospital. He was a friendly guy who said something to me that stuck in my mind, that regardless of the sport, he just wanted his son to become an All-American. I had heard that term before, but it had no relevance for me until I discovered that any finish at an NCAA championship track meet, first to fourth, would entitle that person to an All-American certificate. Before that meet, the best 100-yard time in the country was 9.2 seconds, which was my best time, but no West Coast sprinter, including me, had run that fast that year. So I was thinking that fourth place would make me an All-American.

"One thing about Eddie," Maggard said, "is that he always ran better late in the year. I told Eddie not to worry, that he was [potentially] a champion."

I took four days off from serious training prior to the NCAA Championships in Des Moines, Iowa, in order to rest my body and to rebuild its strength and stamina. It was the perfect strategy: I was reenergized. I couldn't wait to get started in Des Moines. Isaac and I were split up in heats, and we won our semifinal races, posting the fastest times going into the final. Isaac and I shot some pool before heading to Drake Stadium for the showdown—between Isaac and me but also between Mel Gray of Missouri and me. Mel beat me regularly in high school, but this was a new day.

The race was over at the gun. I had the best start of my life, and I got to the finish line just ahead of fast-charging Isaac, in 9.4 seconds. We made history as the first sprinters from the same school to go one and two in an NCAA 100 final. I was now an All-American, in the biggest way. I fared badly in the 220 final; I was disqualified—there's that word again—for running out of my lane. I never liked the 220 anyway. With the temperature at thirty degrees, a downpour occurred as the 440-yard relay got underway. Cal had a slight lead as I got the baton on the final leg. Despite the elements, we put together a perfect relay to take first place

Isaac picked up points in the 220, likewise Rich Dunn in the triple jump, and Cal had enough points to win the NCAA team championship. How was that achievement greeted? With this headline: "Hippie coach wins NCAA." Hippie coach? Dave Maggard was as clean-cut as they come, and he wasn't a radical. Dave took it, outwardly, with good humor, but I knew the phrase upset him.

Cal now had its own "Speed City." Plus we were NCAA champions. Or were we? When we returned to Berkeley, a crowd, including the school chancellor, met us at the airport. All was well, we thought. A few days later, Dave gave everyone on the team a watch. A great moment, we all thought again. There is a song I've sung at church: "Trouble Don't Last Always." Well, good times don't always last either. And so Cal had to forfeit its team championship because of an ineligible athlete: Isaac Curtis.

Eddie Hart wins a relay race comfortably at Cal. (Photo courtesy of Eddie Hart)

Isaac and another football player, receiver Larry Brumsey, had enrolled at Cal without taking the entrance exam. The football staff had crossed the line, and the NCAA put Cal on football probation. Because Isaac was deemed ineligible, our sprint relay team was disqualified—I can't get away from that word—and USC was declared the relay champion. My 100 win was safe—I was eligible—but Isaac forfeited second place. Following the 1971 football season, he transferred to San Diego State, where he became a No. 1 NFL draft pick in 1973.

"Isaac hadn't taken the SAT, and nobody knew that except the football staff," said Maggard. "As a consequence, the NCAA was investigating the football program. As a result of his not taking that test, his points at the NCAA meet were taken away from us, and UCLA and Kansas tied for the title. So he was made ineligible after the fact." Losing the NCAA title was a blow, and it had nothing to do with Dave, who won that championship his first year as Cal's track coach. I felt bad for Dave, but I didn't give back my watch, and guys on the team didn't give back theirs either. None of that, though, changed my primary goal at Cal, which was graduating. That sheepskin was as important to me as an Olympic gold medal. Dave kept reminding me, "You have to graduate." I didn't want anyone saying that Dave had used me. I had to graduate, for the two of us. Dave wanted that degree for me as much as I did for myself.

People don't realize how tough that is, going to school at Cal. Though I was a physical education major, I was competing against premed students. I took chemistry, kinesiology, exercise of physiology—tough classes, and my professors graded on a curve, which meant I was competing against students who didn't have the added pressure of training countless hours in a sport. And PE at Cal was research oriented; it wasn't just "how to coach football." I was down in the labs, experimenting with water and heat, and thinking, "Did I pick the right major?" Cal didn't have a tutoring program for athletes back then. Dave started that program after becoming, in 1973, Cal's athletic director, a position he held for nineteen years after serving as the school's track-and-field coach for four years.

But we're talking about Cal, or Berkeley, a university where academics and even athletics become secondary, in the public's view, to radicalism. At Cal, social causes overlap because they are so numerous. Tables are lined up with activists, recruiting students to join this movement or that protest. Cal is the bastion of liberalism and often plants the seed of some revolution that spreads across the nation's campuses.

My time at Cal, I quickly learned, presented decision-making challenges. Groups and organizations were constantly fighting for my attention. African American groups wanted me to join them and support their causes. I listened to what they all had to say, and some of their arguments were convincing. But I had charted my course before I arrived at Cal, and social activism wasn't part of that course. Graduation! Graduation! Graduation! Some Black Student Union students told me that if I got on the bus that was taking the track team to a meet, I was giving in to the white man, who only was interested in using me. I got on the bus. I stayed on course.

Getting a college degree meant everything to me and to all those people who supported me, mainly my family. Forty years later, I know that I made the right decisions at Cal, thinking of other African American students who got caught up in social causes and flunked out of school. Radicalism became so turbulent my first year at Cal that the university's regents terminated the school year a month early. Students received passes instead of grades in each of their classes.

The radicalism turned so violent that Cal made the news most evenings, often nationally. Squatters set up residence at People's Park, an unattractive piece of land that was university property. When the squatters refused to leave, one of them wound up dead. I watched as the National Guard sprayed pepper gas in order to clear the streets near campus. The City of Berkeley called for a curfew, and violators were told they would be jailed.

The city then developed a volunteer group, the Minutemen, to control the violence, which only led to more violence. The Minutemen were known as the Blue Meanies, and they were mean. We heard stories of how they beat up people for no logical reason. On my way to track practice one day, a kid ran by me, looking back to see if he was being chased. He was, by three or four Blue Meanies, who then beat him with their clubs. I changed my mind and ran back to my apartment—one of the few days I missed track practice. Those Blue Meanies had me scared, and I didn't leave my apartment the rest of the day.

Not all of the Blue Meanies were properly trained, or suited, for this job. One morning as I was walking up the stairs into the gym, a tear-gas canister suddenly flew over my shoulder, followed by a cloud of gas. I raced through the gym and onto the track, looking for cover. I didn't know if the tear gas was meant for me, but I wasn't going to wait around to find out.

From day to day, you never knew what might take place on that campus. All these groups were fighting for your attention: the Hare Krishna, the flower people, liberation groups, and the Black Panthers. These groups had replaced the free speech movement activists of the 1960s, who made Cal the most talked-about university in the country. The Black Panthers successfully advocated having a black studies department at Cal. If you had a cause, and were willing to fight for it, Cal was the place to be, and it still is.

Another image of Cal: the street vendor. Walk north on Telegraph Avenue, while heading toward the campus, and when you pass Dwight Way, you've entered another world. There are street vendors galore, selling everything from handmade jewelry to love beads to tie-dye T-shirts. These sidewalk businesses are set up directly in front of commercial businesses. You might even see nude people walking by or driving by. Where else but in Berkeley?

Crossing Bancroft Way and entering campus, the scene there can be just as weird. Once you pass the food trucks, you come to Sather Gate, where protests, rallies, and even arrests take place. That's just for starters. One day as I was walking through this plaza, a woman was dancing, uninhibitedly, to boombox music. She was under the influence of some substance, for she removed all her clothes and continued dancing. Just another typical day in atypical Berkeley.

My brother John attended Cal and introduced me to Cliff West, who was renting an apartment and needed another tenant. Cliff was a distance runner who roomed with Kerry Hampton, a hurdler, and Mike Lyons, a nonathlete student. That was the start of the "Mad Pad," the apartment we shared on Parker Street, one mile south of campus. We all chipped in on food, and Mike did most of the cooking.

Of the three roommates, I grew closest to Cliff, even though he came from a middle-class home while I came from a poor background. His parents were college graduates with good-paying jobs, wonderful people who made me feel at home whenever I visited. I met Cliff's younger brother, Cornel, a high school honor student who could read a novel in one night. (He is known today as Dr. Cornel West, a college professor, author, public speaker, and television personality, and he wrote this book's foreword.) Cliff and I are still close friends today.

"Growing up in Sacramento, I first saw Eddie in the Woodland Relays in 1967," Cliff said. "He was in high school, and even though he took third to Dave Masters and Mel Gray in the 100, I thought he would be better eventually than the other two. He had the technique, but he wasn't yet big and strong. He had the quick twitch that's so important in sprinting. What I didn't know was the quality of his heart. Eddie is like a relaxed furnace. He's on fire, but he knows how to contain it. That must come from his mother and father. He's comfortable living with that fire, and he knows when to let it out. What balances him is his need to serve. He's first, and foremost, a servant. He emanates something spiritual by the way he serves his fellow man.

"As Cal roommates, and being young men, we ran into some situations. They could have been tragic, but they were avoided because of Eddie's leadership and calmness. He'd say, 'Let's walk away from this right now.' I looked at him as a big brother, so I did exactly what he said to do. You couldn't find a better friend than Eddie, a better friend than he was an athlete, and he was a world-class athlete. My brother, Cornel, is blood, but next to him and my mother, Eddie's the best friend I have, just like a family member.

"I saw him get so focused on track and field at Cal, becoming much sharper and more intense. Isaac Curtis won more dual meets, but Eddie won more big meets. It was his intensity. Isaac was a big, strong guy, probably a better athlete than Eddie. It's like being a prizefighter; you can will your way into a winning situation. And Eddie had that will, that winning gear. He always ate right, treated his body right, and he slept right. He could be a rascal, now, but he didn't drink at all. And this was the 1960s, with drugs and all that was going on back then.

"Eddie is one of the most comfortable people in his own skin I've ever known. He and my brother, Cornel, are very free people. It's just not their self-confidence, but their relying on something greater than themselves. They aren't bothered by what's going on in the room. They're not thermometers as much as they're thermostats. I was at work in Berkeley when I heard what happened to Eddie in Munich. I just remember crying. When I first saw him afterward, he seemed at ease. He took that misfortune to bolster himself, to make himself stronger as an individual. I know this: Eddie and I will be seeing each other this side of time and the next."

Cliff West is a remarkable person and athlete. He almost broke the four-minute mile at Cal, at 4:02. When he was twenty-six, he was timed at 10.3 in the 100-meter dash. How many distance runners can say that? He worked in computer software development. He's recovering from a heart condition with a rehab program he defines as "moderation and balance."

Cliff was a terrific student at Cal. On a couple of occasions, he helped me with homework. In a speech class, I was really struggling with this one speech, and Cliff volunteered to write it. At the time, I virtually had no public speaking experience, so I was terrified. My goal was to speak for five minutes, but I even exceeded that, thanks to Cliff. My instructor said I had room for improvement but that it was a good speech. I wasn't aware then of the subtleties—eye contact, strategic pauses—in giving a speech. But I got a passing grade, so I was happy.

At the Mad Pad, we didn't always have the cleanest apartment. Mike Lyons sort of cleaned. Well, we did have house parties, which presented a cleaning issue. I stayed in the background when there was a party and just went to bed. I didn't want anything to interfere with my goals. Cliff roomed with Mike, who eventually withdrew from Cal, while I roomed with Kerry Hampton. He was

Eddie Hart pulls away from the field while winning a relay race at Cal. (Photo courtesy of Eddie Hart)

a top hurdler coming out of Polytechnic High School in San Francisco, but he put on weight at Cal and never reached his full potential. Yet, he was a good roomie.

My senior season at Cal, in 1971, was set back by injuries. We had a dual meet with UCLA, and we started the meet off well in the sprint relay. Wayne Collett and I were the anchormen, but he didn't have my foot speed, and I won. Then in the 100, I took two or three steps out of the blocks and pulled my right hamstring. That was it for me; I was off for six weeks, missing the conference meet. I returned in time for the NCAA Championships, but then made maybe the biggest tactical mistake of my running career.

I had won all my heats leading up to the finals, when I had a brain freeze and decided to change my start. The gun went off, I got the worst start of my life, and everything looked lost. So I took off in total desperation, and started running by people, even Warren Edmondson. I eventually ran out of real estate and took second to Harrington Jackson of Texas at El Paso. I was devastated, feeling like I had let everyone down, including myself. If I hadn't been such a blockhead in the blocks, I would have been a two-time NCAA 100 champion.

But at least I had managed to alter the perception, along with Isaac Curtis, Atlee Mahorn and others, that Cal was Death Valley for sprinters. And I had proven to myself that I could compete at Cal, intellectually as well as athletically. In my mind, from where I started off in school in Pittsburg, dyslexic, I had become a gold medalist in the classroom, thus worthy of my Cal bachelor's degree.

I wouldn't graduate until I returned from Munich. But for some reason that I cannot remember, I didn't attend my formal graduation ceremony. I went to Sproul Hall to pick up my sheepskin. I wasn't emotional about doing this until I looked at my degree, realizing what I had just accomplished. That's when I felt the tears come, thinking of how proud I had made my family, Gwen, Dave Maggard, and myself. Maybe even Mrs. Mercurio, Mrs. Ascherl, and all my coaches.

I also thought of George Brooks, who taught exercise physiology, one of my toughest classes at Cal. He was a leading professor in this field, having written a few books on the subject. He asked if he could mention me in one of his books. I said yes, of course. I was so honored. I've gone back to see him many times since graduating. I find him a bit eccentric. Once I was having a discussion with him about having children. He shocked me with his answer: A man could kill his wife as a result of childbearing. Wow! A few years later, however, he began having children. As I said, eccentric.

The person I most wanted to make happy with my Cal graduation was my father. No one could be prouder about my degree than my dad. If I had to do it all over again, I would have attended my graduation, just so he could have been there for the ceremony. That was a huge mistake. I am the first generation of my family to finish college. My brother John got his degree from St. Mary's College in nearby Moraga after transferring from Cal. One Sunday in church, my father announced to the congregation that I had received my degree. That was big news in our black community at that time. My father, a third-grade student, had stressed to me the benefits of getting an education. And now I had something to give back to him.

I remember walking out those doors of Sproul Hall as an official graduate. I was now an Old Blue, an alumnus, with a degree. "Eddie's graduation meant more to me than his going to the Olympics," said Dave Maggard. "He didn't grow up with a silver spoon, and so his graduation was an obsession with me. Eddie is a blessing to my family, because of who he is and all that he represents. You can count on Eddie."

After graduating, I thought that if I ever had a son, perhaps he would follow in my footsteps and attend Cal. And that's exactly what happened: Eddie Jr. graduated from Cal, just like his proud father. And there was no way I would have missed my son's graduation. Members of Gwen's family joined mine at the ceremony. Because of the kind of people they are, my parents never complained about not getting to watch me graduate. My father, possibly, was too busy bragging to his buddies at Shell Oil that his son, the Olympian, had received a degree from the best public university in the world. And let's not get my father started on his son's master's degree.

CAT ON THE PROWL

My favorite animal is the fastest animal on the planet, the cheetah. This has nothing to do with my Aunt Cheetah; I'm just fascinated with the cheetah, and I absorbed all I could about this cat, equating his running technique with sprinting.

Any time you find flesh and blood that travels sixty, seventy, eighty miles an hour, you have to be fascinated. That's how I got interested in the cheetah. The cheetah says, "I'm hungry, and there's a wildebeest or antelope over there, and I'll go over there quickly and get dinner." It literally runs down its meal, its gold medal of sorts, and drags it back to feed its young.

There is a correlation between how the cheetah moves and how a sprinter moves. The leg structure is different; the cheetah is a four-legged animal, and its center of gravity is a lot lower. When it moves, it's really not running, but producing a sequence of jumps. Its back legs get into a position to make powerful jumps across the ground at breakaway speed. By the way the cheetah extends its back and bows and contracts as it moves forward, if you cut its back legs off, it still would move at ten, twelve miles per hour. That's no jungle myth; I read that in a science book.

Like the cheetah's movements, sprinting is a science, though I might say it's an art form. The sprinter only has two legs, to the cheetah's four, and the sprinter thrusts off one leg in the blocks, while the cheetah thrusts off two back legs in running down an antelope. But the same idea, force coupling, applies to both feline and human.

What's force coupling? That's the difference between straight-legged and bent-legged running. With a straight leg, you don't get that same thrust. Using a bent leg, when it's time to push forward, the ankle is extended, the knee is extended, and even the hip is extended. How else to run the 100 in 9.2 seconds? And all these forces extended at the same time is known as force coupling. Picture a sprinter coming out of the blocks; that's force coupling. Picture him in full stride; that's force coupling. It's all about extension, getting that thrust.

To explain further, in sprinting, you have a driving phase and a recovery phase. When I push off on one foot, that's the driving phase. Until the foot hits the ground, it's the recovery phase, getting the leg into position to drive off again. Whether you're a cheetah or a sprinter, the period of time you're pushing off decreases as you increase your speed. The faster you go, the less time you have to generate speed. That's true whether your destination is the antelope or the 100-meter finish line.

Whether you're a cheetah or a sprinter, it all comes down to being one fast cat. And with Munich just two years away, I had to be at my fastest, or the cat would be out of the bag, so to speak, an uncoupling of force coupling. Following my junior year at Cal, the National AAU Championships were held in Bakersfield. Though I didn't win the Pac-8 or NCAA 100, my hamstring felt strong, and I was peaking. The AAU 100 had a strong field lined up, including John Carlos and Charlie Greene. That was pressure in itself, but adding further pressure was the challenging format: three sprints, including the final, all on the same day. At the NCAAs, it was three races in two days, a breeze by comparison.

I hung around the hotel lobby with my competition. I was more reserved than the others, who, I discovered, were not only trash talkers but drinkers and smokers. We're talking about world-class sprinters—record holders and Olympians—who dissipated like crazy. Man, I was shocked. My reaction was to take it all in stride, which required some effort. Could abstainers win gold medals? I started to wonder.

I competed alone in Bakersfield; I had no coach watching over me. So I had to be my own coach, from bringing all my running gear to knowing my running schedule. My first race was merely to get the kinks out. I didn't recognize any big names in the first heat, but that didn't change my prerace strategy of talking to no one, regardless of all the smack talk that exists among sprinters. This reckless form of bravado, especially among Americans, extends from the locker room to the starting blocks.

As the quiet American, I got off to a decent start in my first race, accelerated, and coasted to the finish. I easily qualified for the second heat, which involved more effort. This time, after a fair start, there was no coasting, and I worked harder to get a second-place finish and a spot in the finals. John

Carlos required greater effort to qualify for the final, as he was laboring with an injury. The buzz around the track was that he might drop out of the meet.

But when the starter called us for instructions before the final, there was Carlos, walking unsteadily over to join the group. Joining Carlos in the field were Charlie Greene, Ivory Crockett, and Robert Taylor, all top-flight sprinters. What chance did I have? Greene and Crockett blasted out of the blocks as expected, before Greene began to fade as I made my move, catching him at the 90-yard mark. I needed a strong lean into the tape to place, but Greene's lean was stronger, and he finished third to my fourth. Crockett and Ben Vaughan finished one-two. Carlos was, indeed, hurt. He got out of the blocks and jogged to the finish line. It wasn't too long afterward that he turned professional.

Finishing fourth was good enough for me to make my first U.S. national team, as the last man in the sprint relay. Then, suddenly, I was third man, as Greene declined his spot. Robert Taylor, fifth, moved up to fourth. We headed overseas to compete in the Soviet Union, France, Italy, Germany, Sweden, and Finland, on a six-week tour. The team met and trained in New York for a few days before flying to Europe. By this time, I had gotten over my flying jitters, but I still needed to stand up and move about the plane. Sprinters are used to things happening in ten seconds, not eight hours. One person who passed the time easily was women's sprinter Willye White. A veteran of four Olympic Games, she calmly read a book while the rest of us couldn't find enough diversions to speed up this flight over the Atlantic.

Finally, touching down in Paris, we bused to the Hotel Claridge and were assigned roommates. Mine was high jumper Reynaldo "Rey" Brown, a three-time California prep champion who made the 1968 Olympic team while still in high school. Rey didn't talk much, which made him an ideal roommate. Our being paired up was the beginning of a lifetime friendship. Rey had a big heart, and he would go out of his way to help others. He was from a big family, like nine kids, and he was the good son, constantly helping his mom. After getting back to the States, I visited Rey, and we had a wonderful barbecue at his home. His mother was extremely nice to me.

Rey was 6-foot-4, and he could jump a foot over his head. I swear, the man could jump 7-foot-4 in his sleep. He disfavored the Fosbury Flop; Rey straddled his whole career. Because the relay was my only event, I had time to kill. Rey and I went up the Eiffel Tower, we toured the Louvre, saw Leonardo da Vinci's *Mona Lisa,* and we visited the Arc de Triomphe. A hotel doorman gave me a ride on the back of his motorcycle, and that's how I marveled at Paris's spectacular water fountain shows at night. For me, a kid from Pittsburg, California, this worldly experience was one of the best times of my life.

Our team performed well in France, even though a bad pass screwed up our relay. Then we were off to the Soviet Union, not knowing what our greeting would be like. This was the first time a foreign country had visited the USSR for track-and-field competition. And not just any foreign country—the USA, the Soviets' Cold War enemy. I'm sure our meeting had nothing to do with the smoke that entered the main cabin of our plane while the Russian stewardesses moved about as if nothing was amiss. Who was piloting this plane, Leonid Brezhnev?

We landed, mercifully, without further incident. But as soon as our passports were collected, Robert Taylor was pulled aside for questioning. Did TASS think he was a CIA spy? We weren't sure what was happening to Robert, but our coaches assured us that everything would be OK. They were right. Meanwhile, my clothes were circling the conveyer belt, followed by my opened suitcase. I was upset by this sight and even more upset after a supposedly thorough check failed to retrieve some of my belongings, for which I wasn't ever compensated. To Russia with love? Where was James Bond when I needed him?

It grew worse from there. The ride to the hotel took an hour and a half. Where are we, Siberia? We were later informed that the Russians didn't want us to see certain sights. Stalin's grave? Our hotel resembled a college dormitory, and our beds were like stone. I turned on the shower, and the water was brown. When we protested to the desk clerk, he said, disdainfully, "You must let the water run for a while before taking your shower." Bottled drinking water was carbonated, and the food was awful. One entrée was a slab of pork, full of fat and half-cooked. Athletes train on their stomachs, but try training on Russian food!

On the day of our meet, as we were leaving the hotel, some Russian girls were hanging around our bus. I assumed they wanted autographs, but they had no pens or paper. Hmmmmm. As a goodwill gesture, one of our women sprinters handed them pens with "USA" written on them. Seeing that, an armed guard walked over, took away the pens, and returned them to the sprinter. Could Russian hospitality get worse? Yes. The stadium toilets were holes in the ground. "Aim straight," we told one another.

Needless to say, the Russian trip went into the toilet, although we did win the relay. But Russia looked gray and drab, even the people, who told us that there wasn't much to be happy about. Other than the athletes, who had it made, the people enjoyed little opportunity to improve their lives, they said. But even their athletes were indoctrinated early to believe that all their glory was for the good of the Kremlin.

Walking by a construction site one morning, I noticed that most of the laborers were women. Without being chauvinistic, I must say they certainly fit the mold: big, muscular women with biceps the size of NFL linebackers'. These women worked as hard as the men, and the men weren't given preferential treatment. I wondered if I was looking at a training ground for female shot-putters. Was that Tamara Press with a pickax?

Flying out of the Soviet Union, I had no desire to return. I believed the average Russian had little hope. To attend college, get a high-paying vocation, pursue a dream—none of this was readily available in the USSR. How do you fulfill children's hopes in this empty world? Though I grew up with few amenities in Pittsburg, I had a chance to make something of myself, unlike what I saw in the Soviet Union.

Flying into Germany was a return to the real world, even if it was divided. German cities were nice and clean, and devoid of grayness. Hotels were nice, the shower water was clear, the beds were soft, and, compared to the Soviets, the people looked happy. At a train station, twenty of us bought knockwursts—the best hot dog I had ever tasted, on a fresh bun with mustard. I don't normally like mustard, but I love German mustard. One day, I bought two knockwursts. Don't knock the knock!

With some teammates, I went to a discotheque. We enjoyed ourselves, mocking guys' dance moves. Not wanting to be made fun of, I didn't dance. I can dance, but you're fair game on the dance floor. We ran into some Germans whose fathers were American soldiers who had affairs with German women during World War II. These children, now adults, seemed depressed, not knowing their real fathers, their fathers possibly not even knowing of their existences. This made me appreciate my own father even more.

Speaking of World War II, and knockwurst, one incident on that German trip has me thanking God every day of my life. One evening, before midnight, I couldn't sleep. So I went back to the train station to get another knockwurst. I went by myself, and as I passed by an alley, a man stepped out, clearly intoxicated. Startled, I began to say something to him, but he blurted, "I am a Nazi." He reached inside his coat and pulled out a 9-millimeter luger, then aimed the gun at my chest. I could see the headline in the *Pittsburg Post-Dispatch*: "Local Sprinter Killed by Nazi." God must have been with me, because the drunk muttered something, then he stuck the luger inside his coat and staggered back into the alley. I ran back to the hotel in Olympic qualifying time, without telling anybody about what happened. I never left the hotel alone the rest of the trip, even for knockwurst.

After France, Russia, and Germany, team members were given the option of traveling on to Norway and Sweden, then back to Cologne, Germany, or returning home. Ivory Crockett decided to leave, but Ben Vaughan and I stayed. I was a bit rusty, not having run a single 100-meter race in a month, plus I had done very few starts. Thus, my races in Sweden and Finland weren't very productive; I felt uncomfortable in the blocks. Things improved in Cologne after the coaches let me run the second leg of the relay, with Wayne Collett running the third. I ran the best leg of the trip that day, yelling at Wayne to take off sooner so we could have a proper baton exchange. We ran away with the relay, with Ben Vaughan our anchorman.

I really got into the groove in Sweden, becoming faster with each race. Then I had another interesting, but unthreatening, experience on the street. Ralph Boston, the 1960 Olympic long-jump champion, was walking toward me in the company of a tall woman. I could not believe my eyes; it had to be her, and she still moved with the same grace and elegance as she had when she captivated the world with her athleticism. Yes, it was the great Wilma Rudolph, who won three sprint gold medals at that same '60 Rome Olympiad. She mentioned with a sweet southern accent that she had seen me run on television. She had seen me!

I now knew why Muhammad Ali had such a crush on Wilma Rudolph. After winning a gold medal in boxing at Rome, while he was still known as Cassius Marcellus Clay, he drove his pink Cadillac from Louisville to Nashville in search of the comely Wilma. He didn't even get a draw. Wilma was long retired as a sprinter when I met her. Also accompanying our team was Wyomia Tyus, whom we all admired for her spirit and sheer determination. Wyomia had spunk. She grew up in poverty, and won 100-meter gold medals at the 1964 and 1968 Olympics—the first sprinter, male or female, to achieve that in successive Olympics.

After six weeks of traveling in Europe, I needed to get back home, even though the coaches wanted me to stay on another three weeks. But I wanted to see my family and Gwen. On my return, Dave Maggard introduced me to Ralph Anderson, who managed a campus copy center that did printing and copying for Cal. That introduction led to several years of employment, even after I had graduated.

Europe had been a culture shock. Track and field is important there. People mob you for your autograph. Back in the States, track and field receives minimal media coverage, except during Olympic years. I was invited to run the 60-yard dash in an indoor meet at the Oakland Coliseum Arena. Against a strong field that included Lennox Miller and Ronnie Ray Smith, I got off to a great start and hit the tape first. Then, looking into the stands, I was shocked to see Uncle J.D. He had heard that I was running in an indoor meet, and he wanted to see me run. We talked for a while before he said he had to get home to Aunt Cheetah. I was always proud to make my family proud, and I knew Uncle J.D. would let my father know that he had watched his son run and win.

During a U.S. track and field tour through Europe, *from left,* Eddie Hart, Dede Cooper, Cliff West, and an unidentified Italian official pose. (Photo courtesy of Eddie Hart)

Then that hamstring injury pulled the plug on my senior year of track at Cal, making it a season that went down the drain. Basically an absentee the spring of 1971, I received not one offer to run overseas that summer. Of the sprinters who were going abroad, there were guys I knew I could beat and had already beaten. With no meets to run that summer, I lost my edge without competition. No matter how dedicated I was about sprinting, I had to deal with my demons. You can't always have it the way you want in life, and, with an empty summer ahead, I had to find a new form of motivation, for the Olympics were a year away.

I wanted that gold medal more than ever. So I looked in the mirror and said, "Stop feeling sorry for yourself and get to work. Nobody can get you to Munich but you." Thus, I didn't waver, I didn't quit, and I refused to give up. After nine years of endless sacrifice, training hard, and leading a selfless life, I renewed my love affair with track and field and with sprinting. I dedicated myself to training harder, sacrificing more, and being even more selfless. The clock was ticking, one year before Munich, and I wouldn't stop until I got there. I became a driven man.

Watching those international meets on TV the summer of 1971, and seeing runners whom I felt superior to, I refused to let that disappointment distract me. When I'd run alone on the Cal track, I pictured myself beating those same runners. I'd stand atop the medal stand there in my mind and feel that gold being draped around my neck. Thus I punished myself some more that summer and then punished myself even harder over the fall and winter.

Time was running short. This was my one and only Olympic opportunity, and I needed to make it happen. I focused early on distance running, to maximize my stamina. Then I dedicated myself to improving my starts. My early plan was to run the 60 in some indoor winter meets. Cal then scheduled a few all-comers meets, which further prepared me for Munich, even though the competition level was low. I was competing against myself, basically, working against the calendar to become Olympic-ready.

Dave Maggard got me a fifth-year scholarship; that way I could work out with the Cal team, with the added responsibility of coaching Cal's sprinters. I couldn't work out as often as I would've liked; it wouldn't have been fair to those sprinters, who needed my undivided attention. But I also had to train. As I said, time was the enemy; there must be no excuses. I was an amateur athlete, with no professional ambitions. My exit strategy was to retire in 1972, marry Gwen, start a family, and become a coach and teacher.

Cal gave me my first opportunity to coach, a chance to develop coaching strategies and tactics. Unfortunately, my first sprinters weren't very talented or motivated. My best prospect was fifteen to twenty pounds heavier than he had been when Cal recruited him in high school. I worked hard with him, but to no avail; his track interest had faded. He didn't say it, but his lack of motivation gave him away. I had difficulty with his commitment, but it taught me that not everyone had the desire for success I did. That was a humbling time for me, because I thought I could motivate anyone. I had to learn otherwise, that there is only so much you can do with some sprinters if they resist your efforts to help them. I got more into recruiting, which taught me another valuable coaching lesson: the better material you have, the better your chances. Coaches are merely coaches; they don't have magic wands.

After practice ended, that's when I worked out, into the chill of evening. Once the sun dropped behind the east side of Edwards Stadium, the temperature also dropped, significantly. If the track was closed by the time I needed to work out, I climbed over the fence, specifically to work on block starts. Or I'd drive over to the California School for the Deaf, located on the Clark Kerr Campus and named after the late Cal chancellor, and I would train there.

I ran three indoor meets that winter. I traveled to Edmonton, Alberta, for the first one. It was bone-chilling cold outside; I don't know how people live in conditions so severe. I didn't warm up enough inside either, and the result was a poor finish, though I can't blame it on the thermometer. Next up was the Examiner Indoor Games in San Francisco, where the outcome was different, a confidence booster. I got a great start and won going away, though the finish line was tricky. The meet's organizers opened the doors of the Cow Palace, where the meet was held, and allowed the sprinters to run out into the parking lot to decelerate.

I was gaining confidence; all the work I put in was already paying rewards. My first outdoor meet of the season was at the California State University, Hayward, fifteen miles from Berkeley, the same campus where I would earn a master's degree. The 100-meter field wasn't strong, but I had a second strong race and won easily. In March, the Cal track team trained for a week at the UC Santa Barbara campus during spring break. I went along to get in some training. There I heard the team talk about nudists they had seen at the beach. What is it about nudity around Cal's campuses?

After we returned from Santa Barbara, the open track season moved into high gear. My first serious test would be the Mount San Antonio College Relays in Walnut, California. My main competition would be Jean-Louis Ravalomanantsoa of Madagascar, who was competing for Westmont College. He had a rocket start out of the blocks. I'd have to run him down, meaning I'd need a decent start. The race was 100 meters long, though the officials said there would be a string at 100 yards, which was confusing to me, but what could I do? Jean-Louis was out like a shot, typically, but I caught him at 70 meters. At the 100-yard mark, he leaned and stopped. I completed the 100 meters in 10.1 seconds, a personal best. Jean-Louis was declared the winner, somehow, and they gave him my time, a muddled conclusion. I didn't let it bother me; I believed I had won, regardless of what anyone else thought.

My next competition was the West Coast Relays in Fresno, one of the major track-and-field events of the year. There were so many quality sprinters in the meet that qualifying heats were needed to whittle down the field. That gave me a chance to blow it out before the final, and my victorious 100-meter heat time was 10.0 seconds, yet another personal best. Fresno felt like a home meet, because people wanted to talk to me, as if I were in Pittsburg or Berkeley. The danger, though, is that people want to associate themselves with your success. They were successful if I acknowledged them in a personal way, like saying their names or identifying them specifically; once I did that, they affirmed their connections with me, and I became their homeboy. Or they'd provide me with some piece of personal information that connected them to me, like knowing someone I knew. They just want this connection, like they own you, however they manage to get it. It's a slippery slope, so I tried not to offend fans, while keeping them at a safe distance.

Without being rude, folks, I need to concentrate on the 100! Tom Moore was the starter, one of the best there is, which meant nobody would get away with jumping the gun. The winning time of the second heat was 10.1, so it

Eddie Hart edges Gerald Tinker, *center,* and Rey Robinson, *right,* to win the 100 meters at the 1972 Olympic Trials. (Photo courtesy of Eddie Hart)

would be a fast final. I knew if I got another fast start, nobody would catch me. Then I proceeded to get the worst start of my life. I flinched in the blocks and was actually moving backward when the gun went off. The best I could do was to pass a few runners to finish third. The winning time was 10.1, slower than my personal-best heat time. I had taken a step backward, not only in the blocks but also in my training.

My next opportunity was the California Relays in Modesto. I traveled there on the Cal team bus, arriving several hours before my event. I met some folks from the Bay Area, had some friendly conversations, even remembered their names, but then cut off the small talk, remembering my misfortune in Fresno. Ravelomanantsoa was in the Modesto field along with Gerald Tinker, whom I hadn't run against before. My start was only fair, while Jean-Louis bolted from the blocks once again. Tinker was between us as we sped down the track. I caught up to Tinker and passed him, but Jean-Louis was uncatchable.

My start had failed me once again. I was so disheartened, I asked Tom if I could enter the 200, the race I had the least interest in; I needed some salvation this balmy night. He agreed to let me run. Two of my coaches, Bert Bonanno and Dave Maggard, believed my strongest race was the 200. I never argued that point with them; I just didn't like running around curves. But I needed a makeup after my 100-meter screwup. The 220 provided it as I won in a decent time of 20.4 on a chewed-up track. I had a choice of a watch, men's or women's, for my victory. I chose the women's and gave it to Gwen. She was surprised, and happy, which made me happy. All's fair in love and sprinting.

Cal hosted the next open meet, the Kennedy Games. This meant the "Burg" would be there—my homeboys from Pittsburg. I was so nervous about this meet that I didn't sleep the night before or eat anything for breakfast. I sucked on an orange on my way to the stadium. I felt ready, regardless, and decided to run three races—the 100, 220, and the 440-yard relay—while competing for the Bay Area Striders, coached by Nate Slaughter. This time, I didn't talk to anyone at the track, even the folks from Pittsburg. To my surprise, I saw Isaac Curtis warming up. I hadn't seen him in some time. Harrington Jackson, who nipped me in the 100 at the 1971 NCAA meet, also was entered. Tom Moore was once more the starter. I sensed something important was about to occur.

I blasted out of the blocks in the 100 heat, had a comfortable lead by 50 yards, and hit the tape in a winning 9.3, my fastest time ever on the Cal track. I shifted my attention to the 440-yard relay, where the favorite was the Philadelphia Pioneers Track Club, anchored by the dependable Steve Riddick. I got the baton alongside him, then put a couple of yards between us and had my second victory of the afternoon. The 100 final, in a 9.4-second photo finish, made it three wins. Then came the 220, which Larry Black was favored to win. He was given lane five, while I was assigned lane four. I liked that position, because it meant I could see him the whole race. I came around the turn in good position and in the lead, but my body was under great stress from all my sprinting. I felt the others coming on strong, and I lectured myself, "Pump your arms, stay relaxed." I held it together, somehow, and won in 20.7 seconds—my third finals win in three tries, but my fourth overall victory that day, including that blistering 9.3 in 100 degree heat. It was a most satisfying quadruple.

The Olympic Trials were now a month away, and I had never felt more ready than after those Kennedy Games. I was convinced I could defeat anybody in the world. I was like a cheetah, ready to run down and devour my competition.

THE ROAD TO MUNICH

Ten years had shrunk to a matter of months. My boyhood dream of making it to the 1972 Olympic Games in Munich was now right there in front of my nose. All the training, all the commitment, all the endless sacrifice had brought me to this point. It was now or never. No excuses. I'm either an Olympian or I'm yesterday's news. Those ten years had come down to ten seconds, or nine-plus.

There still was work ahead before the Olympic Trials. The National AAU Championships were held in Seattle, where I decided to run the 100 and 200, convinced the latter would improve my performance in the former. Some sprinters were saving it for the Trials three weeks away, thereby passing up Seattle. Isaac Curtis and Robert Taylor weren't among those absentees. I'd see them in the blocks.

The weather was cloudy and cool; conversely, the atmosphere inside the hotel where the athletes were staying was warm and cordial. The anxiety we all felt regarding the high stakes was internalized for the moment with light-hearted lobby conversation. Rey Brown was there after winning the NCAA high jump, and it was good seeing him, as always. I couldn't explain my relaxed mood exactly, as I had the only rare good night's sleep prior to my first competition. Was I too confident? I'd soon find out.

On the bus to the stadium, I knew this would be my last national AAUs. Where did all that time go? I thought of Bert Bonanno; Ray Kring; Jack Albiani; Dave Maggard; and Cal's sprint coach, Charlie Craig. These men with their wise counsel and stopwatches had prepared me for this moment. When we reached the stadium, the skies were clear and the temperature was warm, ideal sprinting weather.

Eddie Hart preferred the 100 over the 200, but he was equally effective coming around the curve in the latter. (Photo courtesy of Eddie Hart)

My first heat in the 100 went off beautifully. I was timed at 10.2, effortlessly. I couldn't believe how loose I felt. A 200 heat was next, and my optimism shifted quickly to pessimism. Given the dreaded lane one, which meant a sharper turn around the curve, I felt a twinge in my right hamstring, the same one I had injured the year before, as I hit the straightaway. I immediately stepped off the track, disheartened.

Disaster had struck. I knew the twinge was serious. I was done for this meet, but was I done, period? It had taken me two months to recover from that last hamstring injury, and I didn't have two months to recover now, or even one month. The Olympic Trials would be in three weeks. I beat myself up, wondering why did I run that stupid 200? Stupid is as stupid does. If I couldn't run in the Trials, how could I go on with the rest of my life? Even if I did run, would I step off the track again?

I sat in the stands at the AAUs and watched Isaac Curtis and Robert Taylor decide the 100 final. Robert won, though Isaac matched his 10.2 clocking. I had run 10.2 in the heat without even breaking a sweat. I knew I would have won that 100 final except for my ill-fated 200 decision. There was nothing left for me in Seattle but to get out of there as fast as my gimpy self would allow.

Track coach Nate Slaughter drove Eddie Hart to the 1972 Olympic Trials in Eugene, Oregon, where he won the 100 meters. (Photo courtesy of Eddie Hart)

I needed some magic to save me, and that magic would have to be the healing hands of Bob Orr, Cal's excellent athletic trainer. He had gotten me through my hamstring pull the year before, and I needed him to do it again, only more quickly. Time was of the essence, and I was so fearful that I hid my injury from my family. I stayed in my room, icing my leg, without anyone noticing my dilemma.

Monday morning, bright and early, I showed up at the Cal training room. Bob assessed my injury and determined that it wasn't as bad as last year's. That was the good news; the bad news was that he was leaving for Texas to visit his family for a few weeks. But he had an exit strategy: heating pads, muscle relaxers, and ice packs. He told me to start off running in the swimming pool before I returned to the track. Good advice. Pushing off my right leg would have been painful on a normal surface, but there was no pain while striding in the pool.

But I had to get back to the track soon, because I needed to run 100 meters, not swim 100 meters. Eventually, I returned to Edwards Stadium and managed to run some 330-yard distances at 60 percent effort. Then I graduated to some 220s at 75 percent effort. Next it was some 165-yard dashes at 80 percent. I was hesitant to attempt anything at 100 percent effort, and even more nervous about settling down in the starting blocks. I wasn't sure of anything as Nate

Slaughter, coach of the Bay Area Striders, drove me up to Eugene, Oregon, for the do-or-die Olympic Trials. Would the Bob Orr plan work? It had to, or else.

Qualifying for the Olympics with no starting blocks preparation was risky enough, not to mention worrying about whether my hamstring would hold up. Thus, I was the most nervous sprinter in the 100-meter field, with the most precarious situation. Nate and I didn't talk much on the drive up, which was fine by me, because my mind was playing games, and I needed to clear it of any impediments. But I couldn't thank him enough for chauffeuring me to Eugene, especially since he was "in the dog house" back home; his wife didn't even want him making this trip. So I owed him a strong 100 meters to make his return trip home pleasant. Mine, too.

The night before the heats, I went over to Hayward Field and discovered Rodney Milburn working out. "Rocket Rod" was favored to win the 110-meter hurdles, but I was surprised to see him training, figuring everyone rested the day before the Trials. We acknowledged each other before he left, then I studied the track and the goal before me: four races in two days to get to Munich, a big risk on a sensitive leg.

My roommate at the Trials was another sprinter from Pittsburg, Ralph Ligons. He was a couple of years younger than me and ran at Sacramento State. He also was competing for the Bay Area Striders. We had a short, friendly, conversation, and then I turned in for the night, not knowing what the immediate future held for either of us.

My first race the next day was at 1:00 P.M. If I qualified, I would run again at 6:00 P.M. I had a decent breakfast, which would hold me through two heats. After breakfast, I returned to my room and found Ralph still asleep. I crawled back into bed, five hours before that first heat, I couldn't get back to sleep, so nervous was I about whether my right leg would hold up. Needing to find out for myself, I got up and headed to Hayward Field. There I did a slower-than-usual warm up, fearing I might reinjure the hamstring before I got to the starting line.

When surveying the 100-meter field, I saw an impressive bunch: Dr. Delano Meriwether, Robert Taylor, Harrington Jackson, Warren Edmondson, Charlie Greene, Mel Pender, Rey Robinson, Gerald Tinker, Ivory Crockett, and Herb Washington—who later had a brief baseball career as a designated runner for the World Series champion Oakland A's. With John Carlos out of the picture, giving the National Football League a try, there was no clear-cut favorite.

I hadn't attempted a start out of the blocks since tweaking my leg three weeks earlier. So I had no idea how the hamstring would respond. Should I fire out of the blocks, or should I leave more cautiously, and would that derail my Olympic goal? I had to find out, so I did a mock start. I got down, without the blocks, and sort of stood up and started running. That wouldn't do, so I got back down and came out with a 25 percent effort. Then I did it a third time, and released at a 50 percent effort. Each time, the hamstring held up.

But would it hold up in the blocks, releasing with a 100 percent takeoff? I would find out soon enough. Robinson, Pender, and Jon Young were the only sprinters I recognized in my heat. I needed a fifth-place finish to advance to the next round. I felt a sense of doom after the gun went off, because I was figuratively out of the race after ten meters, and everyone had a couple of meters on me. I couldn't quit, not after ten years of living for this very moment. I threw off all caution and took off after the field. I ran each sprinter down but one, and I crossed the finish line clocking a wind-aided, yet remarkable, 10.1. At 10.0, Robinson had the best time, but my confidence was renewed. The hamstring had held together. The blocks no longer were the enemy. I felt restored. Thank you, Bob Orr.

I went back to my room to rest, five hours before my second race. Dave Maggard came by to check on me. He didn't stay long, but it was another "I'm with you" visit on his part, typical Dave. Before leaving, he advised me to keep my feet up so that the blood didn't pool in my legs. He took a chair and put it on the bed, and told me to rest my legs on that chair. That way, more blood passed through my body, creating better circulation. I still use Dave's time-tested method today, but in 1972, his advice might have saved the day.

The competition in my quarterfinal heat included Edmondson, Jackson, Riddick, Vaughan, and my roomie, Ralph Ligons. I did a few wind sprints to stretch my legs, and then it was time to get into the blocks. When the gun went off, it was another potential disaster. I was once again at the back of the pack. Edmondson and Ligons were out front after impressive starts, but then the field came back to me. Ligons and Vaughan faded, and I caught up to and passed Jackson and Riddick. Now it was Edmondson and me, and he hit the tape first, though we both were timed in a wind-aided 10.1. But I had achieved an important victory: my leg no longer was a bothersome worry. Thank you, Dave Maggard.

When I got back to the room, Ralph was naturally dejected because he had been eliminated. His family lived on the same street as mine, and I had known Ralph since grammar school. His sister and I were in the same class. Bert Bonanno was Ralph's coach. Ralph was small for a sprinter, but I thought he could improve his time with better conditioning and a more refined technique. He had done better than I had at Pittsburg High, but he leveled off at Sacramento State. Sprinting giveth, and sprinting taketh away. We talked into the night, and then I needed to get some sleep. Ralph's life changed from sprinting into a legal marathon—twenty-five years to life in San Quentin for a third-strike offense. From the starting blocks to a prison block, it was a sad story.

So now it was two down, two to go, but the semifinal field looked formidable. Robinson and Edmondson already had beaten me. Riddick, Pender, Jackson, Norbert Payton and Willie Deckard filled the other lanes. But I only was worried about me. Coach Bonanno taught me that it was a mistake to focus on the opposition, because the only thing I could control was my performance. Wise advice. My main focus, though, still was those starting blocks. This time, to reach the 100 final, I would need a much better start. Robinson and Edmondson had serious speed, and Robinson was brimming with confidence, believing nobody could beat him. Looking into his eyes, I could see why: he was fearless.

As I lowered into the blocks, I heard the crowd's voices rising in pitch. That's because the 100 is one of the more anticipated events, if not the most anticipated, in track and field. That makes sense: the World's Fastest Human might be on the track. At the gun, Robinson, Payton, and Pender were out fast, with Edmondson right behind them, while I brought up the rear once more. I quickly narrowed the gap, overtaking some runners, but the finish line was nearing. Only four men would advance to the final. I found myself in a swarm of bodies lunging for the tape in a blanket finish, where two inches could mean the difference between qualification and elimination.

Maybe even closer than that, as the first five finishers all clocked 9.9, and all five tied the world record, though wind-aided. It was one of the most remarkable 100 meters in history, but how did it shake out? Robinson was the winner, followed by Payton, Edmondson, and yours truly, barely making the final. Poor, unfortunate Willie Deckard ran a 9.9 and was eliminated. Riddick, Pender, and Jackson, sixth through eighth, all ran 10.1. Even that eighth-place time would match the winning time at the Munich Olympics. Unbelievable.

I was just happy to qualify after a third shaky start. Now I had to put the hamstring issue out of my mind entirely if I was going to make the Olympic team. In sports, it comes down to winners and losers, and I didn't want to be a loser, making excuses while joining the also-rans with their woulda, coulda, shoulda excuses. I shoulda done this, I coulda done that—get the picture? Winners win, losers justify; that's how it is, but I couldn't return to Pittsburg empty-handed. The end of my career was at stake, so why hold back? I would be coming out of the blocks at 100 percent with fire in my belly. If I reinjured my leg, so be it; I had the rest of my life to heal. My confidence had been rejuvenated. I felt like that ravenous cheetah, stalking my prey.

After a thousand block starts over the last ten years, including practice, what's one more block start anyway? An emotional burden had been lifted as I settled down into the blocks for the 100 final. I felt a calmness come over me. I knew the routine: lift my hips, keep my head down, inhale, relax, and wait for the gun. Now, here it was. Bang! I had a great start. Bang! Bang! Someone false-started. My world didn't shatter; it wasn't me who jumped. My confidence didn't wane; let someone else worry. I'd gotten off to a great start, for once, so let's do it again. Just tell me when, Mr. Starter.

Bang! Once again, I got the start I wanted. Robinson and Payton had a jump on the field, but I wasn't far behind them. Edmondson, uncharacteristically, was late out of the blocks, and not a factor this day. Payton fell back into the pack, and I took after Robinson, catching him at the 80-meter mark, and then nudging him for the victory, with Robert Taylor edging Gerald Tinker for third place. My wind-legal time of 9.9 seconds equaled the world record, with Robinson matching my time. He no longer was undefeated, and I no longer was an underdog. After three nonwinning qualifying heats, I came through when it mattered the most. I was everything John Carlos, Jimmy Hines, and Lee Evans said I was when they called me the ultimate competitor. And I had every reason to believe them, hamstring and all.

I now was an Olympian. That's what mattered the most, just like I had envisioned at age thirteen. Excitedly, I walked back up the track to pick up my sweats, drinking in the applause and waving at the stands. Dave Maggard suddenly appeared; the biggest Cal Golden Bear wrapped me up in a bear hug. He was as happy for me as I was for him. He believed in me more strongly than anyone. From Mrs. Mercurio to Dave Maggard, and all the people in between, I had a tremendous support system from Pittsburg to Berkeley. I hoped Gwen and my family knew of my victory. Bob Orr, too.

Before returning to my room, I watched the 800-meter final; my Cal team-mate Rick Brown was in the field. I'm glad I hung around, because it was a great race. Dave Wottle finished six meters ahead of the field, in a world-record time of 1:44.3. Jim Ryun finished a disappointing fourth, while Brown finished sixth, but with a personal best time of 1:45.4. Wottle wore a Bowling Green State University baseball hat when he competed. He said it was his lucky hat and that he would wear it in the Olympics.

How does one celebrate a victory of this magnitude? Alone. I went back to the room, took a refreshing shower, and relived the race, smiling at my im-probable win. Not one block start in three weeks, and after nursing an injured leg in a swimming pool, I had just won the Olympic Trials 100-meter final. Somebody up there really does like me. I'm heading to Munich, so how do I come down from the biggest moment of my life? The cheetah was still hungry, so I went across the street to a Denny's to dine on fish. My head was spinning in the clouds, so I can't remember what fish I ate, just that I ate by myself. No party balloons, no confetti, no Cal Straw Hat Band salute, no family hugs, no kiss from Gwen. I wasn't avoiding anybody. I just wanted to savor the moment. So I sat there in my solitude, lingering in my own glory.

Then exhaustion took over. After four races in two days, fatigue hit me like a sledgehammer. Yet as tired as I was, it took a couple of hours to fall asleep. Then morning arrived quickly, with a knock on the door. A photographer from *Sports Illustrated* wanted a picture of me in my track uniform. *Sports Illustrated* wanted me! I told the cameraman I would meet him at the track. After repeated shots of me sprinting, I informed him I was tired, and so the photo shoot was over. Hungry again, probably from all the excitement, I ate, this time at the cafeteria, by myself again, still trying to take it all in. I wondered what people in Pittsburg were thinking. I needed to get home.

So I headed for the airport, where it just happened that Rey Robinson and his coach were waiting for their plane while I was waiting for mine. The coach introduced himself, and then he introduced me to Rey, who congratulated me. I thanked him, and we had a nice conversation before he flew off to Florida. I knew Rey was a formidable opponent, even as a teammate. He had a cockiness and a swagger, because he truly believed in himself. He awaited revenge in Munich.

On my flight home from the Trials in Eugene, a stewardess recognized me. She had seen me win the 100 and wanted my autograph, as did other members of the flight crew. It was becoming harder to travel incognito.

Hail the returning champion? When I walked in the door back home, nobody greeted me. I dropped my bag in the bedroom and went into the living room, where my mom was sitting quietly on the couch. In my house, the main concerns were about people, not trophies. Winning an Olympic berth was fine, but Mom was more focused on how I was feeling rather than any race I might have won. "Oh, you're home," she said, smiling. She loved me, that was the important thing, and she was always happy to see me. She said she had heard about my win on the radio, while in bed with my dad. She said he was proud of me. Then she and I shared a victory hug.

With six children, my mom was a hard-working individual, always washing, cleaning, shopping, and cooking. Nobody ever awarded her a gold medal. But life was changing in the Hart household. My siblings Catherine and John had moved into separate apartments. Alfred now was at Pittsburg High, while Evelyn and David were attending Village Elementary School. And my father

Dave Maggard, who recruited Eddie Hart to Cal and who comforted him after his disqualification in Munich, poses with Paris, Eddie Jr., Eddie Sr., and Gwen Hart. (Photo courtesy of Eddie Hart Sr.)

had received an advanced position at Shell Oil, now that he was out from underneath a supervisor who didn't like him and had been holding him back, even though my father's work was widely respected. I couldn't wait for him to come home, to see the happiness in his eyes. I was eager to see Gwen that evening, because I soon would be off again on another long trip, hopefully to Olympic glory, yet another separation that neither of us liked.

Hanging around the house, though, I felt stir-crazy. After talking with Dave Maggard, I flew back to Eugene to see the 200-meter final at the Trials. I thought Warren Edmondson had a good chance of winning, because he had run some impressive 200s. I was surprised when he didn't make the final, which Charles Smith won in 20.4, followed by Larry Burton in 20.5 and Larry Black in 20.6. I then watched the finals in the 400-meter run and 110-meter high hurdles, which Tom Hill won in 13.5; Hill soon would be my roommate in Munich.

I was heartbroken that Rey Brown didn't qualify in the high jump. The next morning, I went back to Denny's, and who walked in but Steve Prefontaine, the local kid who had won the 5000-meter run at the Trials. We were on the

1970 national team together, and he came over and said hello. He was a lively guy, obviously full of energy, and with the same hearty appetite that all distance runners possess. I had seen Cliff West wolf down sixteen or seventeen pancakes at one sitting, while I topped out at nine or ten. So I wasn't amazed at the amount of food that Prefontaine consumed that morning. He ate like a man three times his size.

I could have flown home again, but some people generously offered me a ride in their compact car. I accepted, but what was I thinking? I was cramped the whole way and couldn't stretch my legs. The people were unbelievably nice and kept offering to buy me food at every stop, when all I wanted to do was sleep. We drove straight through the night. They were going to San Francisco but graciously dropped me off at my parents' home in Pittsburg.

I needed to increase my training before leaving for Bowdoin, Maine, where the Olympic track team would gather before flying to Munich. So I called Coach Bonanno. Though he hadn't coached me in ten years, he recommended that I run a series of 330-yard dashes to keep my stamina strong for the 100. We experienced some extreme heat, but I kept at those 330s and felt myself getting stronger. I used the starting blocks without any complications. My hamstring injury was a thing of the past. My parents and my siblings were gone on a family visit to Alabama, so the house was empty.

I spent more time with Gwen, who really balanced me. She was as easy to be with as ever, as she wasn't the least bit affected. She didn't talk a lot, but, then, neither did I. Looking back on our dating years, I see that Gwen might have thought I took her for granted. It wasn't that at all; my mind was just preoccupied with track and field and that Olympic gold medal. I thought some things between us were simply understood, which was naïve. I was one of those men who believed that actions speak louder than words. Our relationship just sort of grew without our really having a conversation about it. I liked being with her as much as she liked being with me. She was just a good person. I loved that about her and knew that she would make a great wife and mother. Did I get down on one knee and propose? No, it wasn't like that. We just assumed that we would be together forever. She was my first gold medal, but, I hoped, not my last. So one last kiss, and I was off to Maine, and then onto Europe, and the subsequent adventure awaiting me.

The people in Bowdoin were the friendliest I had ever met. There seemed to be a social event every day when we were there. Maine lobsters are the best in the world. Now, I do know something about lobster because it's my favorite food. We were in Maine two weeks, and I ate nine lobsters and hundreds of clams. I drew closer to my teammates now that we were less adversarial. We still competed against one another in our training in Bowdoin, but we were all working toward the same goal, establishing American supremacy in track and field.

Tom Hill went undefeated in the 110-meter high hurdles throughout the Olympic Trials, including his victory in the finals. We remained roommates through Munich. And in Bowdoin the groundwork was laid for the 400-meter relay team. Rey Robinson would run the lead, followed by Robert Taylor, Gerald Tinker, and me as anchor, because Robinson had the best start, Taylor was best on the straights, Tinker was an excellent turn runner, and I was the fastest on the anchor leg. Stan Wright was named the sprints coach, and he emphasized the baton pass as crucial to the team's success. So we used the same relay pass that he had at the Mexico City Games four years earlier. His attitude was "why tamper with success?"

I made the mistake of training with Larry Black, our 200-meter man. He wanted me to run some 300s, and he asked Coach Wright to time us. Only, Black was out for blood, it seemed, because he clearly was in a race mode. He ran as fast as he could, and I was forced to do the same, and we hit the finish in thirty seconds, which would have been a world record in a sanctioned event. When Black asked me to run it again, I thought he was out of his mind. I was done for the day.

Wayne Collett suggested we go to a movie that evening. We saw *A Clockwork Orange,* this crazy movie about kids going around and terrorizing people, not my kind of show at all. The background music was classical, and Collett hummed the score quietly, moving his arms as if he were directing a symphony orchestra. He, obviously, was into classical music and probably saw himself as the Beethoven of quarter-milers.

Some of the runners liked working out in groups, while I preferred training alone. All I needed was a stopwatch, and I was happy. My conditioning was fine, and I felt myself peaking at the right time. I was a little apprehensive because we were heavily invested in training, and competitive sprinting was still two weeks away in Europe. But Stan Wright had an eagle eye. He was right there when we worked on the relay. He had this calm way of coaching, never yelling or losing his composure. His criticisms were constructive, he was quick with adjustments, and he was a perfectionist, making sure we flawlessly executed our baton exchanges. I liked him a lot and believed the two of us were developing a lasting relationship.

Our first stop overseas was Oslo, Norway. Not every runner got to run his specialty there. Quarter-milers ran the 200, and 200 men ran the 100. I decided to run the 200, and I won easily, clocking a solid time of 20.4, without pulling any leg muscles. Rey Robinson was having difficulty. His times in the 100 had fallen off, and he ran a poor relay leg. Stan Wright made a quick decision to replace Robinson with Larry Black as the leadoff man on the 400-meter relay. Wright's thinking was that we'd lose a little at the start, but Black was a better turn runner than Robinson, who didn't seem to resist the change. The rest of the relay team thought Stan Wright made the change correctly and with integrity. Maybe he decided that Robinson had taken his pre-Olympic training too casually or that an injury was bothering him. I wasn't sure of the reason, but life moved on.

Though we all became friends, the sprinters regarded the running track as a war zone. Sprinters are like gun fighters. After Robinson and I had dominated in the Trials, we now had targets on our backs, with Taylor and Tinker taking aim. I'm sure their Oslo times—Tinker ran a 9.9, Taylor a 10.0—had given Robinson pause, but he just didn't look right in training. Normally he was a nightmare for other sprinters: he now seemed his own worst nightmare.

Certainly, Rey could straighten out by the Olympics, but he'd better hurry. Time was short, and who could predict what uncertainty awaited us in Munich?

BLAMED, BUT BLAMELESS

I'm going to say it right now, flat out: I don't blame Stan Wright for the 100-meter foul-up at the Munich Olympics. Everyone has his or her opinion about what went wrong, and I get that. But nobody else was there that day at the starting line except Stan Wright, Eddie Hart, Rey Robinson, Robert Taylor, and the German race official. Just the five of us knew what occurred. I wish I had that official's name, but I don't, and he might be hiding in a witness protection program for all I know, to escape the controversy that resulted from the disqualifications of Rey Robinson and me.

Nevertheless, Stan Wright did no wrong, regardless of what Howard Cosell and thousands of others thought, including some Olympians who offered their opinions when interviewed for this book. But nobody was damaged more by that terrible misunderstanding than the three of us: Rey, me, and Stan. Especially Stan.

"Stan was haunted by that for the rest of his life," said George Wright, who coauthored Stan Wright's autobiography but isn't related to Stan. "There is no debate in my mind about that. After his wife, Hazel, died [in 1997], the two setbacks in his life from which he couldn't recover were the loss of Hazel and not allowing Eddie Hart and Rey Robinson to get to the starting line. He never found absolute peace with that, I can assure you. He felt sad about those losses, and he felt culpable about what happened in Munich."

That troubles me deeply, because Stan Wright didn't deserve to be haunted, or hounded, for others' mistakes. Just as I didn't deserve the blame of those who thought I needed to be more responsible for knowing my race time. Must a NASCAR driver steer the racecar and pump its tires, too? Listen, race times weren't my responsibility. They belong to coaches, their organizations, and Olympic officials.

Sure, I could have memorized the schedule. I also could have known what time our Olympic team flew to Europe, where our next stop was, where were we going to stay, and what time we ate, all that minutia. Only that's not the athlete's responsibility. But I'm not piling the blame on Stan Wright. Whatever happened, unfortunately, I had to deal with it. I'm still dealing with it in a new century.

George Wright wrote Stan Wright's biography, showing a very proud and successful, but saddened, track coach. (Photo courtesy of George Wright)

However, to set the record straight, Stan Wright walked up to that German official after my first qualifying race to confirm the time schedule Stan had in his hands for my next race. The official confirmed the wrong time schedule—not once but twice! What more could Stan have done? The two men were facing each other. I stood there right next to Stan. You could have passed a body between the two of us. There was no way Stan could have thought he had the wrong schedule, unless he considered the judge a liar. How much more proof did Stan need? How much more proof do his critics need?

Numerous people are put into positions of authority to take care of these Olympic scheduling matters, and it's conceivable that some of them failed when it came to the 100-meter dash in Munich. But it wasn't Stan Wright who failed. The German race official certainly is culpable. And what about the USA head track-and-field coach, Bill Bowerman? Stan was merely his sprint coach. And what about the U.S. Olympic Committee officials? They had powers of oversight; why didn't they use them? Why did this entire controversy fall squarely on Stan Wright's shoulders?

So what about those USOC officials? Ollan Cassell knows the whole story, the true story, of what really happened to Rey Robinson and me, and it involves a USOC official, George Wilson. Ollan was executive director of the Amateur Athletic Union (AAU) from 1970 to 1980. He attended the Munich Games, and he's aware of Wilson's involvement in our disqualifications, and it was all the result of a controversy—I learned, finally, forty-four years later—at the pole vault pit.

Wilson was in charge of Army athletics in 1972, serving in the Pentagon. He was named manager of the USA track-and-field team in Munich and was directly responsible to the USOC regarding any issues connected to our team. Unfortunately, he was a one-man operation, and because of that, Stan was left holding the bag.

"George was following pole-vaulter Bob Seagren's protest over not being allowed to use the poles that he brought over from America," Cassell explained in a March 2016 interview for this book from his home in Indianapolis. "A team manager has all of these duties, thus George didn't know that the revised schedule for the men's 100-meter heats was sitting in his mailbox." Why wasn't it delivered, instead, to the sprint coach? That's mind-boggling.

So Stan didn't receive that revised schedule, yet he accepted the blame for Rey and me not making it to the track on time. Bowerman, our head coach, could have accepted responsibility, because it was on his watch, but he held himself blameless. And Howard Cosell, who then hung Stan from the gallows, never used his journalistic skills to discover what really happened.

"ABC offered Stan $50,000 not to sue them for slander," said Cassell, regarding Cosell's interview with Stan and subsequent commentary, both carried by ABC. "But Stan wasn't interested in doing that. And Bowerman didn't take care of Stan—Bowerman took care of his athletes."

Cassell's and Wright's relationship preceded Munich. Cassell attended the University of Houston when Wright coached at Texas Southern. The two schools were a few blocks apart, so Cassell, a quarter-miler, sometimes trained with Wright. Cassell twice won the 440-yard dash at the AAU Championships, and he was a member of the USA 1600-meter relay team that won the gold medal at the 1964 Olympics in Tokyo, in a world record time of 3:00.7.

Cassell recalled the staged election where Bowerman beat out Wright by one vote to become the head coach in Munich. "Stan and I were really good friends," said Cassell. "We watched the Olympic massacre together in Stan's room at the Village. I'll say this about Stan: he had more integrity and honesty—he was a straight shooter—than any man I've ever known."

That's how I knew Stan: very detailed, very diligent. He struck others, including Ollan Cassell, the same way. Stan wrote things down. He had things in order. He was very organized. Stan and the sprinters became a family in Munich. The four of us were happy to win the gold medal, but we were just as happy to win it for Stan, because that gold medal was like salve to the wound. It would have been devastating had we not won—both to Stan and us. But I truly believe Stan Wright didn't recover from that 100-meter mistake until the day he died, in 1998.

Look, so much went wrong in those Olympics besides the massacre: the gold medal basketball game controversy, Rick DeMont, Bob Seagren, the Eastern Bloc and steroids, and our disqualifications. But one of the bright spots was that relay team. We won, and we broke the world record, lessening all that negativity in Munich.

What saddens me to this day was how painful those disqualifications were to Stan Wright. They just ate at him. I agree with George Wright in that regard. But the man Stan was, he placed it all on himself. I could understand Rey's hostility back then; we were going through the same disappointment. I'm not judging Rey; he dealt with a personal crisis in the way that made the most sense to him. Rey and I still are friends today; Munich didn't change that. It has been my hope that Rey would come around in time, without feeling the same anger toward Stan that he did in 1972. I'm sure that wasn't the first, or last, setback in Rey's life.

I've had setbacks, too, since Munich. And I've certainly made mistakes that have disappointed people. I would hope that they would be forgiving, for these mistakes weren't intentional, just as what happened to Rey and me wasn't intentional. But can you believe it, people coming up to me, saying what happened in Munich was intentional on Stan Wright's part? How can people think that he would intentionally hurt us? That wasn't true then, and it isn't true now. Other people wondered if we were asleep and missed our race. No way. Some people even thought Rey and I were boycotting the race. No way. Just how specific can I be about all those suppositions, except to say that it wasn't our fault, and it wasn't Stan Wright's fault, and there was no evil intent anywhere you look leading up to our disqualifications.

Here's is Stan Wright's exact account of that 100-meter quarterfinal situation, taken from his autobiography: *Stan Wright—Track Coach: Forty Years in the "Good Old Boy" Network:*

The first round of the men's 100 meters was scheduled for Thursday morning, August 31. I knew this because I had referred to a schedule that had been provided to the coaching staff in Oslo as part of an "Information and Instruction" packet. The packet had been distributed by George Wilson. Daily heat sheets were supposed to be available each morning at the information center in the Olympic Village. George was supposed to obtain that information and distribute it to us. He did provide the staff with copies of the heat sheets for the session on the morning of August 31.

There was no schedule of the afternoon's session printed on that sheet. According to the schedule I had, the second round of the 100 meters was scheduled that afternoon immediately after the first round of the men's 10,000 meters. The 100-meter semifinals and finals were to be run the following day. At the start of the morning competition, I was under the impression that heat sheets for the afternoon session would be available around noon. At around noon, I met Eddie, Rey and Robert [Taylor] after the first heat and we began to leave the stadium. According to my schedule, it showed: 3 p.m.—Men's 800 meters, first round; Men's final 20,000-meter race walk; Men's 10,000-meter heat; Men's 100-meters, second round; Women's long jump final; Women's 800-meter heat. To make sure that I had the correct time for the second round of the 100 meters, as we left the stadium I showed the schedule I had to a German official at the stadium. Speaking in perfect English, he told me that the schedule I had was the one that was in effect for today's competition. I felt sure that things were going well.

But what that German official didn't know, just as Stan didn't, was that the revised schedule was in George Wilson's mailbox. Stan Wright even asked that same official again to confirm the schedule, and he received the same affirmative answer. Still, everyone was in the dark. Stan's account of how I happened to notice back in my room that his schedule didn't match the one I had in my information packet, that was correct. That's when Stan thought we should gather up and get to the stadium in a hurry. In his autobiography, he picks up what happened next.

The worst feeling I ever had in my life came over me. Things began to feel like a blur as I tried to figure out what was happening and how to react. Several ABC personnel pushed us into a van driven by Bill Norris, a part-time employee hired by ABC. The young man raced to the athletes' entrance of the stadium. I was trying to keep my wits about me, but I kept moaning, "Oh, no! Oh, no!" I was very distraught.

When we arrived at the stadium, Rey, Robert, Eddie and I ran into the tunnel leading to the track. A guard tried to stop us at the gate, but we yelled who we were while rushing past him. We were in the tunnel just as heat two was being called into a set position for the start. Eddie was scheduled to be in that heat; Rey's heat had already been run. Halfway up the tunnel, we heard the starter's gun. The pain I felt for Eddie and Rey at that moment was horrible. As we entered the track, I rushed up to the starter, begging that he let Rey and Eddie run in another heat. I must have run fifty meters up the track while pleading with various officials. I told them that we had gotten caught up in traffic, but my pleas were to no avail. Luckily, Robert was in the next heat, scheduled to run in five minutes. I pleaded with officials to allow Eddie and Rey to run in a remaining heat. Of course, they could not allow that.

In the midst of the most tragic situation I had ever experienced, I was trying to console Eddie and Rey, while trying to give Robert some encouragement for his race in a few moments. I was also crying hysterically. I told Robert, "Just qualify." That was about all I could tell him. Not having warmed up, he peeled off his sweat suit and quickly changed into his spikes. He moved behind his starting blocks and began to run in place, doing several deep knee bends.

Eddie and Rey watched Robert's race from the tunnel near the start. When the race was over, I told them how sorry I was for letting them down, knowing that I could not say anything that could change what had happened. They were both devastated; Rey seemed especially angry. As soon as Robert's race was finished, I went to the Munich officials to try to lobby to get Eddie and Rey into the semifinals. I also issued an appeal to the International Amateur Athletic Federation's jury of appeal. But those efforts were to no avail.

I accompanied Eddie and Rey on the bus back to the dorm. I was feeling very protective of these two young men and, in fact, prevented several reporters from asking them questions. I sensed that they were not up to talking. I was also feeling lower than I had ever felt in my entire life. Even after my mother had died, I did not feel that bad. I had no control over her dying, but I felt responsible for Eddie and Rey missing their races. A large contingent of the United States media was milling around in the lobby of the dormitory. As I entered the lobby, most of them came up to me to ask questions. All I could say was "It was my fault."

Only it wasn't Stan Wright's fault. It was somebody's fault, perhaps an over-worked George Wilson, but not Stan's. He was my friend, and that disqualification didn't change our friendship. "For years afterward," Dave Maggard told me, "Stan Wright would come up to me, throw his arms around me, and say, 'Thank you and Eddie for not blasting me.'" If there was one thing in my life that I could pat myself on the back for, it was how I responded to that one incident. I never wanted Stan to believe that I had any animosity or hatred toward him. I didn't even look at it in those terms; I just didn't. Life does happen, and that [disqualification] was a part of my life that I had to deal with in a specific way. I didn't react to the situation; I responded, and in the right way. I am my father's son, and he taught me how to respond responsibly.

Other 1972 Olympians shifted the blame from Stan onto Rey and me. Well, they know as well as I do, or should know, that there are tons of decisions that have to be taken care of and worked out during an Olympic Games. But the athletes' responsibility is to compete. If we can't trust our team leaders to have these particular things nailed down, we're not going to be an Olympic team. And that's what happened in Munich. Stan Wright wasn't the head of the U.S. Olympic Committee, or the head track-and-field coach (that was Bill Bowerman). Wasn't there someone other than George Wilson in the American contingent to oversee the time scheduling of events, and then coordinate it with the coaches? Or were there too many American officials having a good time, seeing the sights with their families and enjoying a European vacation on Uncle Sam's pocketbook?

So why was it Stan Wright's neck lying on that proverbial chopping block? Why was it just Stan Wright who endured that grueling interview with Howard Cosell? Here is that interview:

HOWARD COSELL: This is Stan Wright, the coach of the United States sprinters and sprint relay team, the key figure in the terrible mishap that occurred today when two very great sprinters, Eddie Hart and Reynaud Robinson, failed to appear on time for their respective heats in the 100-meter dash. Now earlier, Stan, Rey Robinson said you were the culprit, you were the man to blame for their failure to show. Is this or is this not true?

STAN WRIGHT: Well, that's a pretty harsh word, Howard, "culprit." I would simply answer that I am responsible for the sprinters, they have faith in me, and they had faith in me. There was a misunderstanding of time schedules. I assumed one time schedule, and there was another time schedule I had not seen—did not see, and we left the Village together to come over, and the only thing I can do is be a man and take full responsibility as sprint coach for them not being there. It's my responsibility. I'm deeply grieved about it, and will ever, I guess, be sorry on their behalf.

COSELL: Are the athletes in any sense to blame? After all, they're not children.

WRIGHT: No, no, no, no, no, the athletes are not to blame. The athletes are not children. They're men, they're young men, but they put their faith in their coaches. And when I—when we agreed that we were leaving the

Village at a certain time to be over, to run on a certain time, then they go along with me 100 percent. I was going on a basis that the only thing they had on the time schedule was that the 800-meter run went off at 3 o'clock, then the 1,500, and I was going on a basis after that that everything came down the line. And, on a sheet as it came down the line, the 100-meter second round was after the 10,000-meter trials. And, not knowing this, they changed it and put the 100 meters before.

COSELL: But as a matter of accepted routine, with all that's at stake, all the years, really, of work and preparation and so on, don't you check on a given day with the appropriate Olympic authorities?

WRIGHT: Yes, I did.

COSELL: As to the schedule, what happened?

WRIGHT: I checked as to our heats, and I checked the stadium before I left, checked the assembly area, asked them about the schedule I had. They said that's the way it was going to run, to be run, and I left on the assumption that that was correct.

COSELL: I feel deeply sorry for you, but we all have to answer to the American public. Why in the world was America the only country to have the wrong information?

WRIGHT: Well, I can't answer that because those are a little higher up on the echelon, as far as I'm concerned.

COSELL: What do you mean by that?

WRIGHT: Well, I think you know what I mean.

COSELL: No, I don't. I'd like you to tell me.

WRIGHT: Well, I'm not in a position to tell you because I really don't know myself, but I don't feel I have to answer to America. I feel I have to answer to these two youngsters, and this is why I feel so deeply about it. I'm concerned about them. They were the ones that did not make the heat. They were the ones that are suffering the grief of, as you say, long preparation. Great sprinters, outstanding sprinters, representing their country, and they didn't get a chance because there was a misunderstanding on my part on the schedule.

COSELL: I think everybody feels the same way about that, but this other matter you've just implied . . . : some other people. Are you trying to tell me that there are people about you who are responsible for this?

WRIGHT: No, I didn't say other people. I said there might be something in a higher echelon that I'm not—don't quite understand, and why the information didn't get to me, that's what I'm telling you. I'm not blaming anybody else.

COSELL: Do you feel that the breakdown in communications might be attributable to higher authority, not to you?

WRIGHT: No, I'm not saying that either. I'll say this: that there was, perhaps, a breakdown in communications, and I didn't get the information. And I'm not passing the buck, because as far as I'm concerned, the buck stops with me. I'm the sprint coach, and I have to take the responsibility.

COSELL: Final question: do you believe that your young men can still have confidence in you as the coach in view of what happened?

WRIGHT: Well, I think so. They have expressed confidence in me later on after the emotions settled down. I understand that Rey said it was my fault, and I don't blame him for saying that. I think they realize that I'm a human being just like all of us are, and we make mistakes, and it's just unfortunate that this incredible thing happened. I still can't believe it happened.

Stan's interview with Cosell lasted about ten minutes. Rey and I watched it before Cosell interviewed the two of us. Cosell has a law degree, and perhaps he thought that he had Stan on a witness stand, because that interview did feel like it was conducted in a court of law. Later on, after he had interviewed the three of us, Cosell went back on television to offer his analysis of Stan and the topic of our disqualifications:

So that's the headline story in the Twentieth Olympiad, Munich, West, Germany, today from the three principals: Rey Robinson, Eddie Hart, and, finally, Coach Stan Wright. Not a happy story. Frankly, it's a rotten mess and a terrible human tragedy. When two decent young men and two very great athletes spend so many years of their lives for the one fulfillment, the one challenge, and don't even have the opportunity to accept that challenge, it has to be the most frustrating and heartbreaking thing possible to those two young people.

Now what about the coach, who has just openly admitted his mistake, who has made a terrible mistake quite clearly, but who has been a decent man all his life and a very fine track coach? At a press conference just a few moments ago, he alluded to an Olympic authority that he spoke to this morning when he said that he was presented with an old schedule—though he didn't say it was a year-and-a-half-old schedule—in my interview with him as he did at the press conference. It was obviously an old schedule, and the Olympic authority he presented it to was later identified by Stan, in a press conference, as a member of the German

Organizing Olympic Committee. He also said at the stadium later to-day that he had spoken to some Olympic authorities in blue and white uniforms who confirmed that old schedule. But without attacking or unnecessarily pillorying Stan Wright, the plain fact is, for you young people in America, that only the United States of America had the wrong information. It is clear that the *Paris Tribune,* as published today in Munich, had the right time information for those 100-meter heats. It is clear that every responsible reporter in Munich, Germany, had the right time. The American Broadcasting Company had the right information. So, no matter how they try to pass the buck, so no matter how they try to whitewash, our people are to blame. And the ones who suffer are the ones who are supposed to flourish: The two decent young men who've had such dedication and such purpose, and now face such terrible de-spair and disappointment. That's what happened here in Munich, West Germany, today, even as others exulted in Mark Spitz's victory.

Howard Cosell didn't pillory Stan Wright until that wrap-up commentary. But Roone Arledge, head of ABC sports, called Cosell's interview an "inquisi-tion." Bowerman chose not to defend Stan, who found himself an abandoned soldier in the U.S. foxhole. The main point with me is that I trusted Stan Wright. What information could anyone who truly knew the man bring forth that would say that he wasn't trustworthy? He is one of the most organized, structured people that you could ever meet. He was on top of things, 100 percent. You never had to double-check the man.

Cosell interviewed Rey and me right after he interviewed Stan Wright. He was just so easy on us, not the typical Howard Cosell. He had predetermined which individual he was going after, and that was Stan Wright. I wasn't happy that any of this happened, but I wasn't going to blame Stan. Rey Robinson took a totally different tact. I had a good relationship with him. I never had any reason to doubt or distrust this man. Remember, too, that Stan was Jimmy Hines's coach at Texas Southern, and Jimmy Hines is big in my world. Jimmy broke the world record in the 100 meters at the Mexico Olympics in 1968. That was real for me. Stan Wright was solid. Solid!

George Wright began interviewing Stan for their book at Stan's Sacramento home in 1997. The book was completed after Stan moved to Houston, where he died a year later, at seventy-seven. George is a professor emeritus of political science at California State University, Chico, and a passionate track-and-field fan, stemming from his winning the mile run in the Los Angeles City School District's Southern League High School Championships in 1961.

"If I had to describe Stan to someone who hadn't met him, it would be incredibly honest and forthright, really committed to his work passionately," George told me. "He cared about the young people he worked with immensely. He was a by-the-book person; his generation kind of defined that. He also was meticulous with his documentation of everything that he did—copious documentation.

"And related to his MO in Munich, he played by the structure. He had Bill Bowerman as the head coach, George Wilson as the team manager, and Bob Giegenback, chairman of the USOC Track and Field Committee above him. But, as it turned out, Stan Wright really was like a lone wolf."

Speaking of lone wolves: after our disqualifications, Rey Robinson and I didn't hear from Bowerman, Wilson, Giegenback, or any other USOC official about our misfortune. Nobody in the USOC put an arm around our shoulders and expressed their condolences. These people we're supposed to look up to and respect as leaders. But I did receive a letter from President Richard Nixon, saying how sorry he was about what happened to us and that he commended me for how I handled the situation. History has not been complimentary to President Nixon, but he must have had a good heart to care about us with such compassion. Not one word from the USOC, but our nation's president was concerned about us.

Stan Wright had to fend for himself after Rey and I were disqualified. But that wasn't his first career disappointment. As George Wright noted: "Stan applied for the head coaching job at Cal just before you transferred there, Eddie. On paper, he had all the credentials, but Dave Maggard was picked. The door closed on Stan at that point, to be hired by a major university. Part of it was that Stan was black, and that he didn't fit totally into the old boy's network. So he got a job at Sacramento State, which, by comparison, was a second- or third-tier college for athletics.

"From that point on, he dedicated himself to track-and-field administration. He was a chair of the USOC committee that dealt with South Africa. But not getting the Cal job was a major setback in his life, though he was amazingly resilient. He always found a path to go forward. So he became the athletic director at Sacramento State.

"Regarding 1972 and Munich, up until then there was the unwritten policy that the first assistant coach from the previous Olympics would become the head coach of the next Olympics. In 1968, Payton Jordan picked Stan to be his first assistant. But because of politics and, I really believe, race, it came down to a tie between Bowerman and Stan in 1972. Procedure then was broken as the USOC began calling up individuals who were not attending the meetings from which the Olympic coach was chosen, and asking them who their preference was. And Bowerman was picked by one vote, even though he had been anti-AAU and anti-USOC. It was another setback for Stan, who told me, 'I just bit my tongue. I didn't want to be Bowerman's assistant, but I did it because I believed in the system.' It was all about structure, and also that Stan would rather watch the Olympics in Munich than in America."

Failing to become the Cal coach, then getting passed over for the head coaching position in Munich, and then our two disqualifications "didn't make Stan sad in the sense that he was giving up, just sad with grief," said George Wright. Then Stan lost his wife, which made him sadder. But if only Stan had read the morning newspapers that fateful August 31, 1972, day, he would have been saved. "He had the wrong schedule," said George Wright. "The quarter-finals for the 100 meters and 10,000 meters had been switched, and had been printed in the *Stars and Stripes* that morning and also in the *Track and Field News*. For some reason, Stan didn't read either publication. He trusted the people he worked for; he trusted the structure."

So, in that one sense, by failing to read the morning newspapers, Howard Cosell was right in blaming Stan.

"The bitterness that Stan had for a long time," George Wright continued, "was toward Bill Bowerman, who did not stand up for him. That interview with Howard Cosell, Bowerman should have been there with Stan, who had to stand out there on the plank by himself. Stan was so grateful, Eddie, that you and Cliff West went up to see him after Munich. That was very special. Still, Stan lost a lot of sleep over this."

Cliff and I stayed with Stan Wright for a couple of hours. He seemed OK. And I saw Stan after that when I coached at Cal. Then six years after Munich, Stan encouraged me to run again. I knew where that was coming from, possibly that I would have made him feel better about Munich. I was married and a father by then, and I did run again for a year or so, though it wasn't about my coming back to the Olympics, nothing like that. But I think Stan kind of pulled back. There was a chance of his becoming the head coach in Montreal in 1976, but Doc Edwards got it, which disappointed me.

"Doc deserved it in '76," said George Wright, "but it still should have been Stan's position. I think the higher-ups were ready to move on, for reasons I'm not privy to. But while [I was] interviewing Stan for his book at his Sacramento home, he was constantly bombarded with phone calls from people around the country who cared about him. I'm speaking of 1998, the same year that Stan died. But I don't want to give the impression that he died of a broken heart, because of losing Hazel and whatever aftereffects there were from Munich. I can't answer that definitively; I never saw any signs of Stan wanting to give up. His body just gave out.

Stan Wright went to his grave without knowing that he would be absolved of fault for Eddie Hart's and Rey Robinson's disqualifications. (Photo courtesy of Toni Wright Hartfield)

"However, there's something else about Stan that I'd like to discuss. There are a lot of stereotypes about black athletes. I was an athlete once, and I'm also black. But what's interesting about Stan is that he grew up in the 1920s and 1930s in Inglewood, New Jersey. He went to an integrated high school, was the only black on the basketball team and one of two blacks on the baseball team. . . . A line was drawn at an almost all-white school about interracial friendships or dating. Then, after serving in the military and getting a master's degree, Stan couldn't get a job coaching in high school, even at his alma mater. So he, like other black coaches in the 1940s, had to go to black colleges in the South to hone his skills.

"Those obstacles are what drove him, and he became one of the few blacks to break into the bureaucracy of the AAU. He'd bring this little black college, Texas Southern, to the NCAA meet in Ann Arbor, Michigan, and all the white coaches there resented him. But he was committed to integration. I remember talking to UCLA coach Jim Bush about Stan, and Bush spoke disparagingly about him. Stan had strong character. He never brought less than his A game to whatever he did."

To his family, Stan had two roles: father and coach. After losing Hazel, Stan moved to Houston to be near Toni Wright Hartfield, one of his four children, and her family, and that's where he passed away November 8, 1998.

"When I was a teenager," Toni said in June 2015, "I saw my father as strict, because I was the older daughter. But as I grew up, I thought of him as a big teddy bear, very kind and generous. We used to call him 'The Bear.' If I had known when I was younger that I could have pulled something on him, and gotten away with it, I'd have done it. But I was the daughter who was the good student and who did everything the correct way.

"I always tried to please him, but he wasn't one to pass out compliments at all. I can only remember a few times his saying, 'I love you.' Now my mother, she was the warm-and-fuzzy type. I married one of my dad's track athletes at Texas Southern, John Hartfield. When my dad would come to visit our family, it was great. He was the grandfather to my daughter, and great-grandfather to my grandchild. He'd tell that grandchild, 'I love you,' and I'd tell my dad, 'You hardly ever said that to me.' He wasn't warm and fuzzy until much later, but we had a great relationship."

Having spoken with George Wright, I asked Toni if her father's personality had changed after Munich. I guess I was looking for corroboration. "He never talked about it, not with me," she said. "We were devastated, and were trying to find out what happened. I was already married. I lived in Houston when my dad was in Sacramento. We'd phone my mother to find out what's going on, but she protected him. We knew not to bother him or to trouble him with questions. We did send him a telegram after Munich, saying that we loved him. He never said anything to me about it, but I have that telegram because George Wright sent me some things after my dad passed. My dad had kept that telegram.

"A couple of years before, my sister and brother-in-law, Sandra and William Robinson, told me that my dad had actually brought up Munich, and they had a conversation about it. With me, he internalized it. He was quiet at home, but I can still see him sitting in his rocking chair. When he spoke at a banquet, they had to put a timer on him. He could really talk, just not at home. He had a full life, regardless, but he waited too long after my mom passed to move here near his grandkids."

George Wright believes your father was haunted by Munich. Do you agree?

"I don't think he was haunted by Munich, not at all," Toni said. "Like I said, he wouldn't talk about it with me. Whether he talked about it with friends, I don't know. My mother was his rock. If we got angry with him, she was ready to defend him. She was the glue to the family, because my dad was gone a lot. But he had accumulated so much track history around the house that he had his own study, with journals and filing cabinets, like his own museum. I remember at my dad's funeral, so many people came. The love and support was overwhelming. We loved him, and he is loved."

I loved the man, too, and I never had to forgive him for my disqualification. There was nothing to forgive. The sad thing is that Stan went to his grave not knowing who was responsible for what happened to him in Munich. It was George Wilson, if he is to be blamed, though he, also, really is faultless. But, like Stan, he's now in his grave.

Yet the controversy lives on.

LAST LEG OF
THE JOURNEY

Coming back to Munich after forty-three years was everything I hoped for, but not everything that I expected. I knew this trip would be emotional—a reflective, introspective adventure. But I wasn't prepared for the rush of emotions and memories I would feel. Here I was in 2015, standing once again on the track at the Olympic Stadium, where anticipation had turned into devastation and shifted into elation in a matter of days in 1972. My heightened emotions needed calming down, so before I could put into words what I was feeling, I moved down the track for a few minutes to collect myself.

It is more overwhelming than I had anticipated, especially with my son here to relive my Olympic experience and record my return. I was feeling mixed emotions of pride and pain, because half of that gold medal–winning sprint relay team is gone. I didn't go to Larry Black's memorial, and I didn't go to Robert Taylor's memorial either. So returning to this stadium is a memorial of sorts, because it was right here that we broke the world record and received our gold medals in front of seventy thousand in attendance, and before tens of millions on television.

I'm standing on the exact place on the track where I received the baton from Gerald Tinker on the anchor leg of that relay. I'm reliving it all over again, but I'm also thinking of all the changes that have transpired in the forty-three years since I was last here. I've lost two relay partners. I'm a married man of forty-one years, a father of two, a grandfather of three. I graduated from college and got a master's degree. I became a coach and teacher. And I lost a father who taught me how to conduct my life.

I'm also remembering the other people who got me here in 1972: Coaches Bonanno, Kring, Albiani, Maggard, and Craig. I'm not anything like an island. So many people have played constructive roles in my life, like Mrs. Mercurio and my many influential teachers, and especially Gwen, who has taught me about love, relationships, and parenting. I'm digesting it all on this track.

I'm also thinking of Tom Hill, who was my roommate at the Munich Olympics. Today he's Dr. Tom Hill, with a PhD in counseling education, and he's senior vice president for student affairs at Iowa State University. Tom won the 1972 Olympic Trials in the 110-meter high hurdles and took the bronze in Munich behind American Rod Milburn and Guy Drut of France. Tom's son, Thomas Hill, was a star player during Duke's NCAA championship basketball run in the early 1990s.

"Eddie was a steady guy who took care of business, which was good for me, because the two of us weren't flashy guys, just regular folk, and Munich was a once-in-a-lifetime trip for me," Hill told Dave Newhouse in June 2015. "Even though we were on the biggest stage in the world, strange things can happen. I was too nervous at the start of the hurdles final, and it cost me. The only thing I could do for Eddie after his disqualification was to be there for him, even though as roommates, we didn't do much talking. But the way he handled his situation was really with class. To be honest with you, I couldn't have done that. I wouldn't have been calm. But his faith helped him get through that, along with his family.

"You learn what a person is like through difficult times and adversity. I learned a great deal about Eddie's character in Munich. He has great character. If I could support him, I wouldn't hesitate. And he supported me as well. Eddie and I have stayed friends over the years. There's a quiet respect between us.

"We were there during the Munich tragedy, plus all the other things that were going on at that time, like South Africa and its policy of apartheid. We threatened not to compete in the '72 Olympics if South Africa was allowed to participate, and, then, it wasn't allowed. Put that together with everything else that was going on in Munich, all of that helped shape me. You either let it kill you or you grow from it."

Tom Hill's right. We all grew from that tragedy, but that didn't curtail acts of terrorism, an insidious culture that's grown exponentially since Munich. From that crisis to ISIS, it's only gotten worse.

But I'm back in the Olympic Stadium, right here, right now. Amazing! I still can visualize Tinker handing me the baton. "I made sure that I did my part in getting that baton passed to Eddie," Tinker said in May 2015. "That

Tom Hill was Eddie Hart's roommate in Munich, where he won a bronze medal in the 110-meter high hurdles (Photo of Eddie Hart)

was my only race, and I wasn't going to fail at that. My friends told me that I built a five-meter lead; all I know is that it was the greatest race of my life. Eddie told me it was the fastest 100 ever run around a curve. Eddie's a bounce-back kind of guy. He got his gold medal, though not the one he was expecting. Valery Borzov never would have beaten Eddie in the final. Eddie was tenacity. He had the ability and the structure to kick Borzov's butt. No doubt about it. Eddie's a tough cookie."

I've relived what it felt like to be in that Olympic Stadium tunnel, watching my race go off without me. I stood in that same spot, sixty feet from the starting line. From there, I walked to the same starting line on the track where the German official misinformed Stan Wright about the time of that 100-meter quarterfinal. After Stan got that information, we prepared to leave the stadium. Then Stan said, 'Wait a minute.' He walked back to the official. I don't know what made me do it, but I went with him. I heard Stan ask the official again about the quarterfinal heat time. And the official repeated what he said earlier. Howard Cosell obviously didn't know that.

And then it all collapsed. Dave Maggard knows what I was feeling, then and now. "Eddie was at his best then, healthy," he said. "He looked so good in practice. I thought, really truly, that Eddie was going to win the 100 meters. When I didn't see Eddie and Rey at the starting line, I ran right down there. Then at dinner that night, I said, 'Eddie, let it rest, because you're going to win a gold medal in the relay.' I saw Eddie as a real champion. He never bad-mouthed Stan. Never! The way Eddie rose above this, he's more of a champion off the track than he was on."

In a way, coming back to the Olympic Stadium hasn't made this any easier. There is the thrilling memory, and there is the bitter memory. But now, I'm going to heal part of that ugly memory. I'm going to run the race I didn't get to run. There is no gold to be won, but I've got to get this forty-three-year-old albatross off my neck. So I'm stretching on this same track, about to take a ceremonial 100-meter sprint, wearing the same singlet with "USA" across the chest that I wore when I was disqualified and also when I won the gold medal. Talk about a shifting of emotions! But it's cold, man, it feels like winter, and I'm no longer twenty-three. So, what if we make it a ceremonial 50-meter sprint, but not an all-out sprint, for this old man? Is that all right? It's just to say that I was here, and I did it, and who's watching anyway? There are seventy thousand empty seats, except for a few tourists.

Well, here I go, though I'm coasting, not sprinting, this time. I'm not trying to set a world record in the sixty-and-up age group. And it's not Valery Borzov I'm competing against, but Father Time. Only his stopwatch doesn't record seconds, it records a lifetime. Now I'm going to hit that imaginary tape with my once-familiar lean. Done.

I've completed what I set out to do on this trip—see the Olympic Stadium again, revisit that dark tunnel, run that 100, sorta, and clear my head of a long-ago, lingering headache. I've handled heartbreak in the best possible way.

My son and I talked about a lot of things while riding the train around Munich last night. I told him that I felt good about my responses in 1972, how I spoke to Stan Wright, how I spoke about Stan Wright, and how I wanted to assure Stan Wright that I had no ill feelings toward him. Waking up this morning, I realized this trip has been a big confirmation for me in that sense. What's important to me is how I respond to people who are important in my life. My father could look at my actions and say, "Well done, son, you did it the right way." As a representative of my parents, my church, and my community, I believe I conducted myself in 1972 in a way that brought honor to the people associated with me.

In college, I read a book—I don't remember the name—that sheds light on my relationship with my parents. A woman has been called to a mortuary to identify her son, who had been a thief and a drug addict. She looks at the corpse and said, "You've got the wrong boy. This is not my son. My son wasn't like that. My son was a good son, a Christian who went to church." And she leaves, convinced that the corpse isn't her son. Before the story ends, it's revealed that the corpse is, indeed, her son. She couldn't deal with it, so she would rather have the world believe that it was a lie instead of accepting the dishonor that it would have brought her. I never wanted to be that son who brought pain, suffering, and dishonor to his parents. I've tried to live a truthful life.

Though I never had any regrets about my conduct following my disqualification, it took this trip to confirm everything. I just feel good, a comforting feeling. I can look back and see that I did it the right way. On the train ride

In 2015, Eddie Hart returned to the scene of his disqualification in Munich and sat in the stands near where he watched the 100-meter final. (Photo courtesy of Eddie Hart II)

last night, I spotted a monument I remembered seeing in 1972. It made me think about other things that happened at those Olympics. I was really anxious about seeing the Olympic Village as well as the Olympic Stadium. And today, when I put on this USA singlet here at the stadium, I thought, "This is the first time I've worn it since the last time I wore it, in Munich in 1972." I knew I was the same size, that it would fit, but wearing it feels just like it did forty-three years ago. I feel good that I've maintained my shape. Borzov can't wear his singlet today.

But it's all still surreal. When I hit that finish line just now, I had this mental flash that maybe this is what it would've felt like to run that 100-meter final in 1972. I know what the feeling of winning is like, though it was emotionally different today—macabre, yet fulfilling. I don't know how else to explain it, but I'm glad I ran today; it was a huge release.

Maybe someone was watching me today and thinking, "What is that old man doing, wearing a USA uniform, and striding down the track, not sprinting, like he's living out a fantasy? Who is that old man, and what is he all about?"

We do relive things, sometimes, in the strangest ways. Did you ever see the movie *Guarding Tess?* Shirley MacLaine plays an ex-president's wife, and the main person who's guarding her is Nicholas Cage. She wants him to take her on a picnic to this same area where she picnicked with her late husband, only it's in the dead of winter. What Nicholas Cage's character doesn't know is that she has terminal cancer. That sort of reminded me of going back to a time when you can't die. I'm twenty-three, my body is in great shape, and I don't have a bald spot or gray hair. Now it's about reliving the past, recalling a happier time, when I didn't drop the baton, and I won the gold medal. But I wish I could have won that 100-meter gold also.

You know, when I finished this ceremonial 100, or 50, I thought: "This probably will be the last time I come back here." But, then, I thought about it some more and, said, "No, this isn't the last time. I going to bring my grandson, Eddie Hart III, here, to show him what Grandpa experienced a long time ago, the gold with the grim."

And if Valery Borzov wants to have a 100-meter showdown, he has all that time to get in shape. I'll be ready. I've been ready since 1972.

EPILOGUE

Eddie Hart and Reynaud "Rey" Robinson were victims of the most famous sprint dis-qualification in Olympic Games history—missing the 100-meter quarterfinal heat at the 1972 Olympics in Munich because of a scheduling misunderstanding. Forty-three years later, on June 17, 2015, they discussed from opposite coasts how that devastating blow affected their lives then and now

EDDIE HART: We have this history between us, Rey. But I really don't know all that much about you. Like how old are you, anyway?

REY ROBINSON: I'm sixty-three. My birthday was on April first. And what about you, Eddie? I don't know all that much about you either.

EH: I'm sixty-six. My birthday's April 24.

RR: I'm an Aries. I think you're into that Taurus thing.

EH: That's right. What about family, Rey? I have five siblings. How about you?

RR: All totaled, I have three brothers and five sisters. Now, that's from two marriages. I've lived with all of them at one time. My parents shared custody of me, moved around a lot. But both family structures were strong.

EH: Moving like you did, how did that shape you as an individual while growing up? Were you dependent or independent?

RR: That's a good question. I never thought about that. I'd say both—independent with my dad, dependent upon my mom. Either way, I was in a protective environment, living in the Fort Meade and Lakeland areas of central Florida.

EH: Did you have family support, like your parents attending your sporting events?

RR: My dad saw me run in my first college track meet. My dad, Booker T. Robinson, was a professional baseball player. He played in the Negro Leagues for the Indianapolis Clowns and Homestead Grays, and so he did a lot of barnstorming.

He was an offensive weapon, an infielder known for his speed. I saw him play in his last game, in his forties, and he stole second and third base. But his real job was at the phosphate mine.

EH: Did your father ever play against Jackie Robinson or Willie Mays?

RR: He knew Jackie Robinson. They didn't play together. My dad was born in 1913. He saw Satchel Paige, Josh Gibson, and Willie Mays play.

EH: As for me, my parents were married sixty-five years. We were a close family, poor and humble. But, athletically, you inherited your father's speed, right?

RR: I only ran one year of track in high school, my senior year. I got into a lot of trouble when I was younger. That's why I moved back and forth between families. I flunked the fourth and eighth grades, hanging out with the wrong crowd. So I had to go to summer school to keep up with my class. My dad was very strict though, zero tolerance. He let me play football, and I rushed for nearly a thousand yards my senior year of high school. My dad told me I needed to get a scholarship, because he couldn't pay my way to college. So I went out for track.

EH: One year of track, and you went to the Golden West meet in Sacramento that year against the top preps in the country. Man, you were an instant sensation.

RR: Not really, Eddie. In my first meet, I tried the 100-yard dash, and I won in 12-point something seconds. That night, I could not go to sleep because it was the first time I had done something by myself. Everyone was patting me on the back.

EH: You were hooked, huh?

RR: From that point on, that was it. I improved three seconds in one season, winning with a wind-aided 9.2 seconds in the 100-yard dash at the Golden West.

EH: Wow! My thing was baseball when I was eleven and twelve. Then I ran in a track meet, and they handed me this trophy. People came up and congratulated me, and my name was in the newspaper. That was like instant gratification. Track was it.

RR: Track was a true blessing. At the Golden West, the man who gave out the MVP trophy was "Bullet" Bob Hayes, the 100-meter Olympic champion at Tokyo in 1964. He was playing wide receiver for the Dallas Cowboys. He gave me the trophy and said, "Son, where are you going to college?" I sat next to him on a flight to Dallas. He recommended his school, Florida A&M. I wound up getting my master's degree there and later was the head track coach at A&M for ten years. I live in Tampa now.

EH: You and I ran one-two at the Olympic Trials, both timed at 9.9 seconds in the 100-meter final. I just nudged you out. Robert Taylor was right behind us at 10.0 to get the third Olympic spot. But weren't you injured at one point that year?

RR: I suffered a strained hamstring in a Los Angeles meet before the Trials, but it wasn't a problem. I just put a "bandage" on it. I ran well in the Trials; the leg thing wasn't a focus.

EH: Three weeks before the Trials, I injured my leg in the U.S. Championships by running the 200. I didn't do any block starts for three weeks going into the Trials.

RR: Really? The Trials was just the second time we faced each other, Eddie. At the Modesto Relays, I took second and you took third in the 100, remember?

EH: I do, but going into the Trials, I was confident I would win the 100. Were you that confident, too?

RR: Of course, of course. I was just as confident after the Trials. I bet Larry Black I could run the 200 under 21 seconds, and I ran a 20.8. I didn't run any time after that. I slacked off with my training, fooled around a bit. But I was ready in Munich.

EH: I was ready, too. I trained harder after the Trials than I did before. Then what happened to us in Munich happened.

RR: My father and great aunt were there in Munich. That was only the second time my father saw me run in person. The City of Lakeland did a fund-raiser to send him there. After [the disqualification], Stan Wright was in the living quarters with us. He was crying and apologetic. Howard Cosell tore into me in an interview. I had never seen my dad so upset.

EH: I know you were a lot angrier with Coach Wright than I was.

RR: Stan Wright was the worst person in the world to me, at that point. I really didn't know him beforehand. I was talking to my college coach, Bobby Lang, from Munich, and he was telling me what to do. I told Coach Wright that I was going to do what my college coach told me to do. From that point forward, Coach Wright had an issue with me. And after that [quarterfinal] race, I was like a powder keg. I just blew up at Coach Wright. I said some things about his professionalism as a track coach, that this was his fault.

EH: How long did those feelings stay with you, Rey?

RR: A long time, Eddie. I mean, years. I continued to run track after Munich, and I made it to the finals of the 1976 Olympic Trials. I was working with Brooks Johnson as my track coach, and I finished fifth in the 100. They were deciding which sprinters to take in the [400-meter] relay. I figured Brooks Johnson would plead my case because of what happened in Munich. But he pleaded for Steve Williams.

EH: How did you find that out?

RR: Coach Wright came to me. It was the first time I had seen him since Munich. He said, "Rey, if you had somebody in that meeting pushing for you, you'd be on this Olympic team." We had a pleasant conversation. I learned over the years that if Stan Wright could have done anything to make up for Munich, he would have done it.

EH: I'm curious about the reaction back home when you returned from Munich.

RR: People started saying that you and I were screwing around, that we were asleep, and that's why we missed the race.

EH: I got that, too, Rey.

RR: Luckily, I had a support group to help me through that, but I had to develop a second skin and let all that negative stuff roll off me. I did some interviews, but some reporters didn't do their due diligence as far as research, so I stopped doing interviews. I just got tired of saying the same story over and over and over.

EH: Some people said, "You're a grown man, and you didn't have a schedule in Munich?"

RR: I heard that one, too.

EH: My whole focus was the race itself and the relay. I've got to run; I'm not a race scheduler. When you're on a plane, you have to depend on the pilot. You have to depend on somebody.

RR: Returning from Munich, it wasn't all that bad. I got a lot of fan mail, including some [faux] gold medals. But when I got back, it was football season at Florida A&M, so I had to switch gears. I was just twenty, and I had two years of college left.

EH: I was twenty-three. I withdrew from college for a while, and I withdrew from life a little bit, too. I hung around the house for three or four months. When people saw me, this cloud came over them, because they were feeling my pain. That was hard for me, seeing the hurt in others. It wasn't all about Stan Wright for me. My father told me he felt lousy for me after Munich. Forty years later, I asked him about it again, and he started crying.

RR: Same thing for me, Eddie. Your father, my father, we come from the same fabric. He always told me, "Just do your best."

EH: That's the same thing my father always told me.

RR: But what really got me past Munich was life itself. Just maturity. When I had that conversation with Coach Wright at the 1976 Olympic Trials, even after all that I had said about him, he had no animosity toward me. We talked and said a few things, and I felt his sincerity.

EH: I know that took a lot of forgiveness, Rey. But what were your feelings when we were there in Munich, and all that went down between the Arabs and Israelis?

RR: That was devastating, unbelievable. I remember those [Israeli hostages] being down on the floor. Catching the flight out of Munich, I saw the wreckage of the helicopter, still on the tarmac. I watched your relay event after I landed in New York. It was a crazy Olympics. Mark Spitz was the golden boy, but I never met him.

EH: He never was with our group. I don't ever remember seeing him at the Opening Ceremonies. At those ceremonies, do you remember that they let the doves go?

RR: Yeah, they crapped all over us.

EH: Some of the girls got blasted. Those doves circled back over us.

RR: I didn't escape either, Eddie.

EH: But not getting an Olympic medal, Rey, is there a little hole in your heart?

RR: There's no hole in my heart. My life has been very successful. I have a wonderful family, three daughters, and a lovely wife. I couldn't ask for anything more. If it wasn't for the Olympics, I couldn't have had this experience.

EH: What do you mean?

RR: Winning any kind of medal at the Olympics would have been icing on the cake. But I've traveled around the world several times, I've met wonderful people in track and field, and I'm still making a living off track and field today, training athletes.

EH: Has our disappointment in Munich helped you in assisting young athletes in dealing with their own disappointments?

RR: Yes, it has. As you know, Eddie, athletes have their ups and downs. You're not going to win every race, or win all the time at anything. That's the best way I can motivate someone, except that I can speak from the standpoint of an Olympian.

EH: I use our missing that 100 all the time when I work with younger people about the struggles in life they're going to face. We're all going to have adversities. My daughter is developmentally disabled. That was a challenge for my wife and me. My daughter now is forty-one. But whether it's the Olympics or just sports in general, I agree, you're not going to win every time. You could have injuries or things that are out of your control. You could run a great relay race, and someone drops the baton.

RR: I hear what you're saying, Eddie.

EH: We were disqualified, but the Israelis lost their lives.

RR: That's so tragic.

EH: We're still alive, but those Israelis had wives and children.

RR: We went through an Olympics, Eddie, that other Olympians haven't gone through. I can say, looking at the two of us, that we handled it with great character. We didn't let it overcome us; it made us stronger.

EH: We endured, and we have a commonality in how we dealt with it. We were just young men, formulating our lives. I'm not glad our misfortune happened; I wouldn't wish that on anybody, even though there are a lot of ways we benefitted from it.

RR: Every time the Olympics come around, there's something that's going to be said about our event. I'm waiting to see an Olympics when they don't mention it.

EH: Your phone starts ringing whenever it's an Olympic year?

RR: Every time. Almost guaranteed. Like, how am I living with it today?

EH: Maybe, Rey, after forty-three years, it's brought us closer together, two strangers from opposite ends of the country who made history together.

RR: We're talking more, Eddie, I know that, and we have nice conversations about what the other person is doing.

EH: I can't remember; did you watch the 100-meter final in Munich? I was there.

RR: Did I watch it? Wait. Yeah, I believe I was there. But I do know this: if the three of us had competed together—you, me, Robert Taylor—we'd have had a sweep.

EH: I believe Robert went through the motions without us in that final.

RR: After he won the silver medal, I don't know if you know this, Eddie, but he wanted to cut it up into three pieces, for you, me, and Robert.

EH: Robert was a good man.

RR: You know why I felt that we would have swept the 100? At the Trials, remember how the three of us hugged and said, "We're all on the boat?" You don't see that often with sprinters. We had the camaraderie. Though we wanted to beat one another, we weren't even thinking of Valery Borzov.

EH: Winning the Olympic Trials was tougher than running in the Olympics. Eighty percent of the world's best sprinters back then were in the United States.

RR: And all three of us—you, me, Robert—were running faster than Borzov.

EH: Borzov ran a 10.14 to win the gold medal. Robert ran 10.24 to get the silver, but that time was child's play for him. He ran 9.2 over 100 yards to win his conference meet. He just wasn't the same without us competing with him.

RR: Eddie, I need to say something about Coach Wright. I've learned over time that it wasn't a lack of professionalism on his part that prevented us from participating in that race. After he told me later on that we had gotten false information in Munich, I finally understood what went on.

EH: I've said this before, and I'll say it again: Stan Wright was not at fault. I love the man, and that's how I want Eddie Jr. to feel and how I want his children to feel about Stan Wright. I want my entire family to fully understand my story, and Stan Wright is a big part of my story. Even my daughter, Paris, with her beautiful take on life in spite of the setback given her at birth, has helped me with my feelings toward Stan Wright. I have no ill feelings, no grudges, toward the man.

RR: I've gotten over what happened in Munich, too. I got that chip off my shoulder. I just outgrew it. I don't blame Coach Wright anymore.

EH: I'm glad to hear that, Rey. But the three of us—Stan Wright, you, and I—are linked by history. We'll be remembered as long as there is an Olympic Games.

NOTES

Introduction
Jimmy Hines, John Carlos, and Lee Evans, interviews, Feb. 7, 2015.

1. Tunnel Vision
Barbara Ferrell, interview, Feb. 7, 2015; Alexander Bock, interview, Apr. 1, 2015.

2. A Massacre Made Easy
Irmina Richter, interview, Mar. 2, 2015; Tom Dooley, interview, May 7, 2015; Shaul Ladany, telephone interview, May 12, 2015; Shlomo Levy, telephone interviews, May 20, 24, 2015; Shaul P. Ladany, *King of the Road: The Autobiography of an Israeli Scientist and World Record–Holding Race Walker* (Jerusalem: Gefen, 2008).

3. Death Lights Up the Sky
Tape of T. J. Hart's memories of Port Chicago, in Eddie Hart's possession; Robert L. Allen, *The Port Chicago Mutiny: The Story of the Largest Mass Mutiny Trial in U.S. Naval History* (Berkeley, CA: Heyday Books, 1993).

4. Gold Medal for Corruption
Mark Spitz, interview, Apr. 21, 2015; Tom McMillen, interview, Apr. 29, 2015; Bob Seagren, interview, May 4, 2015; Rick DeMont, interview, Feb. 17, 2016; Olga Korbut, quotation from David Clay Large, *Munich 1972: Tragedy, Terror, and Triumph* (San Francisco: Rowman & Littlefield, 2012); H. G. Bissinger, *Friday Night Lights: A Town, a Team, and a Dream* (New York: Da Capo, 1990).

5. School Days
Nanette Mercurio, interview, Mar. 10, 2015; Rodell Johnson, interview, May 11, 2015.

6. The Bavarian Perspective
Klaus Wolfermann and Friederike Wolfermann, interviews, Apr. 3, 2015; Michael Gernandt, interview, Apr. 4, 2015.

7. Learning to Sprint
Nanette Mercurio, interview, Mar. 10, 2015.

8. Black and White
Eddie Hart Jr., interview, Apr. 4, 2015; John Carlos, interview, June 10, 2015.

9. The Eagle Flies
Bert Bonanno, telephone interview, June 13, 2015.

10. Post-Olympic Stress Factor
Marilyn King, interview, May 29, 2015.

11. The Turning Point
Jack Albiani, telephone interview, June 6, 2015.

12. I Love Paris
Eddie Hart Jr., interview, Apr. 5, 2015.

14. View from Olympus
John Carlos, Lee Evans, Jimmy Hines, Stephanie Brown Trafton, and Barbara Ferrell, interviews, Feb. 7, 2016; Gerald Tinker, interview, May 9, 2015.

15. The Berkeley Man
Cliff West, interview, May 9, 2015; Dave Maggard, interview, June 22, 2015.

18. Blamed, but Blameless
Dave Maggard, interview, June 22, 2015; George Wright, telephone interview, June 11, 2015; Toni Wright Hartfield, telephone interview, June 24, 2015; Ollan Cassell, telephone interview, Mar. 11, 2016; George Wright and Stan Wright, *Stan Wright—Track Coach: Forty Years in the "Good Old Boy Network"—The Story of an African American Pioneer* (San Francisco: Pacifica Sports Research, 2005); Stan Wright, interview with Howard Cosell, and Cosell commentary from David Clay Large, *Munich 1972: Tragedy, Terror, and Triumph* (San Francisco: Rowman & Littlefield, 2012).

19. Last Leg of the Journey
Gerald Tinker, interview, May 9, 2015; Tom Hill, telephone interview, June 19, 2015; Dave Maggard, interview, June 22, 2015.

REFERENCES

Allen, Robert L. *The Port Chicago Mutiny: The Story of the Largest Mass Mutiny Trial in U.S. Naval History*. Berkeley, California: Heyday Books, 1993.

Bissinger, H. G. *Friday Night Lights: A Town, a Team, and a Dream*. New York: Da Capo, 1990.

Carlos, John, with Dave Zirin. *The John Carlos Story: The Sports Moment That Changed the World*. Chicago: Haymarket, 2011.

Ladany, Shaul P. *King of the Road: The Autobiography of an Israeli Scientist and a World Record-Holding Race Walker*. Jerusalem: Gefen, 2008.

Large, David Clay. *Munich 1972: Tragedy, Terror, and Triumph*. Lanham, Maryland: Rowman & Littlefield, 2012.

Wallechinsky, David. *The Complete Book of the Olympics*. 1984, Reprint. New York: Penguin, 1988.

Wright, Stan, and George Wright. *Stan Wright—Track Coach: Forty Years in the "Good Old Boy Network."* San Francisco: Pacifica Sports Research, 2005.

INDEX

of, 20–21; media coverage of, 27, 43; Munich police and, 1, 15, 22–24, 62–63; Spitz fleeing, 42–44, 54. *See also* Israeli athletes, at Munich Olympics
Thorpe, Jim, 49
Tinker, Gerald, 133, 156, 169; on 400-meter relay team, *9, 10,* 11, 13, 168, 186–87; at Olympic Trials, *156,* 161, 164; post-Olympics, 14, 126
Tokyo Games 1964, 126
track and field, 52–53, 104, 108, 163; interest in, 98, 105, 152
track-and-field programs, 90, 91, 134; Bonanno's, 90–91; at Contra Costa Junior College, 105, 109
track team, U.S. Olympic. *See* U.S. Olympic track team
Trafton, Stephanie Brown, 126, 129, *132*
training: Olympic Trials: Hart training for, 160–61
training, Hart's, 7–8, 107; intensity about, 153–55; for Olympics, 154–57, 167
trash talk, among sprinters, 148
Turner, Nat, 80
Tyus, Wyomia, 152

UC Berkeley. *See* Cal (UC Berkeley)
United States: 400-meter relay by, *13;* boycotting Moscow Olympics, 28, 54, 96; loss of basketball game, 4, 42, 44–47, 54, 67, 96–98; possible collusion against, 67, 132; refusing silver medal for basketball, 4, 47
U.S. national track team, 122, 149–51, *153*
U.S. Olympic Committee (USOC): on loss of basketball game, 96–98; not defending athletes, 49–51; responsibility for disqualifications, 3, 171, 176
U.S. Olympic track team, 167–68, 172, 180

vacations, 110–11, 117
Vaughan, Ben, 149, 151, 162
visualization, in achieving goals, 89

Waite, Warren, 86
Wallace, George, 77–78
Washington, Herb, 161
Way beyond Sports, 96
Weinberger (Weinberg), Mosche, 18, 20

West, Cliff, 93, 136, 142–44, *153,* 167, 181
West, Cornel, 78, 142–43
West Coast Relays, 155–56
White, Willye, 149
Wilkins, Mac, 91, 126
Williams, Randy, 126
Williams, Travis, 106
Williamson, Buddy, 54
Willie Davenport Track and Field Clinic, 126
Wilson, George, 171–72, 174, 180
Winter, Bud, 87
Winter Olympics (2018), 65
Wolfermann, Friederike, 64–65
Wolfermann, Katherina, 64
Wolfermann, Klaus, 16, 62, *63,* 64
"World's Fastest Human" title, from winning 100-meter dash, 2, 7–8, 13–14, 84
Wottle, Dave, 42, 75, 81, 164
Wright, George, 170, *171,* 173, 179–80, 183–84
Wright, Hazel, 170, 181, 183–84
Wright, Stan, 108, *182;* biography of, 170, 173, 179–80; blamed for Robinson and Hart's disqualification, 53, 93, 108, 132–33, 176; Bowerman and, 172, 181; career of, 180–81, 183; as coach, 132–33, 168; Cossell blaming for disqualifications, 132, 176–79, 181; effects of disqualifications on, 132, 183–84; explanations for disqualifications, 12, 173–75; given wrong times for quarterfinal heats, 2, 8, 67, 187; Hart not blaming, 3, 16, 170, 175–76, 188; Hart's friendship with, 5, 168, 175, 181, 184; Jimmy Hines and, 127, 132, 179; Maggard and, 175, 180; not responsible for disqualification, 67, 131–32, 187; race and, 180, 183; Robinson blaming, 176, 178–79; as sprints coach for U.S. Olympic track team, 6–7, 168–69; trying to find open lanes for Robinson and Hart, 7, 17, 174–75

Young, Jon, 162
Young, Kevin, 126

Zeno, Charlie, 88